ROUTLEDGE LIBRARY EDITIONS:
TAXATION

Volume 10

TAXING PERSONAL WEALTH

TAXING PERSONAL WEALTH

An Analysis of Capital Taxation in the United Kingdom—History, Present Structure and Future Possibilities

C.T. SANDFORD

Routledge
Taylor & Francis Group
LONDON AND NEW YORK

First published in 1971 by George Allen & Unwin Ltd.

This edition first published in 2019
by Routledge
2 Park Square, Milton Park, Abingdon, Oxon OX14 4RN

and by Routledge
711 Third Avenue, New York, NY 10017

Routledge is an imprint of the Taylor & Francis Group, an informa business

British Library Cataloguing in Publication Data
A catalogue record for this book is available from the British Library

ISBN: 978-1-138-56291-2 (Set)
ISBN: 978-0-429-48988-4 (Set) (ebk)
ISBN: 978-0-8153-4970-9 (Volume 10) (hbk)
ISBN: 978-1-351-10705-1 (Volume 10) (ebk)

Publisher's Note
The publisher has gone to great lengths to ensure the quality of this reprint but points out that some imperfections in the original copies may be apparent.

Disclaimer
The publisher has made every effort to trace copyright holders and would welcome correspondence from those they have been unable to trace.

Taxing Personal Wealth

An analysis of capital taxation in the United Kingdom – history, present structure and future possibilities

C. T. SANDFORD

London · George Allen & Unwin Ltd
Ruskin House Museum Street

First published in 1971

ISBN 0 04 336034 3

Printed in Great Britain
in 10 point Times New Roman type
by Unwin Brothers Limited,
Woking and London

To my Wife Evelyn

Contents

Acknowledgments

I am very grateful to Bath University for the two terms of sabbatical leave, Autumn 1968 and Spring 1969, which enabled me to make more rapid progress with the research and the book. Part of this leave was spent studying the Swedish system of wealth taxation; and I acknowledge, with sincere thanks, the research grant from the Nuffield foundation to meet the expenses of this study visit. The many people in Sweden who entertained me and gave me the benefit of their knowledge and wisdom is too large for individual mention; but I should like to express particular thanks to the Swedish Institute for arranging much of my programme; to Mr Gösta Eckman, Head of the Legal Department at the Royal Ministry of Finance, for so freely making available to me the expertise of his department; and especially to Professor Göran Englund, University of Lund, for hospitality and friendship, for information and advice, for checking my text for innaccuracies and for keeping me up-to-date with subsequent developments in Swedish wealth taxation.

Much of this book is a development of ideas first published in 1965 by the Institute of Economic Affairs as a Hobart Paper, *Taxing Inheritance and Capital Gains*. I wish to thank Arthur Seldon, the Editorial Director, for the help and encouragement he gave me with that Paper and the Institute for permission to reprint the substance of chapter III of the original paper as section v of chapter 3 in this book. I am grateful to *The Banker* for allowing me to reprint, in Appendix A, material first published (with P. M. Wright) in that journal as 'Estate Duty: Inflation and Capital Gains', March 1969. I also thank Sweet and Maxwell Ltd for permission to reproduce, as section (iii), chapter 2, the substance of an article, 'Estate Duty versus Inheritance Taxation, 1894', from *British Tax Review*, January–February 1968.

I gratefully acknowledge the help of Mrs P. M. Wright who undertook the calculations for the Property Price Index (Appendix A). A number of friends and colleagues, Mr P. N. Dean, Mr John Hughes, Dr A. A. Tait, Mr M. J. Sargent and Mr D. J. Ironside, kindly read and commented on all or part of the typescript and I thank them, together with Mr J. F. Turner, the Manager, Estate Duties Investment Trust, who as well as reading part of the typescript, took considerable trouble to provide me with statistical data about EDITH. To exonerate all those who have given me their comments, I should no doubt add the usual affirmation. I alone am responsible for the opinions and the errors.

As far as possible I have acknowledged my debt to other authors in footnotes. To my former teachers, and to colleagues and students past and present, I am conscious of a debt none the less real for being imprecisely definable. I have a continuing obligation to Miss Muriel King for her own unique brand of secretarial efficiency. And it would be ungenerous not to thank my publishers for their forbearance despite a long overdue typescript.

September 1970. C. T. SANDFORD

Introduction

'The voluntary tax.' 'A tax paid by those who dislike the Revenue less than they dislike their heirs.' 'A tax on vice—the vice of clinging to one's property until the last possible moment.' These descriptions have been applied to the major capital tax in the United Kingdom—an estate duty with a nominal severity almost unparalleled, but amongst the easiest of death duties to avoid.

The main purpose of this book is to hasten the end of this inequitable absurdity. But there is another reason to reconsider the death duties in the United Kingdom. Not since Sir William Harcourt's reform of 1894 has their structure been comprehensively reviewed—and the reasons which led Harcourt to choose the estate duty form may no longer be valid, if indeed they ever were.

Two main interrelated developments separate the requirements of Harcourt's time from those of today: a change in effect and our understanding of it; a change in philosophy and the purpose implied by it. In 1894 when the maximum rate was 8 per cent, the tax could be met by economies in consumption which reduced private claims on current output, and the government could, and did, treat its yield as ordinary revenue to be used for current expenditure. Today, when the maximum rate is ten times that of 1894, the tax cannot be so met. Death duties are paid out of capital. Essentially they are concerned with the distribution of wealth. This recognition of their effect has been paralleled by a new philosophy and a new purpose. Since Harcourt's day society has become less willing to tolerate gross inequalities in the distribution of wealth, and the function of the tax is now to diminish such inequalities—which are particularly pronounced and obstinately persistent in Britain.

People differ on how far the equalizing process should be pushed; but few would disagree that the main purpose of a modern death duty is to do something towards evening out inequalities in the distribution of wealth. Death duties have singular advantages for this role; no other form of capital tax can achieve the same effect with less antagonism and less economic disturbance.

The grossest anomalies of the estate duty can be corrected by reducing the rate whilst making the duty effective by means of an integrated gifts tax; but more efficacious in furthering the equalizing purpose would be a switch from estate duty (a tax on the corpus of the estate regardless of its dispersion) to inheritance tax (a tax on individual legacies regardless of the size of estate from which they come). The particular form of inheritance tax recommended is an 'accessions tax'—an integrated inheritance and gifts tax by which duty is levied on the cumulative receipts of legacies and gifts throughout a life-time.

A reformed death duty must be considered in the context of wealth taxation as a whole. The past decade has seen much discussion of an annual wealth tax. The author recommends the use of an annual wealth tax not, like the death duty, as a means of reducing inequalities in wealth holding, but to encourage efficiency. With due caution, because of the administrative difficulties, he advocates a wealth tax at modest rates to reduce or replace surtax and abolish the differentially higher rates of income tax on 'unearned' income.

In short, the proposals are an attempt to change the situation in which, to use the vivid language of Oliver Stutchbury in a recent pamphlet, our tax system is relatively easy on the *conservers* of wealth (those who have inherited or been given it) and 'mercilessly severe on the *creators* of wealth (e.g. managers who have had to make their own money); 'this is to put the weight of the tax burden the wrong way round if the country's efficiency is to be promoted.'[1]

These main recommendations are complemented by more limited proposals applicable under any form of death duty; and suggestions for more radical reform—to enlarge the scope of an accessions tax by including other non-income receipts such as gambling winnings and golden handshakes; and to introduce a negative or reverse wealth tax.

Throughout the book alternative reforms are considered, so that policy guides are available to those whose reform aims are more modest or whose judgments differ from those of the author.

Whilst the main recommendations inevitably reflect value judgments, the author believes that his conclusions are well grounded in the history and the analysis. Fiscal historians, who normally shun an economic treatise, may find something of value in the extended treatment of the history of the death duties and their effects on land ownership. Economists of various specialisms may be attracted by the detailed analysis of some aspect of the subject, such as the effect of estate duty on agriculture and landownership or on the private industrial business. The Swedish wealth tax is often quoted as a model for this country, and the full and up-to-date account and critique of it, a product of the author's study visit to Sweden, may be of particular interest to some. Four detailed appendices of statistical data and calculations support the argument of the main text.

Inevitably the question must be asked: 'What chance of adoption,

[1] *The Case for Capital Taxes*, Fabian Tract 388, December 1968.

in whole or in part, has this radical scheme of reform?' The nub is the change in form of death duty from estate duty to inheritance tax. This idea is not new, and its advocates have included economists no less distinguished than Professor Lord Robbins[1] and Professor James E. Meade.[2] Of the political parties, although it was a Liberal Chancellor who introduced estate duty, paradoxically the Liberals have been the first officially to support the change. By 1938, if not before, in *Ownership for All*, they advocated an inheritance tax instead of estate duty, and they have re-affirmed this preference in subsequent election manifestos. As for a wealth tax, the party has shown interest but shunned commitment. The Labour Party, perhaps surprisingly in view of its declared concern for equality, has never endorsed the proposal for an inheritance tax; but it may do so yet, for the most eminent of its recent tax advisers, Professor Nicholas Kaldor, has stated a clear preference for it.[3] By contrast a wealth tax has had frequent mention in recent Labour Party and TUC discussions and literature, but a wealth tax which would have to be met from capital—not the alternative to surtax and the unearned income differential that we have advocated here. Despite the talk, the Party has given no undertaking to introduce a wealth tax in any of its election manifestos of the sixties. Again, however, the ubiquitous Professor Kaldor can be found to have advocated a modest wealth tax as an alternative to the higher rate of tax on income from property.[4] Experience suggests that the Labour Party is more extreme in words than in deed, so that this more modest form of wealth tax might yet come to fruition under them.

What of the Tories? In a party with a respect for tradition it may count for much that some of the most distinguished Conservatives of all time—Lord Randolph Churchill, A. J. Balfour, Sir Winston Churchill—have favoured the inheritance tax. The change ought to be approved to promote the Conservative ideal of a 'property owning democracy'; as indeed might a negative wealth tax, by which some of the income benefits of the welfare state would be replaced by lump sum benefits leaving responsibilities and initiative in the hands of individuals. For a wealth tax the Tories have shown no enthusiasm. But perhaps this is because their image of it has been that tauntingly dangled before them by the Labour Party. They need to be reminded that West Germany as well as Social Democratic Sweden has an

1 'Notes on Public Finance', *Lloyds Bank Review*, October 1955.

2 *Efficiency, Equality and the Ownership of Property*, Allen & Unwin, 1964.

3 'The Reform of Personal Taxation,' *Essays in Economic Policy*, vol. I, Duckworth, 1964, p. 213.

4 *Ibid.*, p. 213.

annual wealth tax. Indeed, such a tax as we have advocated is precisely in line with the declared Conservative objective of reforming the tax system to reduce the disincentive effects of high income tax and so increase individual effort and enterprise. The Tories have thought to achieve this aim partly by cuts in government expenditure allowing tax reduction and partly by a transfer from income to indirect taxes. Yet cuts in government expenditure are difficult to make; and, besides its likely regressive consequences, the price rises from a switch to indirect taxes are particularly unwelcome in a situation of cost inflation; the more so when entry to EEC brings the prospect of further large price increases. In these circumstances, is it fanciful to believe that the Tories may be led to see the merits of a modest annual wealth tax to ease the burden of income tax? And its adoption would bring a Disraelian bonus—the delight of 'Dishing the Whigs'. Who knows?

Part I

THE TAXATION OF WEALTH

Chapter 1

Why Tax Wealth?

DEFINITIONS AND SCOPE

What do we mean by a wealth tax? A learned judge in a famous judgment once defined an income tax as a tax on income; similarly a wealth tax is a tax on wealth; more usefully, it is a tax levied on the capital value of wealth which may or may not be paid out of wealth, i.e. it may be met from a person's accumulated saving or from his income.

But what is wealth? It is used in this volume to mean the whole generality of net assets, i.e. assets minus liabilities. Our definition thus excludes property taxes of a kind levied on gross value or/and on one kind of property only (for example, real property). True, some kinds of assets may be excluded from the scope of any particular wealth tax—but they figure as specific exemptions to a tax which is intended to be general in its application.

Our concern is with personal wealth taxes, i.e. taxes levied on the value of the net assets of individuals not corporate bodies. A few of the annual wealth taxes in existence are levied both on corporations and on individuals, but this is a form of double taxation usually condemned because the same assets are taxed both in the hands of corporations as real capital and in the hands of individuals as share values. Also capital gains tax may be paid on gains in the assets of corporations. But we shall not here be analysing wealth taxes on corporate bodies. The dividing line in practice is not entirely clear cut. It is in accordance with the principle of a personal wealth tax to supplement an annual levy on the net wealth of persons with a tax on undivided estates, and on the corporate assets held by foreigners in a country. In neither of these cases does the levy of a wealth tax other than on persons result in double taxation.

The term capital could be substituted for wealth in our usage. There is perhaps a marginal preference for wealth because wealth is more often thought of as a store to be drawn on for future consumption and is associated more with persons, whereas capital is more often regarded as a stock for future production and is associated more readily with corporations. But both are different ways of looking at what are essentially the same assets. Another reason for preferring 'wealth' is that most of the recent discussion in the United Kingdom about this form of taxation has tended to use wealth rather than capital and it is convenient to keep to current usage unless there is a good reason to overthrow it. But essentially in this volume we use wealth and capital synonymously.

By taxes on personal wealth we mean, then, taxes which are levied on the capital value of personal net assets of all kinds; unless specifically exempted, the assets subject to tax thus include stocks and shares, quoted and unquoted; the business assets of partnerships and unincorporated businesses; bank balances; real property including houses and the capital value of rights in property; personal chattels such as cars, furniture, works of art, boats, horses, jewellery. It is normal for the state to specify some minimum sum below which wealth tax is not levied.

Forms of Wealth Tax

Forms of tax sometimes referred to as wealth or capital taxes are annual net wealth tax (which Britain does not have but which has been the subject of much recent discussion); death duties (currently taking the form of estate duty in the UK); gift taxes; capital gains taxes; stamp duties and capital levies.

The first three meet our definition without question. Capital gains taxes are more borderline; we shall examine in chapter 7 whether capital gains taxes should not properly be considered as taxes on income. In the United Kingdom short-term gains are treated as income for tax purposes, while long-term gains are taxed on a separate basis; however regarded, long-term gains taxes are so bound up with the other wealth taxes—death duties, annual wealth tax, gift tax—that no attempt to consider the structure of wealth taxation in a country could be complete without an examination of them. We shall therefore briefly examine gains taxes; particularly the tax on long-term gains. Stamp duties are different; in the United Kingdom those relating to capital consist of a motley variety of duties levied on the gross value of various properties at the time of transfer. In many ways they are more akin to taxes on outlay than on capital. They are not an essential part of the fabric of the system of capital taxation of a country and we do not consider them here. Capital levies have more claim to inclusion. The genuine *capital* levy (as distinct from the pseudo levy on investment income like the 'special charge' in the 1968 UK budget) meets our definition: it is intended as a once and for all levy on the value of the whole generality of net assets. After the First World War, serious consideration in Britain and elsewhere was given to the idea of a capital levy, especially as a means of reducing the national debt. But a levy has lost most of whatever attraction it had for this purpose. High rates of income tax have much reduced the extent to which a levy would relieve debt charges as there would be such a loss of income tax from interest on the debt; meanwhile the burden of debt interest has in turn been reduced by inflation. A major levy with the uncertainties it would cause, the depressing effect on asset prices, and the immense problems of a valuation which would have to be carrried out with great rapidity if changing asset values were not to cause gross inequities, is not now being advocated in the UK by any major interest. This is one reason for omitting it; another is that we *do* consider an annual wealth tax of such a size that it must necessarily be paid from capital; and, although in a milder form, the considerations which apply to such a heavy annual wealth tax are almost precisely similar to those applying to a once and for all levy.

Thus, in this volume we are concerned with death duties, annual wealth taxes, gift taxes and taxes on long-term capital gains.

We first examine and analyse most fully, death duties. This prior and most detailed treatment of the death duty is justified both because our particular concern is the capital tax system of the United Kingdom and as there has been a continuous history of death duties in the UK since 1694 there is much material to consider; and because death duties are likely to continue to form the core of any new structure of wealth taxation. Despite difficulties and disadvantages death duties have singular merits as a form of wealth tax. Payment is easier because they are levied at a time of transfer of wealth. The taxation of inherited wealth has a special moral attraction as compared with the taxation of wealth which is a result of the taxpayer's personal accumulation. Death duties are probably more readily acceptable to taxpayers and less damaging to incentives than an annual wealth tax of equivalent yield. The problems of administration associated with wealth taxes are minimized because death duties are levied at a time when an inventory of the property is required anyway for other purposes than taxation and only a proportion of wealth falls liable for death duty in any one year;[1] thus the problem of valuation is reduced to manageable proportions.

[1] In 1967–8 in GB £1,739m. net capital value of estates passed through the hands of the Estate Duty Office of which £1,376m. consisted of estates over £5,000 (then the lower limit for tax); the estimated net total wealth for GB 1967 was £83,600m. of which £59,400m. was in estates over £5,000. (Tables 130 and 139, *Report of the Commissioners of Inland Revenue*, No. 111 (Cmnd 3879, Jan. 1969).

Some clarification on the terminology of death taxation is necessary. We use the term 'death taxes' or 'death duties' to apply to any taxes levied on the transfer of properties as result of a death. An 'estate duty' is a form of death duty levied on the total property left by the deceased regardless of its distribution amongst heirs. The term 'inheritance tax' is used in its strict rather than its general sense to mean a tax on what is inherited, i.e. a tax on what the beneficiaries receive, regardless of the size of the estate from which it comes. A 'legacy duty' and a 'succession duty' are generally used synonymously and are inheritance taxes; but when we consider the British legacy duty (1780–1949) and succession duty (1853–1949) we have to distinguish between them because, broadly speaking, the legacy duty applied only to personal property and the succession duty to real property.

Along with death duties we consider gift taxes. A *form* of gift tax grew up with death duties in this country and first appeared in 1881, under the name of account duty, as an adjunct to the death duties, applying initially to gifts made within three months of death. At the time of writing, since the 1968 budget, gifts made within seven years of death are taxed as part of the estate duty provisions. There has also been another element of gift taxation in the UK since the introduction of the long-term capital gains tax in 1965 by which gifts counted as 'realization'. Thus, the capital gains element, if any, in gifts is now taxed. Because of the way the so-called gifts inter vivos provisions have been linked historically with death duties in the UK, and because we shall argue that no reform of death duties would make sense without a comprehensive gift tax, we shall examine gift taxes mainly in chapter 4 when we consider the possibilities of death duty reform.

From death duties and gift taxation we turn to consider the annual wealth tax. To try to give realism to our study we look not only at the theoretical considerations for and against an annual wealth tax, but also at the tax in practice, examining closely the Swedish wealth tax, the example most often quoted by advocates of a wealth tax in the UK.

In our penultimate chapter, we consider in somewhat less detail the capital gains tax. The brief history of this tax in the UK gives us little experience on which to draw in this country and features of gains taxes elsewhere will be considered.

In the earlier chapters we suggest ways in which death duties might be reformed, consider the desirability of an annual wealth tax and how it might be introduced, and suggest modifications to the capital gains tax. In the final chapter, we examine the wealth taxes together and present a more radical scheme for reform which not only requires the integration of wealth taxes but develops the idea of a negative wealth tax. Taxation is a branch of political economy in which practical suggestions almost inevitably involve value judgments. Proposals to improve the individual wealth taxes may be accepted by some who may find the more radical proposals of the final chapter too much to swallow or who may consider them, though desirable, too difficult to implement. Hence, the dual approach to the issue of reform.

PURPOSES OF WEALTH TAXATION

Equity, Efficiency and Equality

Why tax wealth at all? Is it not sufficient for a State to confine its taxation to income (including corporate profits) and expenditure?

There are three main arguments for taxing wealth and one subsidiary argument. The latter is that of administrative efficiency; a wealth tax, by providing information on capital values, can act as a cross-check to the accuracy of the returns of that part of income derived from property and even as a check on income from all sources (e.g. is the taxpayer's income enough to have enabled him to have increased his assets as much as he has since the previous assessment?). It thus supports the income tax and helps to protect it from evasion.

The main arguments can be summed up under equity, efficiency and equality. By equity we mean what the tax economist generally refers to more precisely as 'horizontal' equity—the equal treatment of those of similar taxable capacity. Under efficiency we are concerned with the effectiveness with which resources are used—in particular minimizing the price distortion of taxation. Under 'equality' we consider the question of 'vertical' equity—how *differently* should people of different taxable capacity be taxed. At this point we shall consider the first two only briefly because subsequently we analyse their application in detail to the various kinds of wealth tax.

The equity argument is that we need a wealth tax to supplement income tax. Wealth yields benefits over and above the income derived from it. It gives its possessor security, a source of spending power to meet contingencies, or the opportunity for a spending spree. It provides additional economic opportunities to its possessor. In short, whether or not the wealth yields a money income, it confers upon its possessor an additional 'taxable capacity' which equity requires to be taken into account.

The second argument is that of efficiency in resource use. Briefly a wealth tax is likely to result in less disincentive effect than an income tax of equivalent yield because the tax base is related to past and not present effort. At the same time, to tax wealth irrespective of its yield (especially when the alternative to wealth tax is a higher income tax) may provide a stimulus to use capital as productively as possible.

Equality is here used as a convenient shorthand for a reduction of inequality. Perhaps the main argument for taxing wealth is to reduce inequalities in its distribution. These inequalities may arise from different rates of saving out of earned income. But, especially when rates of income tax are high, the biggest reason for inequality of wealth holding is differences in inherited wealth. Many of the inequalities in the distribution of wealth, perpetuated by inheritance, stretch far back into history, some with their origin in acquisition by conquest—which would not nowadays be thought to constitute a morally strong claim!

The argument for reducing inequalities in wealth distribution is moral rather than economic. It thus rests on a value judgment which not all would accept. Nevertheless, in principle, this purpose was accepted with Sir William Harcourt's estate duty in 1894, which was the first consistently progressive tax in the United Kingdom; and though not all Conservatives at that time agreed with the principle of progression, or graduation as they more generally called it then, all the main political parties today would accept that taxation should be used to diminish the inequalities of wealth and income in the community, though they differ in how far the process should be pushed and what form the redistribution should take.

There is no clear-cut theoretical formula to determine how far the process of evening out the distribution of wealth by taxation or other means should proceed. This is a matter of moral judgment and political and economic expediency. What is not open to doubt is the high degree of inequality in the distribution of wealth in the UK today. There is a long way to go before we need concern ourselves greatly about where the process of diminishing inequality should stop. But let us look at the evidence.

Distribution of Wealth in Great Britain

Official statistics on the distribution of personal wealth in Great Britain are published annually in the Reports of the Commissioners for Inland Revenue. Table 1.1, which provides an estimate for 1967, is derived from Table 139 in the 111th Report published in January 1969.

The method by which the estimate is compiled is important for assessing the validity of the statistics. The basic principle is that the sample of estates passing through the hands of the Inland Revenue in any one year because of possible liability to estate duty, is an accurate representation of all estates of each age–sex group. To obtain the number of estates and the total property in each property range possessed by each age–sex group in the *whole* population, the *sample* of estates and total property for each group and range is multiplied by the reciprocal of the mortality rates for that age–sex group. Supposing, for example, that in the year in question five estates in the range £100,000 to £200,000 totalling £800,000 owned by women aged 85 to 86 became liable to death duty. If the mortality rates for that year for women 85 to 86 were two hundred per thousand (one in five) then it is assumed that there were twenty-five (five by five) estates in the population as a whole amongst women 85 to 86 of a size £100,000 to £200,000 and that these estates together totalled four million pounds (£800,000 × 5). These calculations are carried out for each age–sex group and then the number of estates and aggregate size of the estates are totalled for each property range. Because mortality rates differ according to occupation, to try to increase the accuracy of the calculation the rates appropriate to managerial and professional classes (Registrar-General's social classes I and II) are used in the calculations for estates over £3,000 and rates midway between them and those for the population as a whole for estates under £3,000.

There are a number of difficulties and deficiences in this method of estimation. The figures do not cover the whole population; the Inland Revenue figures are derived from 'grants of representation' taken out as a result of a death and in more than half the deaths in 1967 no grant was taken out because the assets were small and of a kind which could be transferred without a grant. Some forms of property holding are omitted from the statistics, in particular settled property passing at the death of a surviving spouse and property held under discretionary trust. The method also is liable to give rise to sampling errors; for example, the total number of large estates is small and those large estates falling liable to death duty in any one year may not be representative; in particular, large estates possessed by those dying young may be unrepresentative for their age and sex group (for which the mortality rates are low and the reciprocals therefore high). There is a valuation discrepancy in that life insurance policies on the life of the deceased are valued for estate duty at the sum assured plus bonus, if any; but the grossing up of this valuation to obtain the wealth holdings of the population as a whole over-values the insurance policies of the living who would not be able to cash their insurance policies at as high a sum.[1]

The overall effect of the deficiencies is almost certainly that the figures under-estimate the degree of the inequality of wealth. Although the omission of the small amounts of wealth exaggerates

TABLE 1.1. *Estimated Total Net Wealth by Size of Holding in GB in 1967*

Numbers: thousands. Amounts: £ thousand million.

Range of Net Wealth		Wealth-holders		Wealth	
Over	Not Over	No.	%	Amount	%
—	1,000	5,398	31·2	2·8	3·4
1,000	3,000	5,273	30·5	9·8	11·7
3,000	5,000	2,966	17·1	11·6	13·9
—	5,000	13,637	78·8	24·2	28·9
5,000	10,000	2,177	12·6	15·3	18·3
10,000	15,000	620	3·6	7·6	9·1
15,000	20,000	270	1·6	4·8	5·7
20,000	25,000	157	0·9	3·4	4·1
25,000	50,000	279	1·6	9·9	11·8
50,000	100,000	109	0·6	7·5	9·0
100,000	200,000	37	0·2	5·1	6·1
Over 200,000		14	0·1	5·8	6·9
Over 5,000		3,663	21·2	59·4	71·1
Over 1,000		11,902	68·8	80·8	96·7
TOTAL		17,300	100·0	83·6	100·0

the degree of inequality in the figures, this is likely to be more than counter-balanced by discrepancies working in the opposite direction. Insurance policies are a much larger proportion of small than of large estates so that their over-valuation creates an appearance of

[1] These are not the only deficiencies; a fuller account of the statistical limitations is given in the *Report of the Commissioners of Inland Revenue*, No. 111, pp. 211–13. A number of the issues, including the validity of the mortality multipliers used by the Inland Revenue and some estimates of the size of the omitted items of property, are considered in J. Revell, *The Wealth of the Nation*, Cambridge University Press, 1967.

less inequality. Discretionary trusts in 1967 were one of the recognised means of estate duty avoidance and settled property is much more likely to occur in large than in small estates. Unofficial estimates of the distribution of wealth by J. Revell[1] and *The Economist*[2] paint a picture of a more unequal distribution of wealth than that of the Inland Revenue statistics.

TABLE 1.2. *Distribution of Personal Wealth in GB, 1967*

Cumulative ranges of net wealth £	Wealth Cumulative %	Wealth holders Cumulative %	Total Population Cumulative %
Over 200,000	6·9	0·1	0·03
,, 100,000	13·0	0·3	0·1
,, 50,000	22·0	0·9	0·3
,, 25,000	33·8	2·5	0·8
,, 20,000	38·7	3·4	1·1
,, 15,000	43·5	5·0	1·6
,, 10,000	52·7	8·6	2·8
,, 5,000	70·9	21·2	8·9
,, 3,000	84·8	38·3	14·4
,, 1,000	96·6	68·8	24·3
,, 0	100·0	100·0	100·0

Bearing this probable under-estimation of inequality in mind, let us examine the Inland Revenue statistics more closely. In table 1·2 we present the same information as in table 1·1 but in a form easier to assimilate. By reading horizontally across the table we can see what proportion of wealth is possessed by what proportion of wealth holders and what proportion of the total population. Thus, in round terms, over 20 per cent of the wealth is possessed by less than 1 per cent of the wealth holders and by 0·3 per cent of the population. Again, over half the wealth is possessed by 8 per cent of the wealth holders and under 3 per cent of the population. At the other extreme over 90 per cent of the population and almost 80 per cent of the wealth holders possess less than 30 per cent of the wealth; and 75 per cent of the population less than £1,000.

In interpreting figures of wealth concentration, we need to bear certain factors in mind. Thirty-eight per cent of the population in

[1] For example, J. Revell, *Changes in the Social Distribution of Property in Britain during the Twentieth Century*, a paper presented at the Third International Economic History Conference, Munich, 1965.

[2] 'Taxing Britain's Wealth: the Indefensible Status Quo', *The Economist*, January 15, 1966.

1967 were under the age 35 and little wealth holding would be expected from that age group. Even if inheritance were completely abolished and there were no big inequalities in income distribution we should expect quite substantial wealth inequalities in a community; wealth ownership is generally positively correlated with age because older people have had longer in which to accumulate. To put the same point in a different way, many of those who at one point of time rank as negligible wealth holders will, at a subsequent point (say, 20 years later) have become quite substantial wealth holders. Nevertheless, even when allowances have been made for these factors, the ultimate picture of wealth distribution in the United Kingdom remains one of marked inequality. The distribution of wealth is, indeed, more unequal than in the USA. The authors of a comparative study of income and wealth distribution in the two countries in the mid-1950's concluded: 'When we turn from a comparison of income distributions to a comparison of the distribution of capital, it is the British distribution which is more unequal than the American—and quite substantially so. More Americans directly own physical assets, such as their own homes, businesses, farms or other real estate. Even within the group of financial assets, the distribution is more unequal in Britain than in America.[1]

Some reduction in inequality of wealth distribution does appear to have taken place in the twentieth century. Estimates by Mr Revell[2] suggest that the proportion of personal wealth in England and Wales possessed by the top one per cent of the population over 25 fell from 69 per cent in 1911–13 to 42 per cent in 1960; that of the top 5 per cent fell from 87 per cent to 75 per cent over the same period. Mr Revell suggests four reasons for this trend. The growth of a salaried middle class which has been accompanied by a growing owner-occupation of dwellings and saving through insurance. Second, changes in land and other real property prices which fell during the twenties, lessening the concentration of wealth; but which, rising in recent years, have also paradoxically lessened concentration because of increased home ownership and because of the growing owner-occupancy in agriculture. Third, demographic factors, notably a tendency for the redistribution of wealth within the family to its younger members probably as a form of death duty avoidance by gifts inter vivos; and also an increase in the proportion of wealth held by women—probably because of inheritance from their hus-

[1] Harold Lydall and John B. Lansing, 'A Comparison of the Distribution of Personal Income and Wealth in the United States and Great Britain', *American Economic Review*, March 1959.

[2] *Ibid.*, table 6, p. 15.

bands resulting from increased female longevity. Finally, the fourth factor, the effect of estate duty.

Estate duty has had important indirect effects through its influence on the distribution of income; but its direct effects have been less than might have been expected in view of the very high rates which have applied for more than a generation in the United Kingdom. Wealth generates wealth because large wealth owners obtain a much higher return on their wealth than small wealth holders; a larger proportion of large wealth holdings is in the form of income-yielding investments and also large wealth holders can afford the best advice on where to invest, either for high yield or capital gains; thus it is not too difficult for estate reductions resulting from estate duty to be made good in a generation. Further, estate duty is widely avoided. Again, as we shall subsequently argue at length, the estate duty form of death duty is not that most appropriate for diminishing inequalities in the distribution of wealth.

THE PROBLEMS OF WEALTH TAXATION

If wealth taxes carry the merits we have outlined, promoting equity, efficiency and equality, they also pose problems. These are mainly two-fold. First, a possible detrimental effect on saving, affecting both the capacity of individuals to save and their incentive to do so. Second, the administrative effects of wealth taxes, most notably the problems raised by valuation; whilst valuation of some assets, such as quoted stocks and shares, raise no difficulties, valuing other assets except at a time of sale is difficult and costly, e.g. the valuation of real property, unquoted shares, the assets of unincorporated businesses, and personal chattels such as jewellery and paintings.

Both these problems are severe. There is some level of wealth taxation which, through its effects on private saving, would be incompatible with an expanding economy based in important part on private ownership of the means of production. The administrative problems are such that a wealth tax can never be a simple tax to administer nor one which can be entirely free from inequities. We shall examine these problems in subsequent chapters as we look in detail at the various forms of wealth tax.

A Comprehensive System of Wealth Taxation

The merits and problems apply to all wealth taxes but in different measure depending on the form and weight of the particular wealth tax. Thus, the equity argument applies most strongly to an annual wealth tax and the capital gains tax. If we wish to tax inherited wealth more heavily than wealth accumulated from personal effort, then death duties are the most important medium for satisfying this particular argument for equality. Similarly, both an annual wealth tax and a death duty may affect the willingness to save, but whilst the former might reduce private savings under-taken for a variety of motives, a death duty will only affect savings undertaken from a desire to bequeath. The administrative problems likewise apply to all wealth taxes but vary in severity according to the size, nature and frequency of the tax; a small annual wealth tax on large fortunes is easier to administer than a large annual tax with a low exemption limit and both are more difficult than a death duty which necessarily only affects a small proportion of wealth each year.

Because of this similarity of purposes and problems but with important differences arising from the nature of the particular kind of wealth tax, such taxes need to be reviewed together, to be considered as a coherent system. Because of the link between wealth and income, both because a wealth tax is a supplement to income tax and because it may be an alternative to a differentially high rate of tax on investment income, wealth taxes need to be viewed in the context of the tax system as a whole. Our final chapter is concerned particularly with this comprehensive approach to a system of wealth taxation.

Part II

DEATH DUTIES

Chapter 2

History of Death Duties in the United Kingdom

(i) INTRODUCTION

A study of the history of the death duties fulfils two main purposes. First it helps to explain the present. For example, in re-assessing the current estate duty, it is useful to know why estate duty became the dominant and ultimately the sole form of death duty in the United Kingdom. Second, the history of death duties throws light on the contemporary scene—its social theories and customs, its economic and political conflicts and development, its fiscal and administrative limitations and necessities.

The reader who is not interested in fiscal history for its own sake can skip sections (ii) and (v) of this chapter, but is advised to read section (iii), the debate on the reform of 1894 (which contains much of relevance to current proposals for estate duty reform) and the latter part of section (iv) (covering the weight of death taxation, estate duty concessions and avoidance) which must be appreciated for an understanding of the following chapters on the incidence and reform of estate duty. The student of fiscal history will, it is hoped, also find the remainder of the chapter worth while, though in parts (especially section (ii)), by its very nature, it is somewhat heavy going.

The history divides itself clearly into three, with the reform of 1894 deserving a section to itself as the watershed separating the early death duties from the modern. The chapter concludes with an attempt to draw from the earlier detail some historically significant generalizations.

(ii) THE OLD DEATH DUTIES, 1694–1894

Probate and Administration Duty

In the two centuries before Sir William Harcourt introduced the estate duty essentially in its modern form, a patchwork of death duties grew up in the United Kingdom, in 'a series of successive expedients'[1] becoming ever more cumbersome, complex and anom-

[1] Winston S. Churchill, *Lord Randolph Churchill*, Macmillan, 1906, vol. 2, p. 193.

alous. The first, the probate and administration duty (usually referred to as the probate duty) was copied from the Dutch and followed in the train of William of Orange. Stamp duties were relatively easy to administer and initially the probate duty of June 1694 was one of a series of stamp duties imposed to meet the financial strain of the French wars. The probate duty was imposed as a flat rate tax of 5s, increased to 10s in 1698, payable on estates in England and Wales[1] over £20; the stamp had to be fixed before the will could be 'proved' or letters of administration granted (for intestate estates). The tax applied only to personalty for there was no need for realty to be proved. The 10s rate remained for over 80 years; no figures are available of the yield of probate duty over this period for the returns were not separated from the general stamp duties until 1805.

Legacy duty

In 1779 Lord North introduced three rates of probate duty according to the value of the estate, the maximum being £2 10s on property of £300 and upwards. The following year, seeking new taxes to meet the cost of the American war, North introduced a further death duty, a legacy duty, which also may have been copied from the Dutch for North is believed to have derived the idea from Adam Smith's account of the succession duties in the Netherlands.[2] The legacy duty was also introduced as a stamp duty, on lines similar to the probate duty; stamps were to be affixed to receipts for legacies or shares in the personal property of the deceased. The amount of duty also depended on a threefold classification of property by value, the maximum rate being £1 on £100 or upwards. The legacy duty did not apply to realty nor to property passing under settlement. The rate of duty was increased in 1783 and again in 1789, but the tax was ill-conceived, for the stamp was to be affixed to a receipt which it was not legally necessary to give or to demand. Hence not until Pitt recast the tax in 1796 did its yield become significant.

Pitt's modifications marked a new departure of principle. Although it remained a stamp duty in form, in reality Pitt converted the legacy duty from little more than a nominal levy into a proportional inheritance tax graduated according to consanguinity. At first

1 The probate duty was applied to Ireland by an act of the Irish parliament in 1774, but the rates remained lower than in England until 1824 when they were brought into line. Attempts to apply the duty to Scotland were of doubtful success, because of evasion, until Spencer Percival's Stamp Act of 1808. By this Act an inventory of the property had to be stamped before the executors or administrators could have their authority confirmed: hence in Scotland the duty became known as an 'inventory' duty.

2 *Wealth of Nations*, Book 5, Chapter 2, part 2, appendix to articles 1 and 2.

descendants in the direct line were exempt, but they were brought within the tax net in 1805 and legacy duty then applied at the rate of 1 per cent on legacies to children and their descendants rising to 10 per cent on legacies received by people outside the family. The year of Waterloo saw a further increase in rates and the application of the tax to parents of the deceased, widows remaining the only untaxed successors. To secure effectiveness the 1796 tax made the executor or administrator liable for payment. In the years after 1796 the yield of the tax increased rapidly and in 1822 the gross receipts from legacy duty in the UK exceeded £1 million. At the same time the probate duty was annually yielding £700,000–£800,000 and the two death duties together contributed just over 3 per cent of the public income.

TABLE 2.1. *Increases and Extensions in the Legacy Duty, during the Revolutionary and Napoleonic Wars*

	Percentage rate of duty			
Where a legacy shall be £20 or more	1796 1804	1804 1805	1805 1815	1815
1. To father, mother, or any lineal ancestor	—	—	—	1
2. To children and descendants	—	—	1	1
3. To brother or sister or descendants	2	2½	2½	3
4. To uncles and aunts or descendants	3	4	4	5
5. To great uncles and great aunts or descendants	4	5	5	6
6. To any other collateral relative or strangers in blood	6	8	10	10

The scales of probate duty were increased no less than six times 1783–1815, the last of these additions, by Lord Vansittart, introducing a distinction between the rate chargeable on probate and that on letters of administration so that estates of intestates bore a 50 per cent higher rate than those of testators. Before the 1783 increase the maximum rate of probate duty had been £6 10s 0d; in 1815 the maximum tax (for the estate of an intestate) was £22,500. In 1859 a proportional rate of tax was imposed for every £100,000 of property by which an estate exceeded £1,000,000, which had borne the maximum levy in 1815. The first concession in the tax came five years later when the exemption limit for the probate duty was raised from £20 to £100.

Succession Duty

When Pitt had submitted the recast legacy duty to the House of

Commons in 1796, he had attempted at the same time to impose a parallel succession duty taxing successions to real property. He secured its passage through the House, but only by means of the casting vote of the Speaker. In view of the intensity of the opposition he decided that the wise course was to withdraw the bill and real property remained untaxed at death until 1853 when Gladstone secured the enactment of a succession duty. Gladstone's duty was calculated on the value of the succession and was leviable on all kinds of property other than those covered by the legacy duty, with the exception that leaseholds, technically personalty and previously taxed as legacies, were in future to be ranged with and taxed as land. The value of the succession was taken to be the capitalized value of an annuity equal to the net annual value of the property, for the life of the heir, or for any less period during which he might be entitled to enjoy it. Thus although the rates of duties on legacies and successions were nominally the same, in fact the burdens differed considerably. Furthermore, duties on real property could be paid by means of eight half-yearly instalments if the owners desired.

The background of the succession duty is of interest to the fiscal historian. The introduction of the succession duty was in part an attempt to bring about a result similar to that required by the principle of income tax differentiation according to source; the favoured treatment of realty in valuation and method of payment was justified by reference to the problems of local government finance. In 1851 a Committee of the House of Commons had been appointed to investigate the short-comings and inequalities of the income tax. Although the committee failed to return a unanimous decision,[1] a strong body of opinion was advanced in favour of income tax differentiation according to source: it seemed unjust that a 'temporary' income such as that derived from the professions, dependent on the health and ability to work of the individual concerned, should pay the same rate of tax as income from a 'permanent' source such as that from the ownership of land. From the former (earned) income, allowance would have to be put aside for sickness and old age. Gladstone sympathized with the principle of this argument but was unwilling to tamper with the basis of the tax. He regarded the income tax as a temporary form of revenue; in his budget speech of 1853 he presented a scheme of finance for the next seven years which would culminate in the abolition of the income tax in 1860, if all went well. He feared that any alteration of the framework of the income tax would weaken it in an emergency—

[1] B. E. V. Sabine, *A History of Income Tax*, George Allen & Unwin, 1966, pp. 67–71.

which he considered the proper occasion on which to use it.[1] Thus he attempted to remedy the iniquity by resort to other means. Personalty was already taxed at death but not realty. The taxation of realty by the new succession duty was an attempt in a rough and ready sort of way to achieve the same ultimate effect as would have been attained by income tax differentiation according to source. But Gladstone was impressed by the argument that real property bore all the burdens of local taxation, and therefore he did not wish to make the additional tax too onerous—hence valuation on the life interest only.

The yield from the succession duty (at £600,000) proved much lower than the Inland Revenue had estimated (£2,000,000) which in turn had been lower than the estimates of many members in the Commons debate. Reasons for this over-estimation of yield, subsequently suggested by the Inland Revenue officers, were an over-estimation of the amount of settled property, insufficient allowance for the charges and encumbrances of real estate and the fact that successions to land were generally more 'direct' than legacies and hence subject to the lowest rate of duty. The over-estimation by members of the Opposition may have been deliberate tactics.[2]

For nearly thirty years after the introduction of the succession duty no major alterations were made in the system or rates of death taxation. Between 1858 (when, allowing for payment by instalments, the succession duty might be regarded as fully operative) and 1880 (when the next increase in rates took place) price fluctuations tended to cancel out. Death duties were roughly proportional so that no changes in the distribution of property would much affect their yield. Thus the growth in yield over this period is a fair indication of the growth of national wealth.[3] In fact the yield of both probate duty on the one hand and legacy and succession duties on the other

[1] 'I believe it to be of vital importance, whether you keep this tax or whether you part with it, that you should either keep it or should leave it, in a state in which it will be fit for service in an emergency; and this it will be impossible to do, if you break up the basis of your income tax.' Gladstone, *Financial Statements*, p. 47.

[2] See J. F. Rees, *A Short Fiscal and Financial History of England*, Methuen, 1921, p. 118.

[3] As the increase in yield is of similar magnitude for both probate duty and the legacy and succession duties there can be little question of variations in custom in the disposal of property (e.g. by a larger proportion passing to strangers or distant relatives who paid the higher rates of duty) affecting the yield appreciably. Indeed as life expectations were rising, and as payment in instalments would always cause revenue from the succession duties to lag slightly in an upward trend, the growth in national wealth is likely to have been more than proportional to the rise in revenue.

just about doubled. In 1858 they produced just over £3 million, in 1880 over £6 million. Over the same period the proportion of total revenue contributed by death duties rose from under 5 per cent to approximately 9 per cent, total Exchequer receipts varying between about £65 million and £80 million, with a decidely upward trend in the latter half of the period.

If the thirty years preceding 1880 was a period of little alteration in the death duties, the fifteen years succeeding were full of modifications and extensions. In 1880 Sir Stafford Northcote abolished the distinction in rates between testate and intestate property which had existed in the probate and administration duty since 1815. At the same time he increased the rates of duty on the larger estates. In the following year Gladstone swept away the lengthy schedule of probate charges and substituted for it a proportional tax of 3 per cent on all estates over £1,000 with those between £500 and £1,000 paying 2½ per cent and estates between £100 and £500 paying 2 per cent. This represented a rather higher average rate on all property subject to the probate duty than before, but no great increase in total revenue from death duties was anticipated because at the same time an exemption from legacy and succession duties caused a corresponding loss of revenue; all personal property, including leaseholds passing under wills and administrations, which would previously have been liable to a one per cent legacy or succession duty, was wholly exempted. This considerably simplified the administration of the death duties. About half the property subject to legacy duty had previously paid at the one per cent rate after already having paid probate duty by a separate transaction. The payment of one duty meant a relief to executors in time, trouble and legal expenses. At the same time an allowance for debts was introduced into the probate duty, so that the levy was calculated on the 'net' property: previously the charge had been determined by the gross value of an estate and a repayment on account of debts had been obtainable only after submission of a claim. For small estates the 1881 act made additional facilities available: estates under £300 gross value could satisfy all claims for probate and legacy duty by payment of fifteen shillings for probate court fees and thirty shillings for stamp duty.

Account Duty

The Act of 1881 also included provisions designed to protect the revenue from probate duty, and subsequently known as account duty: stamp duty at the same rate as probate duty was to be paid on gifts made less than three months prior to death, a period extended to twelve months in 1889. The number of 'accounts' subject to this duty was never large, but the duty was preventive and anticipates the gifts inter vivos provisions of the estate duty of 1894.

Local Taxation Accounts

In 1888 a peculiar arrangement affecting the revenue from death duties was introduced under the Local Government Act and the Probate Duties Act. A proportion of the yield of the probate and account duty of the UK (one-third for the first year and thereafter one-half) was to be transferred to Local Taxation Accounts created for the purpose at the Bank of England; the sum thus allocated was to be divided between the three parts of the Kingdom—England (with Wales), Scotland and Ireland—in agreed proportions, (80, 11 and 9 per cent respectively) in lieu of certain funds previously voted annually by parliament in aid of local government expenditure. Partly its purpose was to provide local authorities, at a time of rising local expenditure, with a growing income in a manner less threatening to their autonomy than grants, but without increasing the range of local taxes; but it was also a clumsy device to share the burdens of local taxation between the owners of personal and real property instead of leaving them wholly to the latter. When the probate duty was superseded by the estate duty of 1894, which applied equally to personal and real property, the same intention was continued with even less justification and more complication, by allocating a proportion of the net receipts from estate duty levied on personalty to the Local Taxation Accounts. From 1890 the receipts of certain excise licences and duties were also earmarked for the Local Taxation Accounts, and a further contribution from the estate duty on personalty was levied in aid of the rates on agricultural land in England and Scotland, 1896. From 1888 to 1907 the payments to Local Taxation Accounts were made directly, without passing through the Exchequer at all: but the Finance Act of 1907 ended this practice —described by Asquith in his budget speech of 1907 as a 'head-splitting condition of chaos and confusion'[1]—by providing that this revenue was in future first to be paid into the Exchequer, which would then make the payments to the Local Taxation Accounts out of the Consolidated Fund. The provisions for the payment of revenue from excise duties and licences to the Local Taxation Accounts were altered by the 1907 Act, but the proportional contribution from the death duties remained substantially the same until, under the provisions of the Local Government Act of 1929, contributions to the Local Taxation Accounts ceased altogether after March 31, 1930.

[1] Quoted in Sir B. Mallet, *British Budgets* 1887–1913, *Macmillan*, 1913, p. 271.

Along with the new system of 1888 for allocating revenue between the local and central government must be considered the additions made at the same time by Mr Goschen to the rates of succession duty—½ per cent on successors in the direct line and 1½ per cent on all other categories. If the former was designed to equalize the burden of *local* taxation as between personalty and realty, the latter was an attempt to raise the contribution from realty to national taxation to bring it nearer to that of personalty. Probate duty applied only to personalty; as the contribution of the probate duty to the Exchequer had now been reduced from a rate of 3 per cent to 1½ per cent, and an additional half or 1½ per cent added to the tax on successions to realty while the inheritance tax on personalty—the legacy duty—remained unaltered, there was a specious equalization.[1] But this equality of rates was more apparent than real. Succession duty on real property was calculated on the value of the life interest, while the duties on personalty were calculated on the capital values.

Temporary Estate Duty

The following year, although it was widely recognized that a complete re-organization of the death duties was overdue, Goschen contented himself with the introduction of yet one more duty 'Not so much to reform the death duties as to get £800,000 into the Exchequer'.[2] This was a levy at the rate of one per cent on all estates exceeding £10,000 in value. As with existing duties realty was valued on life interest, personalty on net capital value. Known at the time as the 'estate duty', to avoid confusion with the subsequent estate duty of 1894 it is convenient to follow the practice of the Inland Revenue after 1894 and refer to it as the 'temporary estate duty'. Expected to raise £1 million in a full year, the temporary estate duty brought the yield of the death duties to about £10 million or over 10 per cent of Exchequer receipts from taxation.

The budget of 1889 was in many respects a distinct forerunner of that of Sir William Harcourt, five years later. The debate on the proposal for the temporary estate duty brought to the fore once

[1] The rate of probate duty was 3 per cent over most of its range: as half the receipts were now paid to Local Taxation Accounts the contribution to the national Exchequer could be said to be 1½ per cent. An increase on succession duty of 1½ per cent was supposed to offset this for successors not in the direct line.

Successors in the direct line already paid one per cent, whereas inheritors of personal property, in the direct line, paid no legacy duty if probate duty had been paid. Hence to 'equalize' the burden, an increase in succession duty of ½ per cent was required.

[2] Goschen's budget speech of 1889, quoted in Mallet, *ibid*, p. 32.

again the inequality of treatment between personalty and realty in national taxation. Goschen defended the favourable treatment accorded to realty on a new ground—as a compensation for the failure of the income tax to provide a depreciation allowance for real property, which meant that the owner of real estate paid on the gross, and not the net, annual value of his property. Sir William was to sweep away any justification for this complaint. Significant too was the large exemption limit of the temporary estate duty, which had a hint of graduation or progression about it. Harcourt could and did claim that he was but following in the footsteps of his predecessor at the Exchequer when in 1894 he introduced the first consistently graduated tax into the fiscal system of the United Kingdom. If Goschen missed the opportunity to introduce a large-scale reform, at least, unwittingly, he opened the way for Sir William Harcourt.[1]

(iii) THE REFORM OF 1894

The Aims of Harcourt's Reform

'Wonderfully free from any electioneering taint' was how *The Economist*[2] described the budget introduced by Sir William Harcourt in 1894. Facing a four million pound deficit Sir William proposed to amend the sinking fund, increase the beer and spirit duties and, most important, carry through the long overdue reform of the death duties.

When Harcourt rose to address the House there were five death duties in all. They presented an 'extra-ordinary specimen of tesselated legislation'.[3] The probate, account and temporary estate duties were levied on the property of the deceased regardless of its destination. The legacy and succession duties were both inheritance taxes, acquisition duties on the beneficiary, graduated according to consanguinity. The probate, account and legacy duties applied almost entirely to personalty: the succession duty to realty, settlements taking effect on the death of the settlor, and to lease-holds—tech-

1 Omitted from this account of the pre-1894 death duties is the corporation duty, introduced in 1885, as a 5 per cent levy on the annual net income of corporate and unincorporate bodies but with many exemptions including religious, charitable and business institutions. It was imposed by way of compensation for the non-liability of these bodies to death duties and was classified with death duties in the Inland Revenue Reports. Its yield was always miniscule; it was eventually abolished in 1959.

2 April 21, 1894, p. 476.

3 Harcourt's Budget speech, *The Times*, Parliamentary Reports, April 17, 1894.

nically personalty but ranged with and taxed as land. The temporary estate duty taxed both realty and personalty. The first of Sir William's aims was to simplify this complicated structure.

In their liability to national taxes owners of real property were favoured compared with owners of personalty. Besides concessions to realty in the method and timing of payment, real property was exempt from probate duty and enjoyed advantageous methods of valuation under the temporary estate duty and the inheritance taxes, paying on the life interest instead of the net capital value at which personalty was assessed. Additional rates of succession duty, imposed by Goschen in 1888, did not fully offset these advantages. Harcourt's second aim, therefore, was to equalize the burden of taxation on the owners of personal and real property respectively.

Third, Harcourt wished to introduce a tax which was boldly and openly progressive. Graduation in the rate of tax according to the value of the estate appealed to Harcourt as the application of that elusive principle of taxing according to 'ability to pay'. As long as taxation was proportional, aggregation of property was unnecessary: but the logical application of progressive rates of taxation automatically involved the aggregation of all property for the purpose of calculating the rate of duty.

With these three objects in view the Chancellor proposed to sweep away the probate, account and temporary estate duties, replacing them by a new estate duty levied according to the aggregate principal net value of all property, real or personal, settled or unsettled, which should pass on the death of any person, whether by a disposition of the deceased or by a settlement made by others. The rate of duty was to vary from one per cent on an estate between £100 and £500 value, to a maximum of 8 per cent on an estate of over £1,000,000 value. Settled property was to pay the estate duty only once during the continuance of the settlement, but as a partial compensation to the revenue it was to pay an additional duty of one per cent called 'settlement estate duty' (also payable once during the continuance of the settlement with an exemption for a surviving spouse).

At the same time Sir William provided for the assimilation of the mode of valuation and rates of the legacy and succession duties so that they became virtually identical in their effect. Acquisitions of realty or personalty were thus taxed at a proportional rate on the net capital value of the devise or bequest, with graduations according to consanguinity as before. The additional half and 1½ per cent on the rates of succession duty, imposed by Goschen in 1888, were abolished and the one per cent duty on successors in the direct line was taken to be included in the estate duty charge. Further, no legacy or succession duties were to be payable when the estate from which the bequest or devise was made was under £1,000 in value.

Duties on personal property were payable in a lump sum within six months of death. Because of the more limited marketability of much real property, the duty on that might be paid in eight yearly or sixteen half yearly instalments, with interest from the date at which the first instalment became due, twelve months after death.[1]

Harcourt could sum up the changes by the claim that, 'There will be two duties instead of five duties, and two equal duties in place of the chaotic inequality of incidence which now prevails.'[2] His budget also provided for depreciation allowances for realty under schedule 'A' of the income tax (approximately ten per cent for land and sixteen per cent for houses), thus partially compensating for the increased burden of the reformed death duties on land and remedying an injustice.

Opposition to Progression

The Opposition attacked the new provisions on many and varied grounds. They revived the argument that, looking at taxation as a whole, the new proposals far from equalizing the burden of taxation between real and personal property owners, constituted a discrimination against the former because of their additional burdens under local taxation. Mr Goschen felt it necessary to 'protest against these enormously high rates' because they would 'frustrate the object aimed at' by setting everybody thinking how they could evade the duty; and the warning that large-scale evasion was likely to result was frequently given to the Government by Opposition speakers.[3] The difficulty, if not the impossibility, of securing an equitable valuation of realty on the new basis was stressed.[4] Some extreme critics almost went so far as to foretell the doom of English landlords

1 This was a doubling of the time previously allowed (under the succession and temporary estate duties) on payment by instalments of duty assessed on real property.

2 *The Times*, Parliamentary Reports of the Commons debate of April 17, 1894.

3 See Goschen, *The Times*, Report of Commons debate of May 9, 1894; Mr Jeffreys: 'Everybody who had to face this increased death duty began to think of how he could possibly avoid it; Finance Bill in Committee, *Hansard May* 29, 1894; or the comments of Mr J. Chamberlain, Finance Bill in Committee, *Hansard*, June 4, 1894.

4 For example, Mr A. J. Balfour, *Hansard*, Parliamentary Debates, Finance Bill, May 10, 1894, cols. 877 and 878.

and the virtual extinction of English farming.[1] But the most significant debates were concerned with two different questions—the equitability of graduated taxation and the form of the new death duty.

Graduation, or progression, was not entirely new in English finance, but Sir William Harcourt's estate duty represented the first attempt to apply the principle completely and consistently.[2] Sir Willaim himself was fully aware of the importance of the occasion, and could proclaim that: 'The most remarkable circumstance in the history of these financial problems will be the decision of the House of Commons on the general principle of graduation. No doubt it will be the turning point in the history of the finance of this country'.[3] The Opposition members, if they shared with Sir William the realization of the momentousness of the occasion, did not all share his enthusiasm for progression itself. Mr Chamberlain, leader of the Liberal Unionists, openly welcomed the principle, although he disapproved of the particular form of application. The Conservatives were divided: some gave their approval, others were strongly opposed.[4] Their leader in the Commons, Mr Balfour, avoided a direct expression of opinion when an amendment raised the issue in committee on the grounds that it was certainly not the function of a Committee of the House to debate academic issues of a broad and general nature. He did, however, give a warning against the danger of graduation, a warning which had already been delivered with clarity and force during the Second Reading debate by Mr Goschen, who plainly repudiated graduation. Both stressed the point that, once the arithmetical proportion is abandoned, there is no criterion by means of which to determine a 'just' or 'equitable' rate. 'When you embark on this system of graduation there are no stages, no landmarks, nothing whatever to guide you. There is no principle of

[1] For example, Mr W. Long, *Hansard* Parliamentary Debates, Finance Bill, May 7, 1894, cols. 519–522.

[2] 'The two greatest characteristics of the new duty are graduation and aggregation . . . though neither are absolutely novel, they have never, before the act of 1894, been carried out in so complete and systematic a manner in the legislation of this country'. (*Report of the Commissioners of H M Inland Revenue* No. 37.)

[3] Sir W. Harcourt, Finance Bill in Committee, *Hansard*, June 4, 1894.

[4] Mr Chaplin was one of the strongest opponents. He disapproved of graduation on four grounds—the penalization of industry and thrift, the imposition of an exceptional burden on a class which, limited in numbers, was powerless to oppose it; the direct invitation which it gave to evasion; and the belief that it would open the door in the future to the danger of the greatest possible injustice being inflicted on a most limited class at the behest of some needy Chancellor of the Exchequer.

justice—no principle, where you can say you ought to stop; no principle of prudence—no principle whatever . . . Equality of sacrifice will not find correspondence in the geometrical progression of taxation. . . . You have attempted an impossibility if you attempt to reach what is real equality of sacrifice'.[1]

Estate Duty or Inheritance Tax

On the second major issue, and the one which concerns us most, the form of the new tax, the Opposition condemned the Government's proposals because they would have preferred an inheritance tax to an estate duty. The 1894 estate duty was justified by its supporters on a number of counts. First, the legal grounds as laid down by Sir William Harcourt in his budget speech, that 'What power a man possesses to prolong his will beyond his life is a pure creation of the law' and 'the title of the state to a share of the accumulated property of the deceased is an *anterior* title to that of the interest to be taken by those who are to share in it.'[2] If the state had *first* claim on the property, this argument would seem to lead logically to the estate duty form of tax. Further, it was argued that the tax represented a back-tax on the deceased in lieu of income tax, and hence must be on the corpus of the estate and not the shares. This argument took two slightly different forms. It was suggested that a progressive estate duty compensated for the inability of the government for administrative reasons to introduce progression into the income tax:[3] it was also maintained that an estate duty had an effect similar to the result considered desirable 'though administratively impracticable at the time, of differentiating income

[1] Goschen, reported in *The Times* Parliamentary Debates, Wednesday, May 9, 1894. Similarly Balfour: 'It has been laid down over and over again that the only safe and plain principles are in arithmetical proportion, and if these are left then we at once get into an unsound, unsurveyed sea without a compass to guide us.' *Hansard*, Parliamentary Debates, May 10, 1894. The Opposition made considerable play with Gladstone's observance a few years before, that 'I have never been able to observe any absolute rule by means of which that graduation is to be kept within bounds. . . 'e.g. quoted by Mr Chaplin, *Hansard*, Parliamentary Debates, June 4, 1894.

[2] *The Times*, Parliamentary Reports, April 17, 1894.

[3] E.g. Mr Courtney. The income tax in its present form involved the necessity of taxing all income at the same rate; 'The rich man, who died, was therefore in debt to the state. There was an accumulated deficiency in his contributions to direct taxation, and the simple defence of the . . . estate duty . . . was . . . that it was a debt due from the estate of the deceased to the state in consequence of the deficiency of his contributions during his life . . . The duty was a debt which must be paid out of the dead man's effects before they could be distributed'. *Hansard*, Parliamentary Debates, Finance Bill in Committee, May 29, 1894.

tax according to source,[1] i.e. taxing 'unearned' income more than 'earned'. These 'back tax' arguments necessarily implied the estate duty form. The estate duty was supported further on the practical grounds that it was more remunerative to the Exchequer than an inheritance tax, i.e. to obtain an equal revenue from either, the rates of inheritance tax would need to be much higher than those of an estate duty. Finally, in reply to the arguments of the Opposition that an estate duty would be inequitable because it was paid out of the share received and yet might bear no relation to that share, government spokesmen pointed out that it was open to the testator to make his own provisions for the payment of tax in his will, and only in the absence of these provisions would it be assumed that he wished the tax to be levied in the same proportion on all bequests and devises.

The Opposition countered the legal argument by maintaining that, if the right of bequest was a creation of the law, so were most of our other rights: Opposition members did not deny that the law had guarded, limited and regulated the right of bequest, but they did deny that this itself constituted a precedent for taking away a man's property after he had bequeathed it. Mr Balfour exposed a logical flaw in the 'back tax' arguments by showing that their application ought to involve graduation in an estate duty not only according to the size of estate, but also according to the length of time the deceased person had enjoyed his wealth: the poor man who enjoyed a small property for a long time ought to pay more than a rich man who enjoyed a large property for a small time.[2] The opponents of the estate duty emphasized that in practice the incidence of the tax was on the heirs and not the deceased person: the proposed new duty, they argued, was assessed on a fund which bore no relation to what a man got, and it was paid out of a fund which bore no relation to the fund on which it was assessed;[3] and when it was urged that the testator could remedy the injustice by providing that the tax was paid by the residuary legatee or in any other way he determined in his will, they[4] quoted the case of a man with a £100,000 and ten

[1] Sir W. Harcourt: 'The graduated estate duty may be, in fact, reckoned in terms of an annual charge upon the estate, and in that shape may be regarded as a graduated income tax which is levied only upon realised property, and does not fall upon what are called "precarious" incomes. So that, in point of fact, you do arrive at the result which is aimed at in the demand for a graduated income tax, falling upon what are called "spontaneous" as distinguished from "industrial" incomes.' *Hansard*, Parliamentary Debates, vol. 23, p. 489.

[2] *Hansard*, Finance Bill in Committee, May 29, 1894.

[3] Mr Butcher, *Hansard*, Finance Bill in Committee, May 29, 1894.

[4] Speech of Mr Jeffreys, *Hansard*, Finance Bill in Committee, May 29, 1894.

children where each would pay a larger tax on an equal share of £10,000 than would be paid on an estate of £10,000 all bequeathed to an only son—no re-appointment of the tax between the beneficiaries could remove this injustice. 'You have adopted graduation', denounced Balfour, 'because you think it is the method to produce equality of sacrifice. Why have you not the sense or the courage to make your system consistent? I understand the advantage of taxing a man at an increased ratio in proportion to his wealth: I do not understand the advantage of taxing a man exceptionally, not according to his own wealth, but according to his father's wealth, and that is what you do under this Bill. . . . Graduation may be the discovery of the age. It may be the medicine which is to cure all our financial ills, but in Heaven's name apply graduation like rational beings and graduate property in proportion to the amount enjoyed, and not in proportion to the amount left by those who can no longer enjoy it'.[1] Finally, two other advantages of the inheritance tax were claimed by Mr Grant Lawson:[2] an inheritance tax would constitute an encouragement to the distribution of property because 'a testator would have the opportunity by distributing his property of lowering the amount he would have to pay to the state; also it would be administratively superior to the estate duty in that it would expedite the winding up of estates, since many beneficiaries could pay tax on their share without it first being necessary to aggregate the whole estate in order to determine the rate of tax.

The argument of 1894 about the most desirable (or at least undesirable) structure a reformed death duty should take—whether estate or inheritance tax, a duty on the corpus of the estate or on the individual benefits—has been thrown into relief by the publication, after his death, of the budget proposals of Lord Randolph Churchill[3] —'the only Chancellor of the Exchequer who never introduced a budget'.[4] Lord Randolph resigned from Lord Salisbury's government in December 1886 ostensibly because the Prime Minister and other members of the government could not or would not adopt the measures of economy to which Lord Randolph felt himself bound by his election pledges, but fundamentally because his radicalism was out of harmony with the conservatism of his leader. Before he left the Exchequer he had, however, formulated his budget proposals

1 *Hansard*, Parliamentary Debates, May 10, 1894.

2 *Hansard*, Finance Bill in Committee, May 29, 1894.

3 Winston S. Churchill, *Lord Randolph Churchill*, Macmillan, 1906, chapters 15 and 16.

3 Unfortunately, since the death of Mr Iain Macleod, July 1970, this quotation is no longer true.

which envisaged a reform of the death duties more sweeping than, and very different from, the reform of Sir William Harcourt. Lord Randolph planned to abolish all the existing duties and replace them by a single inheritance tax graduated according to the value of the individual succession. Realty and personalty were to be put on an equal footing and the principle of graduation according to consanguinity was to be discarded: the testator, Lord Randolph maintained, in disposing of his property would naturally favour those nearest and dearest to him, so interference by the state was pointless. A liberal system of discounts was to hasten the departure of the probate, account, legacy and succession duties, and the whole scheme was designed to serve the dual purpose of increasing the revenue from death duties and simplifying their operation.

The Finance Bill of 1894 passed into law on August 1 of that year having successfully emerged from the Second Reading by a majority of 14 votes. Let us conclude this section with the comments of Winston Churchill on the structure of death duties as they were after Harcourt's reform compared with that proposed by Lord Randolph. In place of one single duty graduated according to the value of the succession, 'We now enjoy a duty called "estate duty", an extra duty levied in certain circumstances on settled property called "settlement estate duty", and finally, the legacy and succession duties, depending on the consanguinity existing between the donor and donee. We now assert the vicious principle of taxing property instead of persons. We try to tax the dead instead of the living. The state refuses to consider for purposes of graduation anything so personal as the sacrifice of heirs and bases itself on the mass of the inheritance. Conjoined with this in utter contradiction we have a cumbrous and elaborate recognition of such a purely personal and private principle as consanguinity.'[1]

To this question of the most appropriate form of death duty we shall perforce return when we have completed our survey of the history of the death duties in the United Kingdom and analysed the incidence of estate duty.

(iv) DEATH DUTIES SINCE 1894

The story of death duties in the United Kingdom since 1894 has three main strands. First, the abolition of settlement estate duty and legacy and succession duties so that the estate duty emerges as the sole representative of the species. Second the ever-increasing nominal

[1] *Ibid.*, p. 196. This was written in 1906. Settlement estate duty was to be repealed in 1906 and the legacy and succession duties in 1949.

weight of duties—a product both of increasing rates and of rising prices which assimilate estates of the same real value into higher tax brackets. Finally, a direct consequence of the second development, the growth of avoidance to such a scale that estate duty is widely dubbed 'the voluntary tax'.

The first two aspects are considered in this chapter, together with an outline of the main concessions to the taxpayer and the legislative aspects of avoidance. An attempt to analyse and assess the significance of the phenomenon of avoidance is included in chapter 3, section (ii).

The Revenue Hey-day of Death Duties

Sir William Harcourt had estimated that his changes would permanently increase revenue from death duties by some three to four millions, although it was not expected that the full increase would be realized for some four years because of payment by instalments on realty and anticipated valuation difficulties. In the event less difficulty was experienced than had been expected in the payment of duty on realty,[1] the majority of which was paid as lump sums, with the result that the expected increase was reached in the financial year 1895–96 and by 1898 the yield of the death duties had risen to over £15 million, of which the new estate duty produced nearly £12 million; in this year total death duties exceeded 15 per cent of the Exchequer Receipts from taxation.

Harcourt's successors in the Liberal governments in the decade before the first Great War were the first to take advantage of the revenue potential of the new tax. In 1907 Asquith increased rates on the larger estates to provide a budget surplus for reducing the national debt to increase the country's credit and to assist in building up a fund for his Old Age Pension Scheme—to be introduced the following year. A heavier and more general increase followed in Lloyd George's famous 'War budget . . . for raising money to wage implacable warfare against poverty and squalidness'[2] [*sic*]. Lloyd George also used the occasion to reimpose legacy and succession duties on successors in the direct line and for the first time extended them to spouses (but in both cases only where the amounts were considerable) and increased the legacy and succession duties on collaterals. Five years later, in the last pre-war budget, Lloyd George again steepened the progression of the estate duty, raising the maximum rate from 15 to 20 per cent.

1 *Report of Commissioners of H M Inland Revenue No. 38.*

2 Lloyd George's Budget statement, *Hansard*, Parliamentary Debates 1909, vol. 4, col. 548, April 28, 1909.

These years also saw the abolition of the settlement estate duty. Originally fixed at one per cent, the duty raised was to 2 per cent in 1909, but then abolished in 1914, together with the partial exemption from estate duty enjoyed by settled property. Lloyd George, proposing the abolition, held that any distinction between settled and unsettled property was anomalous. Where settlement estate duty had already been paid on any property it was to be allowed (with simple interest at 3 per cent) against the next payment of estate duty. Since then, the only privilege or exemption in relation to settled property has been for the benefit of a surviving spouse.

During the two or three years preceding the first World War the death duties were annually realizing over £25,000,000 of which the estate duty contributed about £20,000,000. The total yield from death duties in these years represented between 13 and 14 per cent of Exchequer Receipts from all sources, and well over 16 per cent of total tax revenue. (See table 2.5 p. 68).

The World Wars and their Aftermath

During the first Great War, although nearly all other forms of revenue were strained to the uttermost—at least in the later war years—the death duties remained unchanged. The reluctance to increase death duties, 1914–18, was characteristic of almost all the belligerent countries; it appears to have resulted from the popular assumption, particularly in the first year or two of the war, that the war would be short and that its expenses could be met by ordinary revenue and by indemnities from the losers, combined with the conviction that it would be unjust to use a death duty as a war tax, i.e. a tax to be increased *temporarily* for the period of the war.

This explanation gains credence not only because Lloyd George clearly had no inhibitions in the use of death duties in general, but also from the remarks of Austin Chamberlain, who, when introducing his budget of 1919, gave support to the policy of his predecessor on the grounds that death duties were unsuitable for meeting a temporary emergency; by 1919 however he believed the time had come for a permanent increase of revenue from this source.

The increases which Chamberlain proposed clearly reflected the revolution which the necessities of war finance had produced in fiscal thinking. He proposed to obtain a further £10,000,000 in a full year from the estate duty by steepening the rates on estates over £15,000 to give a maximum rate of 40 per cent on estates of £2,000,000 —exactly double the previous maximum. This, in the light of past experience, was a startling step for a Conservative to take; but with a capital levy looming in the background the measure appeared comparatively mild to contemporaries. *The Times*, which had shown no enthusiasm for Harcourt's measures, could support the Chancellor of 1919 and comment that the death duty was 'the best kind of tax upon capital'.[1] In 1925, another Conservative, Mr Winston Churchill, further increased the rates of estate duty in the middle range of estates, to offset a reduction in the super tax which he hoped would restore incentive and introduce a healthy buoyancy into the economy.

With Philip Snowden in charge of the Exchequer and the national finances running a deficit, death duties again became the target. Under the 1930 Finance Act estate duty rates were raised on medium and large estates to bring the maximum rate of duty up to 50 per cent. Between 1931 and 1938, the annual yield from death duties in Great Britain averaged about £80,000,000.

In the years 1939 and 1940, three changes followed each other very quickly, the first associated with pre-war armaments expenditure, the others with the arrival of war. It should not be inferred however, from these war-time increases of estate duty, that the arguments which had prevailed upon politicians to leave the death duties untouched during the first World War had been entirely discarded. Rather the experience of the previous war may have warned ministers of the futility of anticipating a short conflict, and the folly of trying to make the defeated powers pay. It was probably realized that an increase in duties would not be temporary—that the need for greater revenue would outlast the war itself. Even so it is perhaps significant that the largest increase followed the end of the war when Dr Dalton was at the Exchequer. In April 1946 the Labour government's Finance Act increased the rates of estate duty on all estates above £12,500, raising the maximum rate of duty by 10 per cent (from 65 to 75) and some rates by considerably more than 10 per cent, for example, the duty on estates of £1,000,000 raised from 52 to 70 per cent. At the same time there was a one to 2 per cent relaxation on estates between £2,000 and £7,500, and the abolition of estate duty on estates below £2,000. The abolition of duty on the smallest estates was fully justified if only on the grounds of administrative economy, since although their total yield to the revenue was small, something like 75 per cent of total estates taxed fell within this category[2] (i.e. £100 to £2,000.)

When in the following year, the Finance Act doubled the rates of legacy and succession duties, taking all death duties together the maximum possible rate to which any property could be subject became 80 per cent—this would apply to an estate of £2,000,000 or

1 May 1, 1919.

2 *Report of the Commissioners of H M Inland Revenue No. 90*, table 12, p. 45.

over wholly bequeathed to someone outside the family. If this rate was conceivable as a limiting possibility when Dr Dalton left the Exchequer, Sir Stafford Cripps's budget proposals of 1949 were designed to make it a practical reality. Sir Stafford abolished the legacy and succession duties, thus leaving estate duty as the sole death duty; at the same time estate duty rates were increased both to compensate for the loss of the legacy and succession duties and to raise a further £20,000,000 from death duties in a full year. To achieve these objects the rate of estate duty on all estates over one million pounds was raised to 80 per cent and there was a general increase in the estate duty scale on all estates above £17,500. The middle range of estates (between £50,000 and £500,000) bore the main brunt of the increases, in some cases amounting to a further 15 per cent of the estate or an increase of 40 to 50 per cent on the existing estate duty rates. Even after allowances for the abolition of the legacy and succesion duties, this represented a very considerable addition. All estates of over £110,000[1] value would in future pay at least a 50 per cent duty. As these swingeing post-war increases indicate very clearly, Chancellors Dalton and Cripps looked upon estate duty as a means of diminishing inequalities of wealth.

The abolition of the legacy and succession duties in 1949 meant the abandonment of tax graduation according to consanguinity which had been a feature of death duties in the United Kingdom since 1796. Objections were raised to the abandonment of this principle in Parliament and in the press and the government was accused of subsidizing immorality since bequests to a mistress were now taxed no more heavily than bequests to a wife. However, probably few people have regretted its departure very seriously. Certainly there has been no widespread demand for its re-introduction. In one sense the abolition of the legacy and succession duties was a distinct improvement for it meant a useful administrative simplification. On the other hand it can be argued that an opportunity for re-examination of the fundamental principles and purposes of death taxation was missed.

The Weight of Death Taxation

The increases of estate duty over the period 1894–1949 are illustrated in table 2.2, showing the changes in rates of tax on specimen estates. The general trend is clearly brought out by the graph showing rates of estate duty introduced in representative years since 1894; this reveals also the increasingly heavy taxation of moderate-sized estates which was a marked feature of estate duty changes during

[1] This allows for marginal relief, see below p. 59.

TABLE 2.2. *Rates of Estate Duty on Specimen Estates, 1894–1969 in per cent*

Net capital value £	1894 to 1907	1907 to 1909	1909 to 1914	1914 to 1919	1919 to 1925	1925 to 1930	1930 to Apr. 1939	Apr. to Sep. 1939	Sep. 1939 to 1940	1940 to 1946	1946 to 1949	1949 to Apr. 15 1969
150	1	1	1	1	1	1	1	1	1	1	—	—
1,050	3	3	3	3	3	3	3	3	3	1	—	—
5,100	3	3	4	4	4	4	4	4	4	4	3	3 †
10,300	4	4	5	5	5	5	5	5	5·5	6	6	6
20,400	4	4	6	6	7	8	8	8	8·8	9·6	12	15
35,500	4·5	4·5	6	6	9	12	12	12	13·2	14·4	18	24
52,000	5	5	7	7	11	15	15	16·5	18	19·5	24	35
78,000	5·5	5·5	8	8	13	18	18	19·5	21·6	23·4	30	45
105,000	6	6	9	10	14	20	20	22	24	26	35	50
210,000	6·5	7	11	12	19	24	26	28·6	31·2	33·8	45	60
370,000	7	8	11	15	23	26	30	33	36	39	55	65
650,000	7·5	9	13	18	27	26	36	39·6	43·2	46·8	60	70
1,100,000	8	11*	15	20	30	30	40	44	48	52	70	80
2,400,000	8	13*	15	20	40	40	50	55	60	65	75	80
3,500,000	8	15*	15	20	40	40	50	55	60	65	75	80

* The rate of duty above 10 per cent was charged on the excess over £1 million at the rate of 1 per cent increase per £500,000 to a maximum of 5 per cent increase.

† This rate was reduced to 2 per cent in 1962 and 1 per cent in 1963.

No allowance is made in this table for marginal relief.

the 1940s. Rates of estate duty have increased during this period of just over half a century by ten-fold at the maximum (from the 8 per cent of Harcourt in 1894 to the 80 per cent of Cripps in 1949) and by sevenfold or more on all estates over £50,000. It is true that the estate duty rates of 1949 included an increase to replace legacy and succession duties previously payable and hence to compare like with like we should allow for these duties in 1894; but if we do this the picture

FIGURE 2.1. Semi-logarithmic graph of rates of estate duty for various years on estates of £10,000 and above

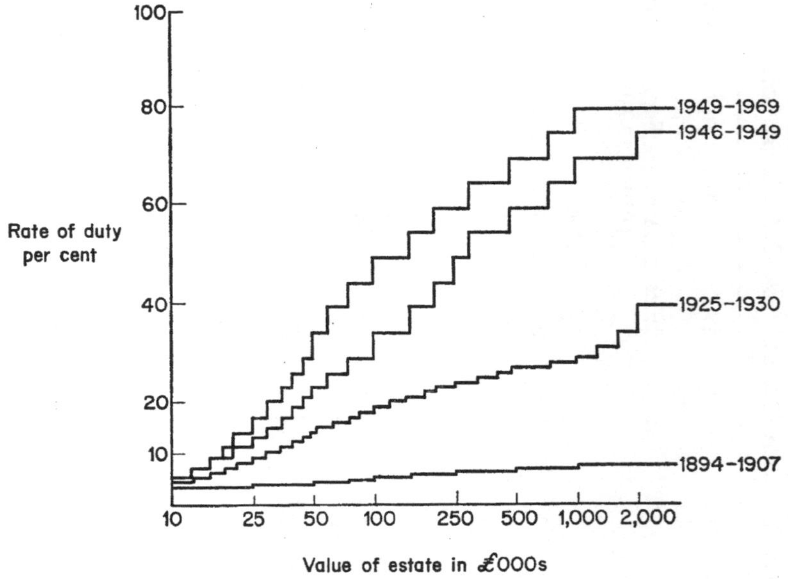

is not much affected for in 1894 no legacy or succession duties were payable on bequests received by husband or wife, parents or children (see table 2.3).

Since 1949 two changes have taken place in the rates of estate duty. First, the exemption limit has been raised in a series of stages, with consequential reductions in the rates of duty on the smallest estates remaining liable to tax; the exemption limit was increased in 1954, 1962 and again in 1963 when it became £5,000. It was further increased to £10,000 in the recasting of the tax in 1969. It was estimated that the 1969 increase would reduce the number of estates liable to estate duty by about 53 per cent (40,000 a year) at a cost in revenue of about £8 million in a full year.

The second change was that, in 1969, Chancellor Jenkins replaced the system of progression by totality, by which duty was charged on

TABLE 2.3. *Rates of Legacy and Succession Duties, 1894–1949*

Consanguinity* of beneficiary to testator or intestate	Rate of Duty per cent		
	1894 to 1909	1909 to 1947	1947 to 1949
Husband or wife	—	1	2
Lineal ancestor or issue	—	1	2
Brother or sister or descendants	3	5	10
Uncle or aunt or descendants	5	10	20
Great uncle or great aunt or descendants	6	10	20
Any other relative or stranger in blood	10	10	20
Charities	10	10	10

* Relatives of the half blood stand on the same footing as those of the whole blood.

Exemption provisions (1947–1949):

1. No duty payable on bequests from an estate under £2,000.
2. No duty payable on individual bequests of less than £100.
3. No duty payable at the 2 per cent rate on bequests from estates under £15,000.
4. No duty payable at the 2 per cent rate on individual bequests of under £2,000.

the whole estate at a single rate (sometimes referred to as the 'slab' basis) by progression by brackets (sometimes called the 'slice' scale). This needed reform abolished the necessity for marginal relief[1] which had meant a marginal rate of tax of 100 per cent. The intention of the change was to leave the weight of the tax approximately the same (except for the higher exemption limit and the consequential reduction of duty on the very smallest estates). Table 2.4 sets out the new scale introduced in April 1969 and figure 2.2 compares the rates of duty before and after the Finance Act 1969.

If rates of duty have remained more or less the same in monetary terms since 1949, the more or less continuing inflation since then has increased the real rate of duty markedly, for inflation has the effect under progressive taxation of assimilating the same real value of estate into ever higher tax brackets.

There is no wholly satisfactory way of assessing the increased weight of estate duty attributable to inflation. Between 1949 and 1967 the index of retail prices increased by 95 per cent. If we were to assume that the inflationary increase in the monetary value of estates as a whole was similar, then an estate valued at £10,000 in

[1] See below p. 59.

TABLE 2.4. *Estate Duty Rates Applicable from April 16, 1969*

Slice of net capital value: Over £	Slice of net capital value: Not over £	Rate of duty when death occurred after April 15, 1969
—	10,000	Nil
10,000	17,500	25
17,500	30,000	30
30,000	40,000	45
40,000	80,000	60
80,000	150,000	65
150,000	300,000	70
300,000	500,000	75
500,000	750,000	80
750,000	—	85*

* With a ceiling of 80 per cent of the total estate.
Source: Report of Commissioners of HM Inland Revenue, No. 112, Table 36.

1949 and paying 4 per cent duty would have been valued at £19,500 in 1967 and have paid 12 per cent; an estate of £100,000 in 1949, paying 45 per cent, would in 1967 have carried a value of £195,000 and have paid 55 per cent. An estate of £1 million in 1949 paying 75 per cent would have moved up into the maximum bracket at 80 per cent.

But a price index, based on changes in the monetary value of a particular combination of consumers' goods and services, cannot accurately reflect inflationary changes in the value of assets which comprise estates. In Appendix A details are set down of an attempt to construct a property price index. The main components of estates (as detailed in the Reports of the Commissioners for HM Inland Revenue) are grouped into four categories, each containing items believed to have experienced similar changes in price. An index of the prices of each of these groups of components has been selected and the four groups combined in a property price index weighted according to the distribution of the various kinds of assets in estates in 1957–58—a year mid-way between 1949 and 1967. This reveals some interesting points of comparison with the retail price index.

FIGURE 2.2. Estate Duty: Comparison of Rates of Duty before and after the 1969 Finance Act

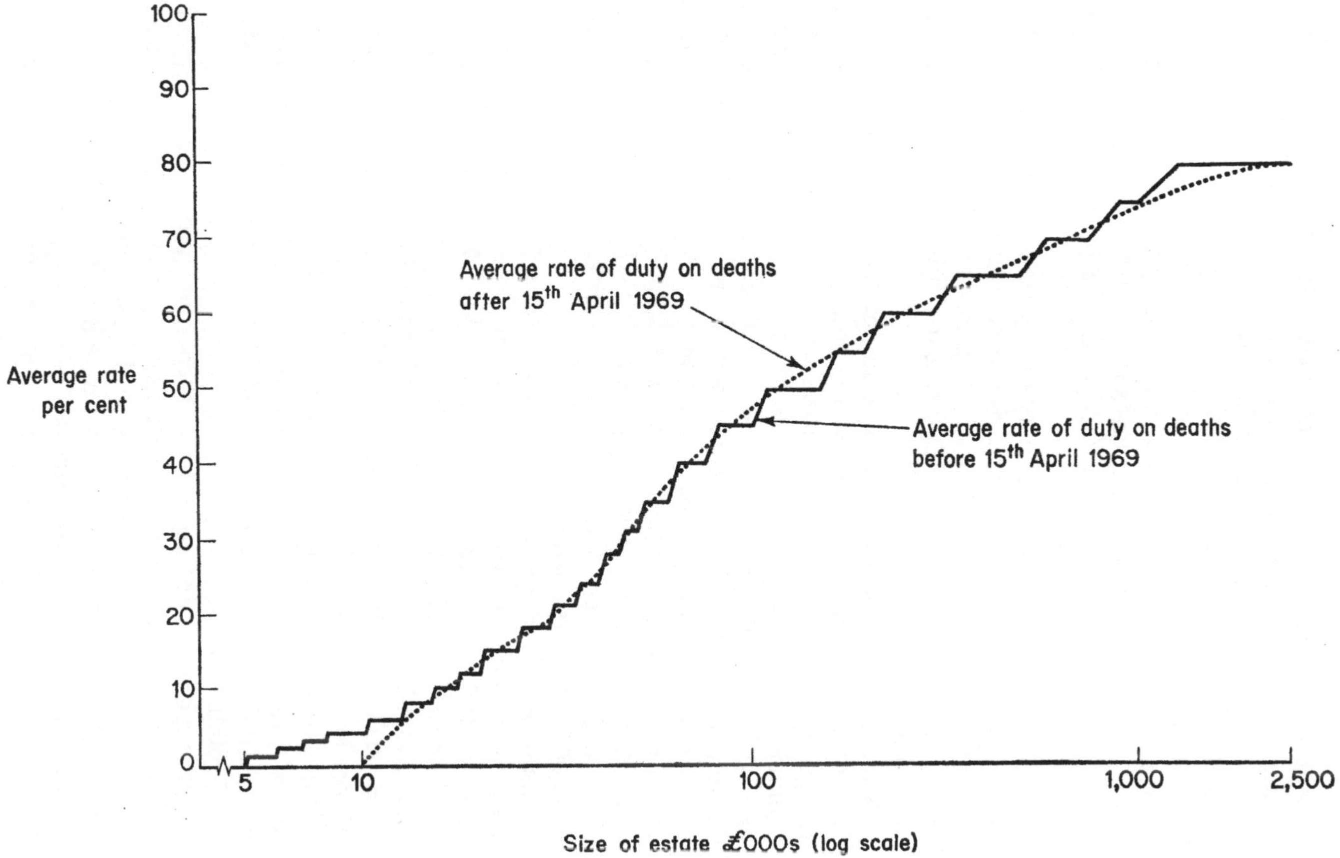

Source: *Hundred and Twelfth Report of the Commissioners of Inland Revenue*, Cmnd. 4262, p. 9.

Over the period as a whole and taking all assets and all estates together, the property index shows an increase of 74 per cent to the 95 per cent of the retail price index over the years 1949–67. But there is much more difference in the movement of the two indices in the two halves of the period. During the first half the property price index rose by only 15 per cent whilst the retail price index rose 52 per cent. In the second half, the relative movements were reversed, the retail price index rising 29 per cent whilst the property price index rose 51 per cent.

Of the individual assets, the outstanding features brought out by the property index are the huge rise in land prices, almost wholly concentrated in the second half of the period; and the large rises in the index of ordinary shares both before and after 1958, but particularly afterwards.

Another point of significance from the property index which is lost by any blanket application of the retail price index, is that the 'growth' assets, those which have risen most in price, figure most prominently in the larger estates whilst 'constant price assets' (e.g. cash, post office balances, government securities) figure most in the smaller estates. If we re-weight assets in the property price index for various estate ranges (see tables 2 and 3 in Appendix A) we find that for the smallest estates, £5,000–£20,000, the property price index shows a rise of only 46 per cent 1949–67, but that the index rises steadily with estate size to reach 145 per cent for estates in the £500,000–£2,000,000 category.

Applying the property price index to a sample of estate sizes, we find, for example, that an estate valued at £21,250 in 1949 might be expected to have a value of about £40,000 in 1967; the rate of duty would have been 15 per cent in 1949, 24 per cent in 1967. An estate valued at £47,200 in 1949 might have been expected to have a value of £100,000 in 1967—with duty at 45 per cent in 1967 against 31 per cent in 1949. Near the top of the scale a typical estate of £510,200 in 1949 would probably have increased in value to £1,250,000 in 1967; rate of duty would have risen from 65·7 per cent to 80 per cent; liability would have been £1,000,000 in 1967 compared with £335,200 in 1949.

Although price increases have been most pronounced for the larger estates, the *percentage* increases in *rates* of tax have been smaller on the larger estates than on the small and middle range of estate values. This apparent paradox reflects two related facts; on the one hand the narrower brackets of tax ranges for estates under £100,000—so that inflation pushes a small estate up through several brackets; on the other hand the height which estate duty rates had already attained even on comparatively modest estates—which limits the scope for increases in *rates* of tax resulting from inflation; to take the extreme case, an estate of £1,250,000 in 1949 was already paying the maximum rate of duty so that no amount of inflation could push it into a higher tax bracket.

However, just as the index of retail prices was an inadequate measure of the effect of inflation in increasing the weight of taxation, so also is the property price index. Changes in the prices of the components of the property price index are the result of a complex of factors. Thus the price of ordinary shares may reveal a secular upward trend because of changes in the quantity and quality of investment; agricultural land may rise in price because of increases in productivity; part of the rise in the price of residential property results from the scarcity of a highly specific factor, site land, at a time of steadily rising demand. These influences would have led to some rise in asset values had the period seen no general price inflation.

The effect of the changing prices of assets is a topic to which we shall return, especially in the context of capital gains taxation and the significance of estate duty as a long term capital gains tax. But no consideration of the weight of death duties would have been complete without reference to the effect of inflation. Although we cannot measure it precisely, there can be no doubt that, where estate duty is not avoided, inflation has increased the weight of the tax very substantially.

Estate Duty Concessions

Inevitably the growing weight of death duties during the present century has led to the development of special legislative provisions along two distinct lines—one designed to alleviate the burden in certain special cases and to facilitate payment without unnecessary hardship or undesirable economic consequences; the other to combat evasion and avoidance of duties. Some of the more important of the exemptions and reliefs are outlined below.

(*a*) *'Marginal' Relief.* The system of progression by totality, which lasted until the 1969 Finance Act, posed the need for marginal relief in computing the estate duty. Progression by totality meant that, unlike the surtax system which is progressive by brackets, the same rate of tax applied to the whole estate. Thus, unless special provisions were made, it would have been possible for the beneficiaries of an estate somewhat in excess of one of the upper brackets in the schedule to be made worse off than if the estate had been smaller. The Finance

Act of 1914 prevented this by providing that the amount of duty payable on an estate was, where necessary, 'restricted to the sum of (i) the duty on the maximum estate in the range below, and (ii) the amount by which the value of the estate extends into the range in question'. An example will clarify the point.

Example of the Operation of Marginal Relief

At the rate of estate duty applicable before the 1969 budget:

An estate £12,500–£15,000 paid at 8 per cent
£15,000–£18,000 paid at 10 per cent
Consider two estates (A) £14,900 (B) £15,100

Without Marginal Relief:

A would have paid £1,192 leaving £13,708
B would have paid £1,510 leaving £13,590

Thus less would have been left of estate B, the larger estate, after tax.

With Marginal Relief:

The marginal relief provisions involve that Estate B pays 8 per cent on £15,000, i.e.

	£1,200	
plus	£100	
Total	£1,300	leaving £13,800

This meant that over considerable ranges of the estate duty scale there was a marginal rate of tax of 100 per cent. Taking the extreme case, on current estate duty rates, the whole range between a size of estate of £1,000,000 and an estate of £1,250,000 was taxed at 100 per cent; in theory therefore, if the man knew that his estate at death would amount to exactly £1,250,000, he could indulge in a gigantic spending spree of a quarter of a million pounds without his heirs being one penny the worse off! The introduction of progression by brackets in 1969 ended this inequity.

(*b*) *Rapid Succession Relief.* Also by the Finance Act of 1914 a rapid succession relief was introduced, applying to certain classes of property. If land, or a private business (not belonging to a company) became liable to estate duty within five years of the same property having paid duty, the duty payable at the second death was to be reduced by up to one half according to the period between the first and second death.[1] This concession was later extended to all property.

[1] If the second death is within:
1 year of the first death, duty payable reduced by 50 per cent. (*cont. p. 61*)

(*c*) *Concessions on Agricultural Property.* The most significant of the reliefs from estate duty has been the concession to agricultural property, first introduced by Winston Churchill in 1925, by which estate duty on agricultural property was to be charged on the agricultural value of the property at the scale fixed by the Finance Act of 1919, and on any excess of the market value over such agricultural value at the current rate of duty. 'Agricultural property' meant agricultural land, pasture and woodland, and included the cottages, farm houses and buildings and mansion house appropriate to the property. 'Agricultural value' meant what the property would fetch if subject to a perpetual covenant prohibiting its use otherwise than as agricultural property. Although Labour and Liberal members denounced the provision at the time as creating a very dangerous precedent[1] for the preferred treatment of a particular class, Mr Churchill's successors, Conservative and Labour alike, continued the exemption and until 1949 the agricultural value of agricultural estates continued to be assessed at the 1919 rates. In 1949 Sir Stafford Cripps altered the form of the concession by allowing an abatement of 45 per cent of the duty chargeable on the agricultural value of agricultural property.

Agricultural estates may also benefit by two other concessions. Special provisions relating to timber were first introduced 1909–10 which, with subsequent acts, established the principle that where an estate includes land with trees, the value of the timber is not taken into account for the purpose of determining the rate of duty to be paid on the estate, and no duty is payable on the timber itself until it is sold. Also, the Act of 1894 retained the provisions which had characterized earlier duties for payment of duty on realty, by allowing twelve months before payment need begin and permitting payment by eight yearly or sixteen half-yearly instalments.

The Finance Act of 1910 provided that land could be given in payment of death duties where the executors and the Commissioners of Inland Revenue agreed. Little use was made of this provision, however, until Dr Dalton infused new life into it in 1946. 'I propose',

2 years of the first death, duty payable reduced by 40 per cent.
3 years of the first death, duty payable reduced by 30 per cent.
4 years of the first death, duty payable reduced by 20 per cent.
5 years of the first death, duty payable reduced by 10 per cent.

In 1958 this relief was extended to 75 per cent when the second death occurred within three months of the first; the 1958 Finance Act also ended the anomaly whereby previously if a husband and wife died simultaneously say in a car crash, and the law assumed the husband died first, duty was payable on both deaths.

[1] For example Lloyd George, 'The principle is a very dangerous one . . .' *Hansard*, Parliamentary Debates, 1924-5, vol. 185, cols. 551-554.

he said in his budget speech, 'that from now on much more use should be made of this power to accept land in payment of death duties. Even as the law stands much can be done. I have instructed the Inland Revenue to keep a constant watch for suitable instances and to suggest the possibility to executors. . . . Further to fortify this provision I propose . . . to carry £50,000,000 in this coming year . . . to a special fund, to be called the National Land Fund. It will be available for a variety of purposes all designed to increase the National Estate. . . . In some cases, where payment of death duties is made in land it may be in the public interest that the land should be transferred to some non-profit making body which may not have the money to purchase it. The National Trust may be such a body or the Youth Hostels Association. . . . In such cases the National Land Fund would be used to reimburse, wholly or in part, the Inland Revenue.'[1] Before 1946, in the previous thirty-six years, only two small pieces of land had come into the hands of public authorities through payment of death duty. Since 1946 an average of some half dozen properties each year, the details of which are recorded in the Annual Reports of the Commissioners of Inland Revenue, have been accepted in payment of estate duty liabilities.

(*d*) *Concession for the Private Business*. The Finance Act of 1954 provided for a reduction of 45 per cent in the rates of estate duty charged on industrial premises, plant or machinery used by the deceased or by a company under his control to which the 'assets' basis of valuation applied; the relief did not apply to other business assets such as stocks. This gave to the private industrial business a concession similar to that applying in agriculture.

(*e*) *Other Concessions*. These are the major concessions, but there are others. Since 1894 a number of provisions concerning objects of artistic, national, historic or scientific interest have been introduced and the general principles had become established that such objects were not aggregated with the rest of the estate, and were only liable to duty when sold, and not even then provided they were sold to the National Gallery, British Museum, a university or comparable institution. The 1969 Finance Act tightened up the provisions effectively to restrict the relief to the enjoyment of the property in kind and prevent them being used as a means of avoidance. Since 1931 gifts, bequests or devises of land to the National Trust have been exempt from duty, provided the whole of the deceased's interest in the land so passed.[2]

[1] *Hansard*, Parliamentary Debates, April 9, 1946.

[2] Under certain conditions exemptions could also be conferred where a gift, devise or bequest in favour of the Trust was subject to one or more life interests.

Another series of reliefs from duty has accompanied the major wars since 1894, exemption or partial exemption being granted where deaths occurred on active service or as a result of the operations of war.

Avoidance and Evasion

When we turn to provisions on avoidance and evasion of death duties we are faced with a whole series of intricate regulations covering a very wide field, many of them well nigh incomprehensible to any but the trained tax lawyer. Little point would be served in reproducing them here; in any case the significance of evasion and avoidance is considered in a later chapter. It is however worthwhile to record the provisions affecting the simplest and most effective way of avoiding death duties—by gifts, technically known as 'gifts inter vivos'. Under the Finance Act of 1894 a gift less than one year before the death of the donor was to be subject to estate duty. In 1910 this period was extended to three and in 1946 to five years. The Finance Act of 1960, however, provided for a reduction of 15 per cent in the principal value of the gift if the death of the donor took place in the third year; a reduction of 30 per cent in the fourth year; and of 60 per cent if death took place in the fifth year. The 1968 Finance Act extended the time period again—this time to seven years, adding two years to each of the qualifying periods for reduced rates. Small gifts of £500 or under to each donee are exempted from duty under the gifts inter vivos provisions. Gifts in consideration of a marriage, whatever their size, were exempt until 1968 when a limit of £5,000 was imposed (£1,000 if the donor was not a party to the marriage or an ancestor of such a party). Gifts for public or charitable purposes are subject to a one (not seven) year gifts inter vivos provision. Also 'habitual' gifts are exempt, although since the Finance Act 1968 it must be shown that such gifts could be met from income if they are to be exempt.[1]

[1] Two other changes merit a footnote in the history of death duties since 1894. In 1909 the Inland Revenue organization was strengthened by the addition of professional valuers. The effect was immediately visible in an increase in the value of property on which duty was assessed—in the first year an increase of over 13 per cent (see *Commisioners of HM Inland Revenue, Report No. 53*, p. 11). The second change relates to the area over which the writ of the Inland Revenue runs. With the establishment of the Irish Free State (Eire), Southern Ireland defected. Further, the Government of Ireland Act 1920—which came into effect November 1921—provided for the collection of certain revenue, including death duties, to be transferred to the Government of Northern Ireland; since then death duties in Northern Ireland have been no concern of the Commissioners of Inland Revenue and have not been paid into the Exchequer at Westminster.

(v) THE HISTORICAL SIGNIFICANCE OF THE DEATH DUTIES

The Use of History

The main purpose of this historical review has been to provide a knowledge of the past to enable us better to comprehend the present. Thus the history offers at least a partial explanation of why estate duty became established as the main and latterly the sole form of death duty in the United Kingdom. Also, particular features of the present estate duty become more meaningful in their historical context—for example the concession to agricultural property, introduced at a time of agricultural depression, of falling prices, profits and rents. But history not only helps to explain; it also points the need to re-examine. Arguments which justified a particular form of duty or a particular concession in their contemporary setting may no longer be valid, or if still valid have changed in relative importance with the changing circumstances. History too suggests useful lessons from the past: one continual theme in the history of death duties from the late eighteenth century onwards has been the interrelationship of taxation—in particular death duties, income tax and sources of local revenue. This is a valuable reminder that in any proposed reform of the tax structure we need to look beyond single taxes to classes of taxation and indeed to consider any reform in the light of the tax system as a whole.

As well as a relevance for the modern tax reformer the death duties have a special significance for the student of history. In isolation, modifications of the death duty structure, a change in the form of duty, the introduction of a new tax, an increase in the rates of duty at the behest of a needy Chancellor—these may appear petty and insignificant: but viewed in the clarifying light of historical perspective such changes take on a new meaning. Studied in relation to each other and in conjunction with modifications in other parts of the fiscal structure, even minor alterations can be seen as part of a general pattern—a pattern which, at times confused and difficult to follow, has woven into it strands of contemporary life; a pattern which reflects the social theories and social customs of the times, its economic struggles and political conflicts, its fiscal necessities and administrative limitations. Thus the fact that the probate duty of 1694 originated as a stamp duty must have been largely due to the administrative convenience of this form at a time when an effective direct property tax on modern lines was an impossibility. The exemption of real property from this duty, and from the legacy duty which followed it, was symptomatic of the disposition of political power in the hands of the Whig landowning aristocracy of the eighteenth and early nineteenth centuries. The recasting of the legacy duty from a regressive into a proportional tax in 1796, and the increases in its rates during the following twenty years, suggest the dire financial straits occasioned by the French Wars: and the form which the recast duty was given—progressive according to consanguinity with as many as five different rates for different degrees of relationship—emphasizes the greater importance of the family bond to an earlier generation.[1] These are no isolated examples. In a later epoch the development of the Labour movement as a political force, the growing emphasis on social ownership of the means of production, the wide acceptance of the need for reducing social and economic inequalities—these, together with the financial exigencies connected with twentieth century wars, are the potent developments which underlie the persistent steepening in the rate of death duty which has been such a marked characteristic of the history of these duties since Harcourt made them into an effective fiscal engine in 1894.

There are three main reasons for believing that the death duties may be more important than any other single tax or branch of taxation in the sidelights they throw on the economic, social and fiscal history of the United Kingdom. First, inheritance is an important element in the structure of property rights, influenced by the social and economic climate and organization and in its turn reacting on them; and changes in the fiscal laws affecting inheritance can be as important, or even more important, than changes in the non-fiscal laws. In terms of social and economic systems some right of inheritance is a pre-requisite of a capitalist or even a mixed economy, whilst a socialist economy would be incompatible with unrestricted inheritance. In agricultural organization the freedom of bequest in nineteenth-century England combined with the custom of primogeniture in the disposal of land supported a structure in which the typical unit of ownership was the large estate owned by tenants. (Contrast France where the *légitim* confined the individual's freedom to bequeath to a certain proportion of his property, the remainder passing at death, irrespective of his wishes, to members of his family according to fixed rules,[2] thereby fostering an agrarian society of

[1] Cf. G. D. H. Cole: 'Even in a capitalist society the family has largely lost its economic significance and become, save in respect of inheritance, mainly a social unit whose bonds have grown far looser even within living memory'. Article on 'Inheritance', p. 43. *Encyclopaedia of the Social Sciences,* edited Edwin R. A. Seligman.

[2] The *légitim* was the legally enforceable claim of widows and children to at least a part of a dead husband's or father's estate. The French Civil Code limited

peasant proprietors and small holdings). During the twentieth-century death taxation in Britain has been an important influence in the break-up of large private agricultural estates and the growth of owner occupancy and public estates (see chapter 3, section (iii)). In industry and commerce the development of the company form of organization made possible the heavy taxation of wealth at death without destroying a capitalist economy, whilst the heavy death taxation itself stimulated the adoption of the company form of organization (see chapter 3, section (iv)).

The second reason for the historical importance of death duties in the United Kingdom is their long unbroken existence. Politicians, in Europe and elsewhere, have for centuries found it convenient to levy taxes on property changing hands at death. A death duty could be supported on the plausible ground that it imposed no burden on the deceased and—especially if a collateral inheritance tax—was a levy on a windfall addition of wealth to the inheritor who would not miss what he had never possessed.[1] Moreover, since the transfer of property as a result of death generally involved documents which could serve as a convenient instrument for tax collection, administration was simple. Feudal dues in Europe, such as the heriot and the rachat or relief and some of the imposts of the church, were a form of death duty; but no continuous link can be traced between those dues in England and the modern estate duty. Rather the origin of our present death taxation is to be found in the probate duty of 1694. Although this was a stamp duty for the first century of its existence and continued to be classified as a stamp duty[2] until superseded in 1894, it developed into what was virtually an estate duty and the continuity between the probate duty and the present estate duty is unbroken. Thus we can survey the continuous development of death taxation over two and a half centuries; few important modern taxes can claim such ancestry.

Thirdly, death duties can take (and have taken during their history in the United Kingdom) a variety of forms. They can be made regressive, proportional or progressive. They can be graduated according to one or more of the following—size of estate, value of

the testator's power by mathematical rule. Thus he might bequeath only one-half of his property, if he left one child, one-third if he left two and so on.

[1] See Max West, *The Inheritance Tax*, pp. 193-4; Jeremy Bentham, *Supply without Burden; or Escheat vice Taxation*, 1795.

[2] All the 'death duties' were sub-classified as such for the first time in 1888 and indexed as 'Death duties' from the following year, in the Reports of the Commissioners of Inland Revenue. Even so they continued to be included in the stamp duty tables until 1896 (*Report of the Commissioners of H.M. Inland Revenue, No. 39*).

the individual inheritance, consanguinity, the number of children of the deceased, and—in theory at least—according to the prior wealth of the beneficiary or the age of the property.[1] Death duties can be made to fall with equal or unequal incidence on different classes of property—realty and personalty—and can be modified to allow special treatment to particular categories, such as agricultural land or the industrial premises, plant and machinery of private businesses. A stamp duty, an estate duty, an inheritance tax, may be the principal fiscal media at different times and in different places. In the structure of death duties, therefore, there is wide scope for the expression of current fiscal theory as circumscribed by administrative practicability —fiscal theory itself reflecting contemporary economic and social beliefs and practice. Particular forms of death duty may be appropriate to particular purposes and the choice of one structure at one time and another at a different time may have a deeper significance than mere fortuitous circumstance. In the remainder of this section we examine interesting historical aspects of the death duties.

The Yield of Death Duties

The yield of death duties both in monetary terms and as a percentage of total public income increased steadily throughout the nineteenth century, rising from about one per cent of public income in the first decade of the century to rather over 10 per cent in the last. After Harcourt's reform of 1894 the increase was still more rapid and in the decade before the first World War over 13 per cent of central government income and more than 16 per cent of income from taxation was raised from death duties. Death duties thus made a not insignificant contribution to the financing of the beginnings of the welfare state.

Thereafter the picture takes on a note of paradox. Before 1914 when death duties were at their high water mark as revenue producers, estate duty was levied on a scale the maximum rate of which was 20 per cent. The end of the war saw a doubling of this to 40 per cent and subsequent increases to 80 per cent, yet the contribution of the duties to revenue has never approached its pre-1914 level. A big drop in yield during and immediately after the first World War (to below 5 per cent of tax revenue) was followed by a gradual rise to over 10 per cent in the decade before the second World War; but this war also was marked by another big reduction and since

1 This is the proposal of Professor Rignano for 'progression in time' or progression according to the number of successors. See Rignano and Stamp, *The Social Significance of Death Duties;* a full account of these proposals is also found in the *Report of the Committee on National Debt and Taxation,* Cmd 2800, 1927.

the second World War the yield has sunk to 5 per cent of the tax revenue with a continuing tendency to fall. This trend is characteristic of other countries besides Britain. Undoubtedly the main reason has been the growth in revenue from other forms of tax, but it is possible that increased avoidance has played some part in recent years.[1] Death duties yielded £365 million in 1969–70—only

TABLE 2.5. *The Yield of the Death Duties and their Contribution to Revenue 1858–1970*

Financial years (ending March 31)	Total death duties GB (average per annum) £m.	Net death duties as percentage of central government revenue from taxation (average per annum)
1858–1867	3	5·8
1868–1877	5	7·9
1878–1887	6	9·6
1888–1897	10	12·6
1898–1907	17	14·4
1908–1915	23	16·1
1916–1919	30	6·4
1920–1922	46	5·0
1923–1932	69	9·8
1933–1938	84	11·3
1939–1942	82	6·7
1943–1946	106	3·7
1947–1948	160	4·9
1949–1958	175	4·2
1959–1964	249	4·1
1965–1969	326	3·4
1969–1970	365	2·5

Notes:

(1) Comparison over this long period of time has involved some changes in definition and base, but the general picture is thereby not affected.

(2) Averages have been chosen instead of selected years because the yield of the death duties in single years is particularly liable to fluctuation. A ten year average is used as a general base, but is abandoned in favour of a shorter period to bring out a particular trend. The best overall picture of the yield of the death duties and their contribution to revenue is obtained by studying table 2.5 and figure 2.3 together.

(3) The figure for 1969–70 is the provisional out-turn from the *Financial Statement and Budget Report*, 1970–71.

[1] See below chapter 3, section (ii).

FIGURE 2.3. Death Duties as Percentage of Revenue from Taxation (Central Government)

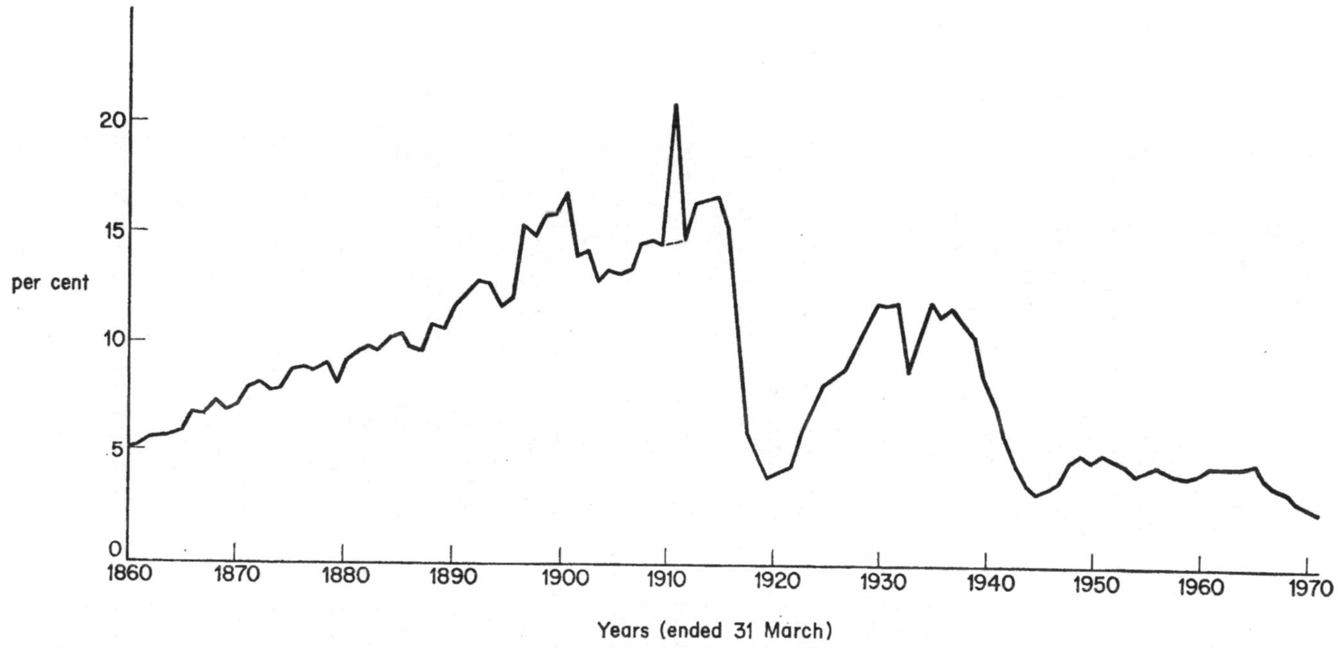

(The peak of 1910 is an abnormality arising from the Lords' rejection of Lloyd George's budget of 1909)

some $2\frac{1}{2}$ per cent of total revenue from taxation. In that year estate duty yielded less than 8 per cent of income tax, less than a third of tobacco tax, 42 per cent of the revenue from spirits, beer and wine duties and 28 per cent of the revenue from oil duties.[1]

With a maximum estate duty rate of 80 per cent (on the totality of the estate) and with estates over £80,000 paying at a marginal rate of 65 per cent or above (an average of 43 per cent or above), it is difficult to see that any further increase in rates is possible. Rather, as we shall subsequently argue, the rates should be reduced but made effective. In any case the days of death duties as really significant revenue producers appear to have gone.

Table 2.5 and figure 2.3 indicate the yield of death duties and their contribution to revenue.

Fiscal Theory and Practice

Eighteenth-century tax revenue came almost entirely from indirect (or outlay) taxes, and with the exception of the period 1799 to 1815 when the war-time income tax was in force, this continued to be true until Britain followed the path of free trade and Peel re-introduced the income tax (1842). Eighteenth-century practice was buttressed by theoretical justifications such as the objectionable and inquisitorial nature of direct taxation. It was only towards the end of the nineteenth century that the revenue yielded by direct taxation began to equal or exceed that from indirect. The change in views and practice on the subject is well brought out by the death duties. The only death duty from 1694 to 1779 was the probate duty and over these years it was levied at a flat rate on all personal property passing by will or intestacy. It was a stamp duty, and resembled far more a duty on a transaction, or a fee for services rendered (i.e. the probate of the will or the grant of letters of administration) than a direct property tax. Fiscal reasons induced Lord North to introduce a schedule of rates in 1799 and compelled increases in rates and extensions in the schedule during the Revolutionary and Napoleonic Wars, so that in fact at the commencement of the nineteenth century the probate duty was beginning to bear the character of estate duty, if a regressive one: but it was not until nearly the end of the nineteenth century that the probate, or any other of the death duties, was classified other than as a stamp duty.

The historical development of the death duties from regressive to proportional taxes and thence gradually to fully-fledged progressive taxes illustrates in an interesting manner the changes which the period witnessed towards general graduation in tax rates. The

1 *Financial Statement and Budget Report, 1970–71*, table 9.

probate duty of the eighteenth century was frankly regressive. North's schedule constituted a first step towards proportionality, but a very small step. By 1815 successive increases had brought proportionality nearer but the rates were still regressive in parts: thus the rates for the estates of testates, introduced in 1815, were £2 on £100 (2 per cent), £30 on £1,000 (3 per cent), £200 on £10,000 (2 per cent), £1,500 on £100,000 (1½ per cent), £15,000 on £1,000,000 (1½ per cent): on any estate above £1,000,000 the duty remained at £15,000 fixed, until 1859 when for testate estates 1½ per cent was charged on every additional £100,000 above £1,000,000. In 1880 a revision of the probate duty scale eliminated some of the regressive elements, but it was not until 1881 that a proportional rate of 3 per cent was introduced for all estates above £1,000, those £500–£1,000 paying 2½ per cent and £100–£500 2 per cent. The legacy duty as first introduced was regressive, but the recast duty of 1796 was proportional to the benefit received (although graduated according to consanguinity) as was the succession duty of 1853. It has been emphasized that the estate duty of 1894 was the first tax in the country to be consistently progressive, but elements of progression had already crept into the tax system in the form of a lower rate on the smallest estates, as with the 1881 probate duty.[1] The very high exemption limit (£10,000) of Goschen's temporary estate duty of 1889 illustrates the same tendency, and a system of allowances had effected a distinct progression at the lower end of the income tax scale by 1894.[2] Nevertheless the boldness of the graduation of Harcourt's estate duty constituted a distinct departure from earlier practice and it was around the estate duty of 1894 that the general theoretical conflict on the question of graduation was fought out. Thus the history of the death duties illustrates the trend of opinion on graduation and foreshadows the lines along which modern direct taxation was to travel.

1 This development is sometimes called 'degressive' i.e. rates embodying a slight graduation but under which the bulk of transfers fall under one particular rate.

2 Sir A. Rollit, Finance Bill in Committee May 29, 1894, *Hansard*, Commons Debates: 'Graduation of taxation was at the present moment in actual operation in this country . . . the principle of graduated taxation was, if the payments were averaged, at present actually applied to the income tax—the very tax to which the Chancellor of the Exchequer denied it could be applied. For the purpose of his calculation he would take the income tax to be 3d in the £1. Then an income of £180 paid ¼d in the £1, an income £250 paid 1d in the £1, an income of £350 paid 1½d in the £1 and an income of £400 or over 3d in the £1. That scale showed that the principle of graduation was really in operation at the present time with respect to the income tax.'

The Economic Basis of Political Conflicts

The death duties illustrate fundamental economic and social developments and the political conflicts these developments engendered. In a somewhat extreme form this line of argument has been presented by a Russian writer, Paul Haensel, who believed that 'the death duties in England and the inheritance taxes in France and other continental countries developed largely as incidental to the political struggle between the old landed aristocracy and the new business oligarchy which the industrial revolution brought to the fore. In England, for example, the eighteenth and early nineteenth centuries which saw the political supremacy of the landed classes, saw also a revenue system based on indirect duties which bore hardly at all upon the landed proprietors and some of which, like the Corn Laws, reacted directly to their advantage. As the industrial and commercial classes gained more political influence, they brought about the abolition of the more obnoxious of these indirect duties and sought to expand the death duties, which would bear more hardly upon landed property than upon capital fortunes. It would be possible for the industrial capitalist whose fortune consisted of securities and other concealable moveables to arrange his property so as to evade death duties, while no such evasion would be possible for the landed proprietor.

The landed interests by no means shorn of their political power, countered by advocating an income tax which would fall upon the large incomes of the rising capitalist classes, but which the agriculturalist would escape to some degree since so much of the income from landed property was psychic income, or disguised as increases in land values, etc., and also by forcing compromises on the issues of the death duties, maintaining the exemption of landed property until 1853,[1] and for many years thereafter maintaining the valuation of land on a capitalization of revenue basis rather than market price. The act of 1894 represented the triumph of the business classes'.[2]

Had Haensel continued his line of argument into a later era he would doubtless have represented the 1925 concession to landowners on the agricultural value of agricultural land as a last fling of a tottering aristocracy: the further progression in the death duties and its extension to income and surtax would have been analysed in terms of the class struggle between Capital and Labour and be called as witness to the growing strength and influence of the pro-

[1] Compare Lord Morley's comments on the 1853 Succession Duty Act, 'The first rudimentary breach in the ramparts of the territorial system'.

[2] Quoted from W. J. Schultz, *The Taxation of Inheritance*, Houghton Mifflin, 1926, p. 101.

letariat. There is a considerable element of truth in this interpretation: for example, few can doubt the important influence on post-1918 death duty legislation of the demand to reduce inequality in the distribution of wealth, which has grown and strengthened with the rise of the Labour movement: but any attempt to explain the history of death duties solely in terms of class struggles—agrarian landowners versus capitalists, or capitalists versus proletariat—would be woefully inadequate if only because it neglected administrative and purely fiscal considerations.

Administrative and Fiscal Considerations

The history of the death duties reveals how much fiscal development is dependent on administrative expediency and financial necessity. The arguments put forward in support of indirect taxation in the eighteenth century[1] were to a considerable extent a rationalization of what was possible. Customs and excise were duties which could be fairly easily and effectively administered: direct taxation would have been liable to extensive evasion.[2] The first English death duty taxed only personalty at least partly because the probate of the will constituted a convenient instrument of taxation; and realty was exempt because it was not subject to probate. It was for a similar reason that settled property on the death of the first heir so long escaped its full share of tax. When realty was taxed by the succession duty of 1853, the preferred treatment given in the valuation of real property up to 1894 may have been at least partly due to the realization of the greater difficulties in valuing land as against most personalty—and the determination to take an easy way out by capitalizing annual values on a life interest basis. Progression was first applied to the estate duty, not because the capital a man left at his death was considered to be a better criterion of his ability to pay than the income he enjoyed during his life, but because at a time when it was believed that a progressive income tax was an administrative impossibility, a progressive death duty was considered practicable.

[1] See J. F. Rees. *Short Fiscal and Financial History of England*, pp. 3–4.

[2] The manner of development of two of the earliest direct taxes is most significant. Both the land tax and the local rate were originally general property taxes. Gradually they became solely taxes on real property because of the difficulty in securing payment on other kinds of property. See J. A. Venn, *Foundations of Agricultural Economics*, chapter 6, e.g. (writing on local rates): 'as was the case with the land tax, all forms of property were concerned at first and gradually all save land and buildings tacitly dropped out of assessment. Again the explanation is the simple one that other forms of property were elusive, and also that the area of lands and the size of buildings, formed an easier criterion by which to assess the wealth of individuals', pp. 129–30.

Harcourt made it quite clear that he believed that progression in the income tax would mean the abandonment of taxation at source, wherein lay its strength as a fiscal weapon. It was because it was felt that progression did not produce the administrative difficulties in the inheritance and estate tax, that a number of dispassionate economists approved of it in death duties but not elsewhere.[1]

We have pointed out how often the changes in the probate and legacy duties in the later eighteenth and early nineteenth centuries, were due to pressure of war finance. Wars have been just as potent a factor in bringing about increases in the duties in the twentieth century. This does not contradict the tendency we have noted amongst politicians to refrain from using death duties as a temporary war tax. Increases in death duties have taken place as a result of the permanently higher level of government expenditure which has followed the two major wars of this country, and which has been at least partly a direct result of these wars. One of the considerations which doubtless weighed very heavily with practical politicians in adopting proportional in preference to regressive taxation and progressive in preference to proportional, must have been the increased yield to be derived from these changes. If the rates of death duty were to remain regressive, or even proportional, and any large increase in revenue to be obtained therefrom, it could only have been managed by an intolerable burden on the smallest estates. If fiscal necessity was not the primary cause of the progression in the estate duty of 1894, it is at least arguable that, with the vast increase in government expenditure which twentieth century conditions necessitated, resort to progression would have been inevitable.

Fiscal Interdependence

Finally, if the death duties reflect in their history the intricate interplay of such varied forces as economic and social conflicts between classes, fiscal theories, changing ethical views and practical expediency, they also emphasize the essential relationship between the different parts of the fiscal structure of the United Kingdom. In particular, we have seen that the history of the death duties cannot be considered in isolation from the problems of income taxation or the difficulties of local government finance. The succession duty of 1853 was in some measure an attempt to achieve indirectly the effect, considered desirable but impracticable directly, which would have followed

[1] Seligman 1908: 'The only important tax to which the progressive scale is at all applicable at present is the inheritance tax.' *Progressive Taxation*, p. 324. Similarly J. S. Mill, *Principles*, Book 5, chapter 2, no. 3.

from taxing 'unearned' income more than 'earned'. The estate duty of 1894 was justified on similar grounds, and also supported by the argument that it was a 'back tax' on the deceased person, compensating the revenue for the lack of graduation in the income tax which was also considered administratively impracticable. Turning to the connection with local taxation, much of the legislation in the forty or so years preceding the reform of 1894 (e.g. the succession duty of 1853, the Local Government Act 1888 and the additions to succession duty of 1888) unsatisfactory 'though such expedients may have been, was undoubtedly partly intended to effect some rough sort of over-all justice on the owners of personal and real property respectively, when local as well as national taxation was taken into account. At the same time the Local Government Act of 1888 in particular was an attempt to satisfy the growing financial needs of local authorities without resort to forms of local taxation other than rates.That the reform of 1894 which equalized the burden of national taxation as regards real and personal property did nothing to solve the local taxation problem, or meet the argument of those who complained that, over-all, realty was bearing an undue weight of tax, is suggested by the events of subsequent years. In 1896 it was thought necessary to reduce to one half the rates on agricultural land, the deficiency being made good by grants to the local authorities out of the yield of that part of the death duties levied on personalty.[1] In 1923 local rates on agricultural property were reduced from one-half to one-quarter, and in 1929 they were abolished altogether. But it must be emphasized that the depressed condition of agriculture during these years was the dominant factor in bringing about rate reductions on agricultural land (which after all is only one section of real property) and not any ethical considerations of over-all equity in tax burdens on the owners of different kinds of property.

The emphasis in this chapter on the history of the death duties has been primarily political and fiscal. Some important historical aspects of the economic and social effects of death duties are considered in the next chapter, in particular their effects during the twentieth century in diminishing the number and size of large private agricultural estates and promoting owner-occupancy in agriculture; and their effects on the organization and life of private industrial and commercial firms. To these matters we now turn as part of an analysis of the incidence of estate duty.

[1] Since the equalization in 1894 this sort of provision was of course even more meaningless than it had been before.

Chapter 3

The Incidence of Estate Duty

(i) INTRODUCTION AND DEFINITIONS

In this chapter we examine the incidence of death duties, with particular reference to the estate duty of the United Kingdom. A substantial proportion of the not very extensive theoretical literature on economic aspects of death duties has been concerned to establish where the incidence of the duty lies—on the deceased or on the inheritor.[1] To some extent this is a semantic dispute which dissolves in an appropriate definition of terms. We shall use the terminology advocated by Lady Hicks,[2] of 'formal incidence' and 'effective incidence'.

Formal incidence is the immediate answer to the question 'Who pays the tax?' It does not take us far with our economic analysis, but it is useful in a social accounting sense. The formal incidence of a death duty is on the inheritor; as Dalton puts it 'the predecessor must be dead before the tax can be levied and dead men, like other inanimate objects, can pay no taxes'.[3]

Effective incidence is an attempt to unravel the full consequences of a tax; it consists, in principle, of a comparison between two situations, one with the tax in force, the other without it, one of these situations necessarily being hypothetical. As will be clear in our subsequent analysis, the full consequences of the tax may affect both predecessor and successor and no useful purpose is served by specifying that effective incidence must rest on one or the other.

We shall look first at those particular parts of the economic system where, because of the nature of the business organization, estate duty may be expected to have most effect, i.e. in agriculture and the private business; then we shall look at the 'macro' picture, the effects on the supply of the factors of production to the economy as a whole, its effect, that is to say, on effort, enterprise and saving.

1 For a survey of the views of various economists on this issue, see J. K. Hall, 'Incidence of Death Duties', *American Economic Review No. 1*, March 1940.

2 U. K. Hicks, 'Terminology and Methods of Tax Analysis', *Economic Journal*, March 1946.

3 H. Dalton, *Principles of Public Finance*, 4th edn., p. 53.

However, there is a necessary preliminary investigation; we must first examine the extent and nature of evasion and avoidance, because the *form* they take may have importamt economic consequences of a macro or micro nature; because substantial evasion and avoidance may have significant effects on the allocation of resources, both the time and effort of the tax avoider and the skilled labour engaged in advising on avoidance; and because they may affect the applicability of any analysis based on the assumption that tax is actually paid.

First, to clarify these terms. As used by tax lawyers, evasion is illegal tax dodging, e.g. a failure on the part of the executors of an estate to include part of the estate in the tax returns.

Avoidance is the adoption of wholly legal methods to reduce liability to tax, i.e. so arranging one's affairs, legally, as to reduce tax liabilities. To quote a famous dictum of Lord Atkins delivering judgement in *Inland Revenue Commissioners v. Duke of Westminster* in 1936: 'The subject whether poor and humble or wealthy and noble has the legal right so to dispose of his capital and income as to attract upon himself the least amount of tax. The only function of a Court of Law is to determine the legal result of his dispositions so far as they affect tax.'

The definition of evasion is unambiguous and appropriate for usage by economists; but that of avoidance is less satisfactory. As it stands it would imply any legitimate activity which would reduce liability. Thus, if as a result of tobacco tax a man gave up smoking and instead ate sweets and consequently paid less tax, this would constitute avoidance on the basis of the tax lawyers' definition; similarly, any reduction in supply of effort as a result of an income tax would constitute avoidance of income tax by the simple expedient of not earning as much income.

Clearly, avoidance, if it is not to be so broad as to embrace almost the whole of the analysis of the effective incidence of taxation, must be more closely defined. At least two distinctions can be made. First, we can distinguish between avoidance where there has been a change of objectives as a result of the tax, e.g. an alteration of a man's consumption pattern to avoid purchase tax; and avoidance where personal objectives have been substantially achieved despite the tax, e.g. that despite estate duty, a man's estate has been handed on largely intact to his son by means of gifts. Second, to 'avoid' some taxes may be to fulfil the purpose for which they were imposed, e.g. a protective tariff or a high purchase tax to restrict consumption of a potentially harmful commodity. (Nor are the examples necessarily confined to outlay taxes: thus, avoidance of estate duty by gifts which were untaxed or taxed at a lower rate would be in accordance with the intention of the legislature *if* parliament had wished to encourage the transfer of property to younger people.)

Henceforth in our discussion we shall seek to confine the term avoidance to the kind of legal re-arrangement of affairs and activities where the 'tax payer' reduces his tax liability without substantially changing his objectives *and* where the intention of the taxing statute is defeated.

This definition is far from perfect; it rests on the meaning given to 'substantially' and is based on an assumption about the intention behind a statute—which might well be a matter of dispute. Nevertheless, it is of more practical use to the economist than the broader definition of the tax lawyer and in most instances there is a clear enough demarcation line between activities which constitute avoidance as we have defined it and other legal methods of reducing tax liability. For example, if, as a result of estate duty a wealthy man decides it is not worth saving for heirs and instead spends some of his wealth in taking his family on a trip round the world, this is an aspect on the effective incidence of the tax on saving but is not avoidance as we are now using the term. If, on the other hand, he were to decide to continue to save but to give his property to his heirs in the expectation that he would live seven years thereafter, this, if his expectation is realized, does constitute avoidance, for he has substantially achieved the object of his saving—i.e. passing on his wealth more or less intact to his heirs—despite the tax.

(ii) AVOIDANCE

How significant are evasion and avoidance as defined?

Evasion

The nature of evasion is such that its amount can only be guessed. Almost certainly the most common form is the failure on the part of the deceased's relatives or executors to reveal or return items of the estate which can be most easily concealed, e.g. cash in the house, small personal effects, jewellery, ornaments. Another area which lends itself to evasion is gifts inter vivos where the donor fails to survive the 'statutory period' and the gift is not revealed. But gifts and items of the readily concealable kind will rarely form more than a small part of a large or moderately large estate, and unless evasion is planned with the connivance of the deceased before his death, a will may prove a highly embarrassing inventory of some of these personal valuables.

There are other reasons for believing that the existence of fraud on a large scale is improbable. Despite a decline in tax morality in Britain, there remain many whose standard of conduct would prevent them from contravening the law. Others are deterred by the fear of discovery and the penalties and ignominy of failure; the Inland Revenue is known to cross-check the capital value of estates with the previous income tax returns of the deceased and to investigate any inconsistencies revealed. Further, the existence of loopholes for avoidance makes illegal action less necessary for the tax dodger. Except where there is collusion between beneficiaries as a body, they have an interest in seeing that all property of the deceased sees the light of day; beneficiaries will want to establish an incontrovertible legal claim to their legacies. Any large-scale evasion would only be possible with the connivance of the executor, who has sworn to the truth of the statements in the estate duty account; unlike the income tax returns, which simply require a signed declaration, estate duty accounts have to be sworn to by affidavit. Moreover, for the larger estates in particular, executors are often professional men, accountants, solicitors, qualified employees of executor and trustee companies, with personal or company reputations to maintain, who have far more to lose than to gain by conniving at illegalities.

A form of partial evasion which may have some currency is the undervaluation of assets. For some years before 1953, the Inland Revenue in their annual reports published a comparison of the value of property in land and buildings for death duty purposes 'as brought in by the accounting parties' and 'as certified by the Valuation Office' and indicated the percentage increase due to the official valuation. Publication of this comparison ceased with the 1953 report, without published explanation; but the figures available, set out in table 3.1, reveal a markedly higher level of undervaluation after the second World War than pre-war and in the early war years. This could be interpreted as evidence of increased willingness to evade by undervaluation; but there are plausible alternative explanations—for example, that the 'accounting parties' were simply not keeping pace with inflation in their valuations. Moreover, market valuation of land and buildings, in the absence of an actual sale, lacks precision and the 'accounting parties' may not have been deliberately undervaluing so much as simply giving the taxpayer the benefit of a genuine doubt.

Much more significant than evasion is avoidance.

Forms of Avoidance

Methods of avoidance can be grouped under six heads: domicile abroad; gifts; trusts; investment in assets which carry reduced rates or are not aggregated with the estate; reduction in the estate duty value of assets; and generation skipping. These methods may be adopted singly or in combination. This account is not offered as an exhaustive statement of avoidance possibilities but as a sufficient

TABLE 3.1. *Valuations of Property (Land, including buildings) for the Purposes of Death Duties, GB.*

Financial year	No. of cases	Principal Value			
		As brought in by accounting parties £m.	As certified by valuation office £m	Increase due to official valuation	
				Amount £m.	Per cent
1938–39	85,091	127·1	132·0	4·9	3·87
1939–40	83,813	113·5	119·0	5·5	4·48
1940–41	89,921	114·8	120·3	5·5	4·80
1941–42	91,808	118·9	125·2	6·3	5·32
1942–43	92,466	130·2	137·3	7·2	5·50
1946–47	94,017	147·6	160·8	13·3	9·00
1947–48	93,960	168·8	187·2	18·5	10·95
1948–49	101,713	211.8	235·2	23·4	11·06
1949–50	91,793	200·1	221·4	21·3	10·64
1950–51	89,568	199·2	220·2	21·0	10·53
1951–52	98,982	225·7	249·6	24·0	10·63
1952–53	93,802	209·4	228·7	19·3	9·21

No figures of principal value are available 1943–4, 1944–5 or 1945–6.
Source: *Commissioners of Inland Revenue, Reports* Nos. 91 and 96, Cmd. 7738 and Cmd. 9030 respectively.

indication of the main methods to enable some assessment of likely economic consequences to be made and to provide a basis for some of the suggestions for reform in the subsequent chapter.

Until the loophole was closed in 1962 immovable property held outside the UK was exempt from estate duty. Since that date however all property, wherever situated, comes within the estate duty net, but it remains open to the tax avoider to become domiciled abroad, exchanging Britain's high death duty for a milder tax climate. Although there are difficulties in removing capital outside the sterling area, Ireland, the Channel Islands, the Isle of Man and places such as Malta are all within the sterling area. Moreover, with modern air travel, a foreign domicile[1] is compatible with the maintenance of business and social interests in this country. But abandoning one's native land or becoming an international commuter is not acceptable to many.

The simplest method of avoidance is to give property away and live seven years thereafter. Provided that the donor still has a considerable life expectation, the risk from estate duty liability can be removed at a modest cost if the recipient of the gift insures the life of the donor for seven years for an amount equal to the contingent estate duty liability. If the gifts are made by someone of advanced age, the premiums might be too high for insurance to worth while; but even if the donor fails to survive the full statutory period, if he lives beyond the beginning of the fifth year the rate of duty on the gift is diminished[2].

On a smaller scale judicious use can be made, over a period of time, of the exemption of gifts up to a maximum of £500 for each recipient within the seven-year period (ignoring gifts which come within the 'normal' and 'habitual' exemption). This provision may be used in conjunction with an insurance policy. Until the budget of March 1968, life insurance policies taken out under the Married Women's Property Act were taxed as a separate estate, thus reducing the average rate of duty; a man at the outset nominated his wife as the beneficiary of this insurance but paid the premiums himself. He can still pay the premiums himself and they can be treated as a gift provided they are not in excess of £500 in a seven-year period: the policy is made over to his wife and, on his death, the maturing policy is her property and does not count as part of his estate.

Clearly, outright gifts have their disadvantages, and gifts *must* be without strings if they are to come within the exemption provisions of the estate duty. One method of giving which may commend itself, therefore, is by means of a settlement which enables a man to continue to exert some indirect influence over the distribution of his wealth although he himself must not benefit from the provisions of the settlement. If, for example, a man is reluctant to make an outright gift of capital to his wife because he fears that, after his death, someone may marry her for her money, or she may marry again and not make adequate provision for his children, then he can make a settlement by which she receives the life interest whilst his children receive the capital on her death. Such a settlement counts as a gift, so that to avoid estate duty on his death the settlement must

[1] Domicile does not simply mean establishing a residence; there must also be present the intention to reside there.

[2] See chapter 2, p. 63.

be made more than seven years before. Again, the possibility of an earlier death can be insured against, but if the settlor undertakes the insurance, the policy needs to cover not only estate duty attributable to the settlement but also the additional duty on the estate resulting from the aggregation of the maturity value of the insurance policy with the remainder of the estate. Even so, estate duty savings from a settlement can be substantial for a man in middle age. On a straightforward settlement of this nature, estate duty remains payable on the death of the widow at the rate appropriate to her estate because a definable interest then passes to the children, unless the settlement has been caught for estate duty on the death of the settlor husband. There is an exemption on the second death of a settlement in favour of a surviving spouse provided that the spouse has no power to control the destination of the capital.

To escape estate duty on subsequent deaths, discretionary trusts carried a distinct attraction until April 1969[1]. Under a discretionary trust the trustees have powers to determine payments of income and capital to any or all of a number of persons or classes of persons (e.g. children, grandchildren). Because the benefits are at the discretion of the trustees, no clear definable interests passed on the death of the beneficiaries until the number of possible beneficiaries was reduced to two. Once the trustees have received their initial instructions, they could be given no further instructions and must be free to use their discretion; but in practice the trustees take into account what they know or believe to be the wishes of the settlor. Discretionary trusts can meet a genuine need unrelated to estate duty avoidance. For example, an oldish widower with several daughters may wish to provide for them according to their individual needs (e.g. whether or not they marry and, if so, whether their husbands are rich) which may not be clear at the time of the widower's death. Nevertheless, Professor G. S. A. Wheatcroft, writing in 1965, hazarded that 'in Great Britain it is probably true to say that 95 per cent of all discretionary and accumulation trusts are created solely for tax saving reasons'.[2] As a result of the 1969 provisions this may soon cease to be true.

A further method of avoidance is investment in assets which carry a reduced rate of duty or are not aggregated with the estate. The

[1] The 1969 Finance Act provided that if an individual had enjoyed income in the seven years ending with his death, there was a liability to estate duty of the proportion of the fund equal to the proportion of its income that he has enjoyed in that period.

[2] *Estate and Gift Taxation; a comparative study*. Sweet & Maxwell, London, 1965, p. 136.

various concessions noted in the previous chapter come within this category. Of these, the most important is the 45 per cent rebate on the agricultural value of agricultural property, which has added to the amenity value of 'living in the country' as well as encouraged 'death bed' purchases of agricultural land. Business buildings and plant, when valued on the assets basis, enjoy the same concessions as agricultural land. Again, properties of artistic, national, scientific or historical interest are not aggregated with the rest of the estate. Before the 1969 budget, no duty was payable on these assets as long as they were not sold; when sold, duty was payable only at the rate previously paid by the estate. Thus it was possible for a man to borrow on the security of part of his estate and to buy paintings with the money borrowed and with the remainder of his estate so that, at death, apart from paintings, his net estate was below the exemption limit for estate duty. Then, even if his heirs sold the paintings immediately after his death, no duty was payable on the proceeds because the rate of duty on the estate had been nil.[1] However, the Finance Act of 1969 restricted this relief. A similar concession still applies to timber; the value of the trees on an estate is not included at the time of death; duty is not paid until they are sold and then they are not aggregated with the estate to determine the rate of duty.

A somewhat different method of avoidance, open to those with shares in private companies, takes the form of reducing the death duty value of the shares. This can be done by obtaining a Stock Exchange quotation for a minority of the equity; then the estate duty office has to use the stock market value for *all* shares ignoring the extra value which the effective control confers and which the family retains.

Finally, there is avoidance by generation skipping. From a family point of view, the weight of estate duty depends on the frequency with which it is levied in any given time period. If B is A's child and C is B's child, estate duty is effectively reduced if property is bequeathed direct from A to C without passing through B. Increased longevity from falling mortality rates together with the trend to earlier marriages, increases the feasibility and attractions of this method of avoidance; there is more chance that C will have reached an age of discretion by the time A dies, and hence A will be more willing to make C his heir and B more willing to let him. Generation skipping with its implications for the age of inheritors is an issue which we shall consider at more depth in chapter 4 when we examine the equity of death duties.

[1] I am indebted to Professor G. S. A. Wheatcroft for this exotic example.

How Much Avoidance?

Listing the main methods of avoidance is not difficult; estimating its extent is little easier than that of estimating the extent of evasion. No assessment of the amount of avoidance can be more than an intelligent guess and a rough guide to its magnitude.

Several general pointers suggest that avoidance is considerable. The financial sections of the daily press, as well as some professional journals, not infrequently carry advertisements from tax consultants of an 'AXE YOUR TAX' variety. In 1959 Mr D. J. Campion could write in the *British Tax Review* that 'estate duty saving has been a thriving industry for many years'. There is little doubt that since the second World War an extensive literature on so-called 'tax planning' and a new class of professional consultants has come into existence. The following quotation from *The Guardian*, February 24, 1967, under the heading Advice on Tax Problems, is particularly interesting as an indication of the range of firms engaged in giving advice on estate duty avoidance.

> 'Twelve major firms engaged in company finance, insurance, agricultural land, forestry and works of art have set up a Capital Protection Consortium to give "package deal" advice to people with estate duty and tax planning problems. The scheme is promoted by three life assurance brokers, Antony Gibbs and Partners, Kirkby Seymour and Partners and H. W. Stutter and Partners, who specialize in estate duty and "tax mitigation".
>
> 'Advice on agricultural land will be given by Knight, Frank and Rutley, on forestry by the Economic Forestry Group and Tilhill Forestry, on works of art by Sotheby's and on private companies by Estate Duties Investment Trust. Four major merchant banks will contribute advice on finance, company reorganization and investment.'

Another indication of the extent, and more particularly the trend, of avoidance, is the figures of gifts inter vivos which become liable to estate duty, i.e. gifts where the donor failed to survive the statutory period. Gifts are the simplest form of avoidance and are likely to be that most widely used. The gifts subject to estate duty are declared in the estate duty account. Even though the donors may have made the gifts without thought of avoidance, yet had the death not occurred during the statutory period the effect of the gifts would have been to reduce the duty payable. Figures of gifts on which duty *was* paid can therefore be considered attempted avoidance which failed. Knowledge of the failures does not provide a precise guide to the extent of success, but it is reasonable to assume that the failures represent a fairly constant fraction of the whole, or at the very least, that the total of gifts inter vivos moves in the same direction as the sub-total of gifts on which duty was paid. We have no consistent figures over a long period but those that are available are interesting. Figures of gifts inter vivos on which estate duty was paid were collected and published in the Inland Revenue Reports for the period 1898-1931, except for the years 1916-1919 inclusive. In 1939 publication stopped, to be resumed on a somewhat different basis in 1961.

Because of the big break in time, the different basis of the later figures, and other factors, notably the change in the length in the statutory period, the information for the two periods is presented separately. Full details for both periods are set out in Appendix B.

In 1898 the gross capital value of gifts inter vivos subject to estate duty in Great Britain was £858,000; by 1931 it was £6 million, having attained a peak of nearly £9 million in 1929. The general growth of capital and price changes make a direct monetory comparison almost meaningless; but these distorting factors are likely to be largely neutralized by expressing the total of gifts subject to estate duty as a percentage of total property subject to estate duty in each year; changes in this proportion can be taken as a guide to changes in the trend of gifts inter vivos. To reduce random calculations the data is presented as a three year moving average (figure 3.1). The big increase for 1910 must be largely attributable to the effect of the extension of the statutory period from one to three years. An interpretation compatible with the figures would be that for the first five or six years of the period little change in rates of giving took place; the five or six years prior to 1910 witnessed a distinct upward trend, perhaps significantly contemporaneous with the reforming Liberal government and associated with the increases in estate duty of 1907 and 1909. After the rise from 1910, associated with the extended statutory period, no further clear trend is apparent before the first World War. When the figures are again published after the war, they show giving established at a higher level than hitherto, with possibly a further slight upward trend. It will be recalled that a big increase in duty took place in 1919, by which maximum rates were raised from twenty to forty per cent.

Turning now to the later period; when figures of gifts inter vivos are again published in 1961 the statutory period had become five years (since 1946); moreover, the figures published by the Inland Revenue from 1961 are the value of gifts *for estate duty purposes*, which is different from the total value of the gifts which become liable to estate duty; under the terms of the Finance Act 1960, where gifts take place in the third, fourth and fifth years before death, their value is reduced for estate duty purposes (by 15, 30 and 60 per cent respectively) and it is this reduced value which the Inland Revenue figures show.[1] Thus, no direct comparison can be made with the

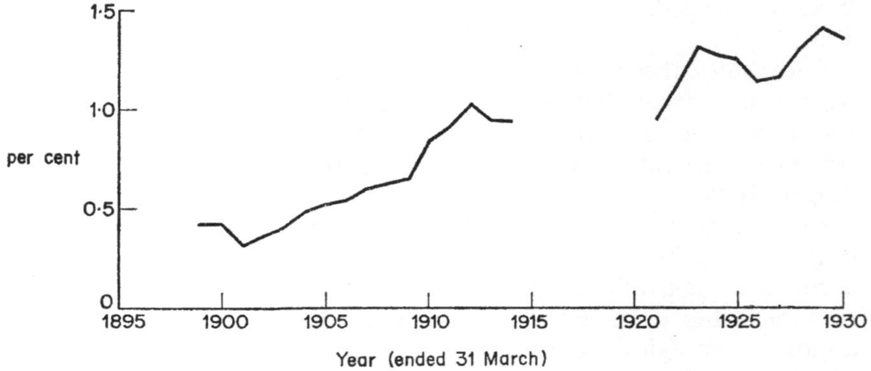

FIGURE 3.1. Gross capital value of gifts inter vivos subject to estate duty as a percentage of gross capital value of all property subject to estate duty in the same year, calculated as a three year moving average. GB 1898–1931

earlier figures. Whilst the extension of the statutory period increases the amount of gifts which become liable to duty, the reduction in the value of what the Inland Revenue call the 'graduated gifts' means that total giving within the statutory period is undervalued in the years 1961–1968.

In 1961, the value of gifts on which estate duty was charged was just over £25 million representing 2·43 per cent of the net capital value of total property subject to estate duty. In 1968, the corresponding figures were £41,500,000 and 3·02 per cent. During these eight years the increase in the value of gifts for estate duty purposes was 64·8 per cent against an increase in total property subject to estate duty of 32·8 per cent. These figures may exaggerate somewhat the upward trend in giving, for the total for 1961 may have been abnormally low; but a steady upward trend is very marked when the data is expressed as a three year moving average (figure 3·2). This

[1] For further details of this and other less important differences in the basis of the statistics of the two periods, see Appendix B.

rise is the more remarkable in that the period saw no increase in estate duty rates.[1]

What conclusions can be drawn from these statistical exercises? In the absence of knowledge of the mathematical realtionship between the total amount of giving and the amount which becomes subject to estate duty, we cannot use this data to establish the extent

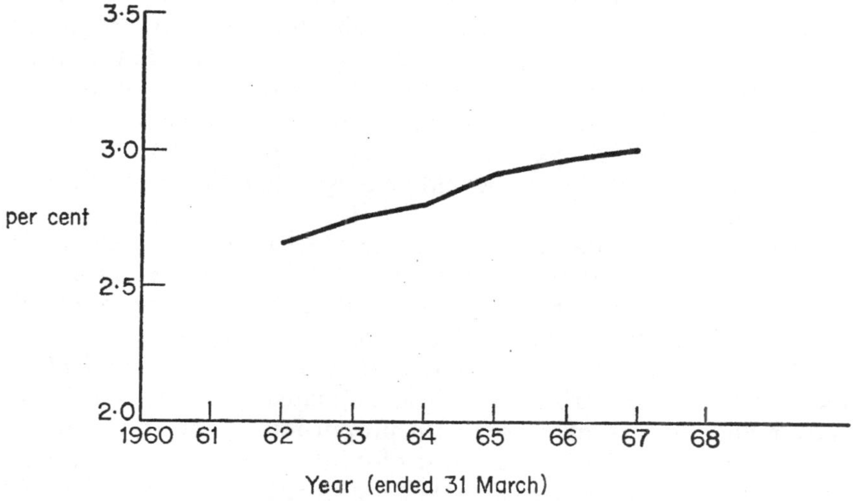

FIGURE 3.2. Value of gifts inter vivos subject to estate duty as a percentage of net capital value of all property to estate duty in the same year, calculated as a three year moving average. GB 1961–8.

of avoidance by gifts.[2] But we can use it for the trend. There has clearly been a secular upward trend in the amount of giving since the introduction of estate duty. There may have been periods of stability in the amount of giving and, because of the big gap in statistical information between 1930 and 1961 we cannot say for certain that there may not have been periods in which giving declines. Indeed, it is not unlikely that the second World War witnessed

[1] The long-term capital gains tax was introduced in 1965 by which death counts as 'realization'; but as gifts also count in the same way, no direct saving of this new tax would result from giving.

[2] In *The Taxation of Personal Wealth*, Appendix II, University of Illinois Press, 1967, Dr Alan Tait attempts to estimate the extent of gifts inter vivos from gifts liable to estate duty by assuming an 'average' age of giving of 60; by using life expectancy figures, the percentage who will probably die between the ages of 60 and 65 can be assessed; multiplying the value of gifts liable to estate duty in any one year by the reciprocal of this mortality rate gives an estimate of total gifts inter vivos. The weakness of this method is the lack of an adequate basis for the initial assumption of the average age of donors.

a decline in giving because of the higher risks of mortality of those who would otherwise have been the recipients. But the overall trend has been markedly upwards and the rise is continuing at a significant rate. There may be social factors at work which have nothing directly to do with estate duty, for example, that with diminishing inequality between the sexes husbands more readily share property with their wives. But whatever the reason, it seems fairly clear that the amount of estate duty avoidance by gifts has grown substantially and is continuing to grow, Indeed, there is reason for believing that our method underestimates the upward trend. The rise in life expectations might be expected to lead to some decline in the proportion of gifts which became subject to estate duty; if so, then the upward trend in total giving would be bigger than the upward trend in gifts on which duty is paid.

One method of attempting to estimate the total of avoidance is to take the figures of estates liable to duty for a year early in the century when death duties were low, and hence when the extent of avoidance could be assumed also to be low, and then to estimate the yield which would result if current estate duty rates were applied to the estates of the earlier year. The estimated yield from current rates could then be expressed as a proportion of the total wealth held in that year. The actual yield of estate duty for a recent year could also be expressed as a proportion of the total wealth for the same year and the ratios of yield to wealth for the two years compared. If there was no avoidance, subject to reservations which we list below, the ratios should be the same. If the ratio is higher for the earlier year, then this would indicate the existence of avoidance and its amount could be calculated, Thus, supposing that the ratio in the early year was twice that of the later, this would imply an amount of avoidance equal to the yield of estate duty in the later year.

Dr Tait has made these calculations to compare 1912 with 1960.[1] Applying 1960 rates to the estates liable to duty in 1912, gives estimated receipts of £79 million. Total wealth in 1912 has been estimated at £9,310 million to £10,500 million. Therefore the proportion of estate duty receipts at 1960 rates to total wealth in that year is 0·75–0·85 per cent. Actual receipts from estate duty in 1960 were £236 million representing 0·56 per cent of the 1960 national wealth. The 1912 ratio thus exceeded that of 1960 by between 1·3 and 1·5 times. The extent of avoidance is thus estimated as equivalent to between 30 and 50 per cent of the yield of estate duty in 1960.

[1] A. Tait, *ibid.*

As Dr Tait points out, the validity of the calculations rests on two main assumptions:

(i) that avoidance in 1912 really was negligible; and

(ii) that the distribution of wealth was similar in the two years compared.

Both assumptions are open to doubt. Our earlier analysis of gifts inter vivos suggest that avoidance by gifts was already in evidence and increasing by 1912; to this extent the estimate of avoidance for 1960 would under-state its amount. On the second assumption, our figures in chapter 1 indicated some shift in the distribution of wealth between 1912 and 1962 in the direction of less inequality; moreover, the estimates of total wealth are themselves subject to the kinds of limitations discussed in chapter 1. A further factor is changes in life expectation; we should expect rising life expectations to result in a decline of the yield of estate duty as a proportion of total net wealth, since a smaller proportion of wealth might be expected to fall liable to duty in any one year. It follows that no great weight can be put upon this estimate.

Nevertheless, although we may not be able to quantify precisely the extent of avoidance, it is notable that all the evidence, the general observations, the increase in gifts liable to estate duty, and Dr Tait's calculations, point in the same direction. There seems little doubt that avoidance is substantial and continuing to grow. It is well within the bounds of feasibility that it amounts to 50 per cent, or even more, of the yield of estate duty.

Consequences of Avoidance

Our knowledge of the forms of avoidance provides pointers to many of its consequences, even though our ignorance of its extent prevents us from assessing their significance. The attractions of a domicile abroad is likely to mean some transfer of wealth and possibly enterprise from the country; where capital remains in the UK and income is transmitted to a foreign domicile, a deficit item enters the balance of payments. Gifts from the older to the younger and generation skipping may have the effect of transferring wealth from those who have become less enterprising to those who are more enterprising; it may also constitute a transfer from persons with high to those with lower propensities to save. The attraction of trusts for estate duty purposes means that more wealth is held in a form which lacks mobility. As a result of avoidance measures, particular forms of investment—e.g. in pictures and insurance policies—are favoured; investment in agricultural land as an avoidance device may reduce the efficiency with which some land is farmed because the owner lacks interest in the activity, and this additional demand accentuates price increases in agricultural land.

In our subsequent analysis of the effective incidence of estate duty, the significance of avoidance must be remembered; for example, when we look at the effects of estate duty on the incentive to save, it seems likely that those who are keenest on saving for heirs will not so much be deterred from saving by the tax as be induced to seek methods of avoidance. Avoidance may therefore modify our conclusions about the effect of estate duty on the supply of the factors of production.

Several broad consequences of widespread avoidance should also be mentioned. As a result of it, estate duty is capricious in its incidence; objectives of the tax—equity, equality and efficiency—are not attained. Further, if the State seeks a given yield from death duties, then the weight of tax on those who do not avoid is increased because of those who do. Again, the more widespread is avoidance and the more complicated the avoidance devices, the more the resources of the community, the time and the effort of the avoider and his advisers and those on the Revenue side who seek to outwit him, are taken up in a communally unproductive activity.

(iii) AGRICULTURE

It is on 'family businesses' that death duties may be expected to exert their maximum effect. Where a business is run as a public joint stock company and provided shares are nor concentrated in a few hands, the death of a shareholder—i.e. one of the owners of the business—will not affect the business. Some change in ownership takes place whether the heirs retain the shares or sell them to pay the duty, but the resources of the company are unaffected by this transfer. Where shares are heavily concentrated, however, where they are unquoted, or where a business is a partnership or an individual proprietorship, then death duties can exercise a powerful influence.

It was the agricultural interest which cried out the loudest when Harcourt introduced the new estate duty in 1894, for agriculture has traditionally been and remains the branch of economic activity in which the family unit has predominated, both in the farming and ownership of land. The World Census of Agriculture[1] 1960–1 recorded that 88 per cent of holdings in England and Wales were

[1] *Supplementary Report to Agricultural Statistics* 1962–3, *England and Wales*, Ministry of Agriculture, Fisheries and Food, HMSO, 1965. For further details of this report, see Appendix C.

occupied by individuals and 10 per cent by partnerships and that, together, these accounted for 92 per cent of the total area; most of the remaining holdings were farmed by companies, institutions and similar corporate bodies. The *ownership* of agricultural land we examine in some detail below.

Broadly speaking two main influences of estate duty on agriculture can be discerned:

(i) Throughout the twentieth century estate duty has been an influence in the break-up of large agricultural and large landed estates, which in turn have been the key factor in two other changes in land ownership, an increasing public ownership of land, and, more important, a growth in owner-occupancy to such an extent that this has become the dominant form of tenure;

(ii) More recently, especially from the late fifties, the striking increases in the price of agricultural land have so increased the value of farms that estate duty has become a serious problem for the owner-occupier of even a small or medium sized farm; the problem has been accentuated since 1965 by the long-term capital gains tax, under which death counts as realization.

Thus a paradox is evident; estate duty, which helped to create the large class of owner-occupiers, has become a threat to their efficiency and even their existence.

But let us examine these changes in more detail.

Twentieth Century Changes in Land Ownership

Our problem is twofold: to identify the changes which have taken place and to assess how far they can be attributed to estate duty.

Decline in Large Private Estates. Reliable data on land ownership is scanty; the latest comprehensive national survey relates to 1873, the so called New Domesday Book[1] and that was the first of its kind for 800 years. But a more limited report published in 1948, *Land Ownership in the Eastern Counties, 1941*,[2] which was a development of information collected for the National Farm Survey of 1941, can be compared with the relevant county returns of the 1873 survey.

There are three principal difficulties in this comparison. First, because the 1941 data covers only a part of the country it may not be entirely typical of the country as a whole, especially as it is

[1] *Population—Owners of Land 1873*, C. 1097.

[2] Report No. 30 Farm Economics Branch, Department of Agriculture, University of Cambridge, 1948.

drawn from one geographical area. Second, the period of the comparison is far from ideal; our first datum line, 1873, is some forty years earlier than we could have wished—it is unlikely that death duties can have affected agriculture significantly before the first World War; for our second datum line, the 1960s would have been preferable to the early 1940s. Third, and perhaps most important, the basis of the returns is in each case different. Broadly the 1873 return can be taken to cover all land, the 1941 figures referring only to agricultural land excluding forest land. In each county therefore, the area covered by the 1873 survey is considerably larger that that covered in 1941, mainly because of urban and forest land in the former. Though there are other small discrepancies in basis, this difference in extent constitutes the principal margin of error in the comparison. We should expect most urban land to be held in small estates (except for the holdings of local authorities): on the other hand forest land will often be in large private or public estates. Our method of analysis will be to distribute this 'excess acreage' (of 1873) over estates of different sizes and categories in 1941, on the basis of different assumptions, to try to obtain the most reliable picture of the changes in the extent of large estates both public and private.[1]

Tables for the six eastern counties where comparison is possible—Bedford, Huntingdon, Norfolk, Suffolk, Essex and Hertfordshire—are included in Appendix C together with a comparison of 1873 and 1936 for Buckinghamshire.[2] For the four eastern counties in which the margin of error is least—Bedford, Huntingdon, Norfolk and Suffolk—the figures of large estates for 1873 and 1941 are shown in table 3.2 below. Table 3.3 shows the decline in the extent of large estates for the four counties combined, on the basis of three assumptions:

(i) that the whole of the excess in acreage (for estates of one acre and above) of 1873 over 1941 consisted in 1941 of private estates over 2,000 acres;
(ii) that the whole of the excess in acreage (for estates of one acre and above) of 1873 over 1941 consisted in 1941 of estates below 1,000 acres;
(iii) that the whole of the excess in acreage (for estates of one acre and above) of 1873 over 1941 consisted in 1941 of estates of all

[1] A fuller account of the statistical data and the problems of comparing the 1873 and 1941 returns is contained in Appendix C.

[2] Data for Buckinghamshire in 1936 is from Thomas and Elms, *The Farms and Estates of Buckinghamshire*, Faculty of Agriculture, University of Reading, Bulletin L1, 1938.

sizes and categories in the same proportion as the estates already analysed for that year.

Assumptions (i) and (ii) are included not because they are at all probable, but because they represent the extremes. The third assumption is likely to provide the estimate nearest the true picture, but there is no reason to believe that this assumption corresponds precisely with the facts.

There can be no doubt that the area of land held in the form of

TABLE 3.2. *Bedfordshire, Huntingdon, Norfolk and Suffolk 1873 and 1941*

Estates over 1,000 Acres

County	Extent of estates in thousands of acres 1873				Extent of estates in thousands of acres 1941			
	one acre and above	over 1,000	over 2,000	private over 2,000	one acre and above	over 1,000	over 2,000	private over 2,000
Bedford	285	161	130	127	244	99	62	38
Huntingdon	225	113	92	89	200	87	67	42
Norfolk	1,232	733	583	564	1,032	487	373	287
Suffolk	909	475	387	382	775	290	226	193
TOTAL	2,651	1,483	1,193	1,162	2,251	963	728	560

Difference in extent between the total of estates of one acre and above for the four counties combined in 1873 and 1941 respectively:
absolute = 400,000 acres
relative i.e. percentage excess of 1873 over 1941 = 17·8

TABLE 3.3. *Percentage Decline in Extent of Large Estates (four counties combined) 1873 and 1941*

Assumption	Over 1,000 acres	Over 2,000 acres	private over 2,000 acres
(i) above	8·0	5·4	17·4
(ii) above	35·0	39·0	51·8
(iii) above	23·6	28·1	43·3

large estates has declined, for even on the most unfavourable and unrealistic assumption (i)–i.e. that all forest, urban land, etc. belonged to large estates in 1941—a decline is indicated. If 1,000 acres is taken as the definition of a large estate then the decline in extent of large estates has probably been rather less (proportionately) than if 2,000 is taken. The most reasonable assumption (iii)–i.e. a proportional distribution of the excess acreage—suggests that by 1941 the extent of large estates over 1,000 acres had decreased by between 20 and 30 per cent, the extent of estates over 2,000 acres probably by an additional 5 per cent. If we look only at private estates over 2,000 acres[1] the extent of the decline seems likely to have been rather more than 40 per cent. Since 1941, factors making for the break-up of large agricultural estates have continued, there is evidence of further growth in large public estates and especially in owner-occupation; thus it is clear that the decline in large private estates has proceeded, possibly at an accelerated rate.

Growth of Public Estates. Our evidence indicated a bigger decline in the extent of large private estates than of all large estates; the other side of this picture is that public bodies have become owners of large estates to a greater extent than before, absolutely as well as relatively. The Eastern Counties Report does not give the details of individual public ownership, but the report for Buckinghamshire in 1936, gives the comparisons of individual holdings by the same authorities and organizations in 1936 and 1873. With the exceptions of Church Lands which do not permit of an accurate comparison between the two dates, all the principal public owners of land had increased their holdings by 1936—the Crown, local authorities (principally through the development of small holding estates) and educational bodies (Oxford Colleges and Eton College); these changes are probably fairly typical of the kind of public bodies whose land holdings had been increasing in the eastern counties.

In the country as a whole, besides those public owners of land mentioned in the Buckinghamshire survey, other public bodies have been acquiring land on a large scale both before and after 1936. By far the biggest single land owner in the country, public and private, is the Forestry Commission which, founded as recently as 1919, began by acquiring traditional Crown forests, such as the New Forest, and went on to buy forests from private land owners and also large tracts of moorland and mountains for planting. The

[1] In comparing *private* estates, 1873 and 1941, the available data only permits a comparison over 2,000 acres; we cannot compare private estates over 1,000 acres.

Commission now holds over $2\frac{1}{2}$ million acres and continues to expand its empire.

In terms of total land area, the next most important land owner is the Ministry of Defence with probably upwards of half a million acres. Post 1945 nationalisation had the effect of bringing into public ownership land previously held privately. British Railways possess possibly a quarter of a million acres; more relevant to agricultural land is the holding of the National Coal Board of about 300,000 acres of which about half is agricultural on the surface and now held by tenants of the Board.[1]

Another large and growing public land owner whose holding is particularly related to the effects of death duties, is the National Trust for Places of Historic Interest or Natural Beauty. The National Trust was founded in 1895; by 1914 the Trust had a little under 6,000 acres of leasehold and freehold land; by 1939 its land holding had risen to 39,000 and by 1945 to 112,000 acres. In a publication of March 1969, the Trust recorded an ownership of about 355,000 acres, in England, Wales and Northern Ireland (there is a separate National Trust for Scotland) and the total continues to mount; besides the gardens and parks which form the setting for its historic mansions and cottages, the National Trust owns forests, downs, moorlands and large tracts of cultivated land; in 1969 it was landlord to about 600 farm tenants.[2]

Increase in Owner Occupancy. The evidence for the third major change in land ownership, the increase in the number of owner occupiers, is also less complete than we could wish.[3] The number of owner occupiers in the country as a whole and the extent of their holdings appear to have remained a fairly constant proportion of total occupiers, and of the total area under crops and grass, for many years before the first World War—probably for most of the nineteenth century. There is some evidence of an increase in owner-occupancy from 1909, slowly at first, then with increasing speed after 1917, with the immediate post-war years showing a veritable buying spree. Agricultural depression in 1921 checked the rise but

1 On this subject of land ownership, where hard information is difficult to come by, reference should be made to two popular studies of interest and value, Mervyn Jones, 'Who Owns Britain?' the *Observer Weekend Review*, March 21 and 28, 1965; and MacDonald Hastings, 'The Profit (and Loss) in Owning Land', *Weekend Telegraph*, December 2, 1966.

2 The 1969 figures are from *Properties of the National Trust*, March 1969. The earlier figures are taken from the Trust's Annual Reports.

3 A full account of the statistical data on owner occupancy is given in Appendix C.

it recommenced in 1924. The figures published annually in Agricultural Statistics are too inaccurate up to 1927 to do more than reveal the trend. In that year, however, the Board of Agriculture and Fisheries made a special effort to obtain reliable returns and the analysis yielded the result that in 1927 over 36 per cent of the total land under crops and grass in England and Wales was owned by its occupiers and the proportion of holdings owner-occupied was 36·6 per cent.[1] These compare with pre-war percentages that were almost certainly below fifteen and may have been less than twelve per cent in each case.

Between 1927 and 1941 there is a gap in reliable information on owner-occupancy for the country as a whole. In 1941, however, approximately 35 per cent of occupiers owned or mainly owned their holdings and 33 per cent of the area of crops and grass in England and Wales was owned by occupiers, according to the *National Farm Survey*.[2] As the 1941 compilation was on a slightly different basis from and was founded on more complete information than that of 1927, we are warned that the slightly lower figures of 1941 cannot be taken as conclusive evidence of a reaction against owner-occupancy. However there is some general evidence, e.g. the number of bankruptcies amongst farmers and reports of land brokers, that the depression of 1929 reduced the number of owner-occupiers, which subsequently started to rise again from about 1934.

Although there is nothing to suggest a post-war spree such as that which followed World War I, owner-occupation grew during and after the second World War. Figures for 1950[3] suggested that about 36 per cent of holdings were wholly owned, whilst a further 15 per cent were part-owned, part-rented. Because the average size of farms owned was lower than that of farms rented, the wholly owned holdings represented 27 per cent of agricultural land; if we add the amount of land under combined tenures which belonged to the holder, then the total agricultural land in owner-occupation was 38 per cent.

Between 1950 and 1960 the rate of growth of owner-occupation appears to have increased compared with the previous decade. By 1960–1, 47 per cent of holdings were wholly owned by their occu-

[1] *Agricultural Statistics*, 1927, pp. 28-9.

[2] *National Farm Survey of England and Wales: A Summary Report*, Ministry of Agriculture and Fisheries, HMSO, 1946.

[3] The 1950 and the 1960 figures are derived from the World Census of Agriculture. The figures of tenure of holdings for both these years are brought together in a Supplementary Report to *Agricultural Statistics 1962–3*, England and Wales, Ministry of Agriculture, Fisheries and Food, HMSO, 1965. For further details see Appendix C.

piers and a further 16 per cent part-owned, part-rented; the amount of land owned by the occupiers (including that under combined tenures) had risen to 49 per cent. During the 1950s, although the trend to owner occupancy is apparent for holdings of all size classes, the biggest increase was in the middle groups (50–250 acres). As some of the main factors promoting owner-occupancy have continued since the 1960–1 census, there can be little doubt that owner-occupancy is now the dominant form of tenure both in terms of numbers of holdings and in area.

Reasons for the Changes in Land Ownership. What has caused the major changes in land ownership in the twentieth century? In particular, what part has estate duty played in this transformation in agrarian society?

The break up of large estates has been a product of many and varied factors. Changes in the franchise in the nineteenth century reduced the political importance of land holding and therefore also reduced the reluctance of large land owners to part with land. Social changes may have exercised some influence, in particular the decline in the custom of primogeniture. The growth of towns and suburbs encouraged or compelled some land owners to part with portions of their estates. The lack of prosperity in agriculture in the later nineteenth century and many of the inter-war years, reduced landlords real income from their estates. Heavy general taxation since World War I has lowered net income and reduced the capacity of land owners to save and recoup large outlays such as estate duty payments.

Whilst these are important underlying factors, impetus to the break up of large estates arose from a combination of market conditions which can be seen best from those periods when owner-occupancy grew most rapidly.[1]

The agricultural depression of the last quarter of the nineteenth century saw large rent reductions. As land prices rose in the period before World War I, rents followed them upwards more slowly. During and after the war, product and land prices continued high. There was a demand for land from investors and the newly rich from the war. The net rents of estates often gave landlords a low return on capital invested and an even lower return on the capital value of the land measured by the market sale price. Some landlords raised rents, patricularly on a change of tenancy; but many took the opportunity to sell.

The later period of most rapid growth of owner-occupancy shows

[1] S. G. Sturmey, 'Owner Farming in England and Wales, 1900-50,' *Manchester School,* vol. xiii, No. 3, September, 1955.

some similarities with the earlier period but also some differences. From the end of 1942, farm tenants were given security of holdings. Whilst this removed a powerful incentive for tenants to purchase holdings, it led also to a shortage of farms to rent, with the result that a new entrant to farming was forced to purchase a vacant farm. Consequently vacant farms fetched higher prices than tenanted, the differences being a vacant possession premium which, between 1946 and 1960, often exceeded one hundred per cent.[1] This premium was a strong inducement for the owner of a vacant farm to sell it rather than re-let, and the rental provisions of the 1947 Agriculture Act reinforced this tendency, for although a landlord could ask what he liked for a vacant farm, he could only be sure of receiving it for three years; after then, the tenant could appeal to arbitration on the rent.

A period of rapid rise in land values, 1939–48, was followed by a decade of approximate stability and then a dramatic price rise after 1958.[2] As in the earlier period of rapid growth of owner-occupancy, price rises exceeded rent increases (partly held back by rent controls); moreover, much of the demand for land and farms was for various general reasons not closely connected with their income potential in agriculture—as a hedge against inflation, for capital gains and perhaps for the value of farm buildings at a time of general increases in house prices. All these factors created market conditions favourable to sale. It is also likely that often landlords and tenants have agreed to share the vacant possession premium if the tenant bought the holding.

The break up of large private estates, the growth of owner-occupancy and the growth of public estates are closely interconnected. Often it is clear that the key factor has been the break-up of estates. Many tenants, particularly during the big increase in owner-occupancy after World War I, bought their farms to avoid having them sold over their heads—although tenants were not invariably reluctant purchasers.

What of estate duty? That it has been a potent cause of the decline in the extent of large private estates appears indisputable. Many illustrations can be given where the immediate cause of the sale of part or all of a landed estate in recent years has been, quite patently, the necessity to meet death duty liabilities. No evidence of the alienation of large estates as a result of death duties can be more direct than details contained in the Annual Reports of the Com-

[1] G. H. Peters, 'Recent Trends in Farm Real Estate Values in England and Wales', *The Farm Economist*, vol. 11, No. 2, 1966.

[2] See the land component of the property price index, Appendix A.

missioners of Inland Revenue of land actually handed over in payment of death duties since 1946. In a negative sense, the growth of public ownership of land has been promoted because public bodies unlike private individuals are *not* subject to death duties. Many of the acquisitions of the National Trust have clearly resulted from the estate duty problems of the erstwhile owners. Estate duty has worked with market trends to promote the break-up of estates; where, as after the first World War and in recent years, the value of agricultural land has exceeded its earning power capitalized at current interest rates, an heir, having to sell assets to meet a claim for estate duty, can retain a larger income by selling land rather than non-agricultural assets.

To disentangle with precision the influence of estate duty is hardly possible. Perhaps those directly affected, as well as the onlooker, may tend to over estimate the importance of death duties as a causal factor in breaking up large estates as they frequently come as the final blow and immediate occasion of disintegration; but a forced sale may be due to the cumulative effects of many factors. Moreover, the favoured treatment of agricultural land under estate duty should be remembered: concessions since 1911 for growing timber; the right to pay estate duty by instalments; and, more important, the lower rate of duty since 1925 on the agricultural value of agricultural property, converted to a 45 per cent abatement in 1949.

There can be little doubt that the market conditions which accompanied and followed both the first and second World Wars would have resulted in extensive sales of agricultural land, much of it to tenants, without any death duties. Estate duty is probably best regarded as a very powerful supporting cause of the changes in land ownership which are outlined, but certainly not the *only*, and probably not the most important cause.

Capital Taxes and the Owner-Occupier

Let us now turn to the second development we noted earlier; as a product mainly of the recent phenomenal increases in the value of agricultural land, the owner-occupiers who as a class in part owe their existence to the effects of estate duty, now find themselves seriously threatened by it, and, since 1965, by a capital gains tax under which death or gifts count as realization. In this chapter we shall concentrate on the incidence of estate duty, but the analysis needs to be conducted against a background appreciation of the capital gains tax, which we consider further in chapter 7.

The clearest way to demonstrate the significance of estate duty for the owner occupier is to give numerical examples on the basis of simple but not unrealistic assumptions.[1] Table 3.4 sets out the estate duty payments on farms of various sizes assuming:

(i) Farms are valued at £250 per acre (i.e. a realistic price for vacant possession farms in 1967; to avoid undue complication the same value has been assumed for all farm sizes, although there are in fact differences in value per acre between farms of different sizes with, very broadly, the larger farms having the smaller value per acre).[2]

(ii) Other farm capital including crops, livestock, machinery, etc., are equal to one quarter of the value of the farm, of which half is taken to be eligible for the agricultural concession. (Data from the Farm Management Survey, *Farm Incomes in England and Wales 1962*, Ministry of Agriculture, Fisheries and Food, HMSO, 1964, suggests that this allowance for other farm capital is almost certainly an under-estimate except for the very largest size of farm).

(iii) No addition to the value of the estate is made for farmers' holdings of cash, insurance policies, stocks and shares, or other property; no deduction from estate value is made for mortgage or other debts. (This omission of savings and debts may well under-estimate the size of estate; the widespread reluctance of farmers to incur debt is well authenticated;[3] by the time of death most farmers are likely to have paid off mortgages and made some saving).

Estate duty is levied at the full market value at the date of death on all property (including the land and farm buildings) aggregated, less any debts; but there is an abatement of 45 per cent on the agricultural value of agricultural land, buildings and machinery but not on live and dead stock.

Table 3.4 demonstrates the seriousness of estate duty payments for the owner-occupier, a seriousness accentuated because the value of the farm is likely to be a very large proportion of the total estate. Even on the estate containing the small farm of 100 acres, after

[1] For some more sophisticated calculations covering both income tax and estate duty liability, see Vivien F. Stewart, 'The Agricultural Problem in Estate Duty Taxation', *The Farm Economist*, vol. X. No. 10, 1965. I gratefully acknowledge my debt to Miss Stewart on this aspect of estate duty. The calculations in Miss Stewart's article relate to 1962 and since then the huge rise in land values has made the problem more acute.

[2] G. H. Peters, 'Recent Trends in Farm Real Estate Values in England and Wales', *The Farm Economist*, vol. xi, No. 2, 1966.

[3] Vivien F. Stewart, *ibid.*

TABLE 3.4. *Estate Duty Payments on Owner-Occupied Farms of Various Sizes, at 1967 rates and approx. 1967 farm values*

(1) Farm size, acres	(2) Value of farm at £250 per acre	(3) Other farm Capital (¼ farm value)	(4) Total capital value (2 and 3)	ESTATE DUTY*							
				Full Rate			Reduced Rate (45 per cent abatement)			(11)	(12)
				(5) Capital value ($\frac{1}{10}$ total)	(6) Rate per cent	(7) Tax	(8) Capital value ($\frac{9}{10}$ total)	(9) Rate per cent	(10) Tax	Total (7 and 10)	Annual instalments over 8 years
	£	£	£	£		£	£		£	£	£
100	25,000	6,250	31,250	3,125	21	656	28,125	11·5	3,234	3,890	559
200	50,000	12,500	62,500	6,250	40	2,500	56,250	22·0	12,375	14,875	2,137
400	100,000	25,000	125,000	12,500	50	6,250	112,500	27·5	30,938	37,188	5,342
800	200,000	50,000	250,000	25,000	60	15,000	225,000	33·0	74,250	89,250	12,821

* No allowance has been made for marginal relief.

Interest rate 2 per cent. (The interest rate on estate duty outstanding was raised to 3 per cent in 1970).

allowance for the agricultural rebate, nearly £4,000 would have been payable in estate duty in 1967; on the estate containing the 400 acre farm the payment would have been nearly £40,000; on that of the 800 acre farm, nearly £90,000.

Payment by instalments over the eight years permitted does not solve the problem for the owner-occupier. Miss Stewart's figures for 1962[1] show that even in that year instalment payments would have taken some 20 per cent of the net of tax income of an owner-occupier of a 100 acre farm and between 100 and 150 per cent of the net of tax income from an 800 acre farm. Since 1962 the rise in land values has increased the discrepancies between the land price and the income from the land, whilst the capital gains tax has added to the weight of taxation on death.

The extent to which the problem has been accentuated by the rise in land values, much though not all of which is attributable to monetary inflation, can be gauged from the fact that in 1949, when estate duty rates were the same as in 1967, farm prices per acre were only one third of the 1967 figure. Using the same assumptions as for Table 3.4 except for the lower price per acre, estate duty payments on the various farm sizes in 1949 would have been as follows:

	£
100 acres	248
200 acres	1,860
400 acres	6,942
800 acres	22,319

Thus for the largest farm size the estate duty payments would have been only one quarter in 1949 what they would have been in 1967 and for the smaller sizes a much smaller proportion. The price rise has not only meant a larger nominal value on which to levy tax, but, because of the progression of estate duty, the assimilation of a particular size of farm into ever higher tax brackets.

Reverting to the 1967 figures, it would not be true to argue that the farms most heavily hit by estate duty are the least important; whilst the *number* of owner-occupied farms in the largest categories are comparatively few, farms over 300 acres contained nearly a quarter of the total acreage owner-occupied in 1960-1 and contributed a proportionately larger share of farm output. The number of farms in this size category was increasing and the category probably contained the most dynamic and efficient farm enterprises.

[1] Vivien F. Stewart, *ibid.*, p. 419.

Economic Significance of the Incidence of Estate Duty on Agriculture

In so far as estate duty has accentuated the break up of large tenanted estates and the growth in owner-occupation, it has helped to end a form of tenure characterized by a division of function in the supply of capital: landlord and tenant each contributed a part, the landlord provided the bulk of fixed capital and the tenant working capital and machinery. Owner-occupation replaces this system by one which makes heavier demands on the occupier; the owner-occupier has all the capital to find and has no possibility of rent reductions to act as a cushion against falling product prices. On the other hand, with ownership comes a security of tenure, possibly a greater incentive to effort and an undivided responsibility; moreover impoverished landlords did not invariably adequately meet their capital contributions. Whilst this might be true of private landlords, the institutional landlords, who, as we have seen, have become increasingly important, and who do not face the same tax bills, appear to maintain very high standards. The conclusions of an analysis of estate equipment in the Eastern Counties Report 1941 was reassuring both on the quality of equipment maintained by public bodies and the ability of the owner-occupiers at that time to find working capital as well as to meet their own mortgage charges:

> 'The highest standard of estate equipment was maintained by the public and educational bodies with owner-occupied estates a close second. In the latter group, the quality of equipment increased with the size of the estate, the largest estates showing an even higher standard than on properties belonging to the public and educational bodies.'

This comment referred to 1941. In assessing it we must remember that most of the present generation of owner-occupiers secured their farms on advantageous terms; they had a relatively low capital outlay and subsequently a substantial capital gain (tax free). The future generation of owner-occupiers will not enjoy the same advantages if they purchase and if they inherit they will be faced by heavy estate duty liabilities. If the farm is small enough, or other assets large enough, for the estate duty bill to be met by instalment payments, it will be at the cost of exhausting liquid assets making it impossible to undertake desirable or necessary investment. (Similarly, curtailment of investment may result from anticipatory measures to acquire liquid assets against future death duty liabilities.) Even the exhaustion of liquid assets for the period of instalment payments would be inadequate to meet duty due on a large farm. A heavy debt may be incurred which will curtail investment for a still longer period. Alternatively, and perhaps necessarily for larger farms, the sale of part of the farm may be required. This fragmentation is likely to reduce efficiency and runs entirely contrary to general agricultural policy in this country which is concerned with building up larger farm units. There is a strong possibility that much of the effect of national policy in supporting the industry by grants will be subsequently dissipated by the effects of tax.

To quote the conclusion of a recent study of the incidence of taxation on agriculture:[1] 'The tax structure inhibits the growth of the farm business beyond a certain size and taking the long term view tax legislation in the UK does not enable a person to have personal wealth on the scale which modern agriculture requires. The intensive capital requirements in relation to output and earnings is such that it cannot, against the present tax pattern of the UK, even maintain the existing position which has been achieved due to fortuitous circumstances. . . . The shadow of 'corporation' farming lies across the career path of everyone associated with agriculture who is 45 years old or under.'

In our next chapter on reform of estate duty we shall consider modifications to tax law affecting the position of the owner-occupier; but, apart from tax changes, one action which might have some ameliorating effect is the development of a form of credit institution specifically designed to meet the problems raised by payment of estate duty. Currently, the Agricultural Mortgage Corporation does not fully meet this need; whilst the AMC is prepared to consider granting loans for the purpose of paying estate duty, it offers no specialist advice on estate duty problems and its loans for this purpose are on the same terms as any other loans it makes.[2] Moreover, any assistance is by *loan*, not a share in the profits of the business; and loans in mid-1969 carried a rate of interest of 10¼ per cent. In these ways it differs significantly from the Estate Duties Investment Trust, which evolved specifically to meet the estate duty needs of the private business in industry and commerce; consideration of this problem occupies the next section of this chapter.

[1] Ancrum F. Evans, 'The Impact of Taxation on Agriculture', *Journal of Agricultural Economics*, vol. xx, No. 2, May 1969.

[2] The main conditions are: loans must be a first mortgage; the amount must not be more than two-thirds of the value of freehold property assessed as a farming unit; and the AMC must be satisfied that the applicant will have enough free capital to maintain the property and stock and run the farm. (See AMC explanatory booklet issued by the Agricultural Mortgage Corporation Ltd).

(iv) THE PRIVATE INDUSTRIAL OR COMMERCIAL BUSINESS

The Nature of the Problem

The incidence of death duty on the *unincorporated* industrial or commercial business is not dissimilar to that on agriculture. The business owned by an individual propietor or partnership might be affected in various ways: payment of duty might deplete liquid assets, require the sale of part of the capital equipment or the raising of a heavy loan or mortgage. These results might restrict development and even cripple the business. Alternatively, the business might be sold as a whole or additional partners might be introduced into it to provide the necessary liquid capital.

On the *incorporated* business the repercussions are somewhat different. A public company with readily marketable shares is largely or wholly immune from the effects of death duty. The private company is much more vulnerable. If the shares of a small shareholder in a private company have to be sold to meet estate duty liabilities, they can probably be bought by the remaining shareholders without much difficulty and even should it be necessary to introduce a new shareholder there need be no change in control; the beneficiaries of the deceased might have to accept a low price from a forced sale, but the business would be little affected. The position may be very different on the death of a major shareholder. The typical case is the family business where the majority of the shares are held by a small number of close relatives who comprise the board of directors. If on the death of a director/shareholder, estate duty liabilities have to be met from the business assets of the deceased, the other shareholders might not have the means to buy his shares. Then an outsider, if he could be found, would have to be let into the business, possibly on terms unfavourable to the family interest and resulting in some change in control and perhaps of policy. Outright sale of the business might be preferred to this alternative and the family might accept the first reasonable offer of take-over. A further possible effect of the forced sale of a large proportion of the shares of a private company, or even a small public company, is that the low price that they may fetch in these circumstances, besides harming the beneficiaries of the deceased, may also prejudice the terms on which new capital can be raised in the future should the business wish to go to the market shortly after.

Measures in anticipation of death duties may also have repercussions. They could lead to the sale of the business; they might hold back business developments because the proprietors were attempting to accumulate liquid assets against future liabilities; and a private might be converted into a public company to minimize the embarrassments of future estate liabilities of shareholders. A particular problem is the uncertainty surrounding the valuation of shares assessed for duty.

These are the *possible* effects of estate duty on the private business. We must attempt to assess how frequently death duties *in fact* impinge on the private business and how serious the results might be for the efficiency of the business and the economy.

The significance for the private business of estate duty payments rests on various considerations including how many dependents the deceased leaves, whether there are descendants keen to maintain the business, how far the deceased has considered the convenience of his associates in framing his will, anticipatory provisions (if any) made against estate duty liabilities, and possibly the conditions of any partnership arrangements entered into. But besides such details affecting each particular case, there are two important general considerations:

(i) the size of the deceased's share in a particular enterprise;
(ii) the relationship between the value of the deceased trade assets and his total estate.

The Inland Revenue Investigations

Both the size of the deceased's share in a business enterprise and the proportion of trade assets in the total estate must be considerable before there is much likelihood that payment of estate duty will significantly affect the business. The relationship between trade assets and total estate lends itself to statistical treatment and the Inland Revenue department has twice investigated it—or more specifically the relationship between non-trade assets and estate duty liability. The first occasion was in 1927 at the request of the (Colwyn) Committee on National Debt and Taxation.[1] The second was a special enquiry in 1951.[2] The investigations followed broadly similar lines, but with some important differences.

The study undertaken for the Colwyn Committee consisted of an analysis of all estates over £10,000 which passed through the hands of the Inland Revenue during the first three months of 1922. Of these estates all with 'trade assets' (taken to comprise shares in private companies, interests in partnerships and the business assets

[1] The full details of the investigation are contained in Appendix 20 to the Report.

[2] *Estate Duty and the Family Business*, Report on Statistical Investigation by the Board of Inland Revenue, Cmd. 8295, July 1951.

of individual proprietors) valued at over £1,000 were further examined, to establish the relationship between, on the one hand, the estate duty payable, and on the other (i) the gross cash and liquid assets[1] of the estate, (ii) the non-trade assets, assuming debts[2] charged proportionally against all assets, and (iii) the non-trade assets assuming all debts charged against the non-trade assets. This third

TABLE 3.5. *Summary of Results of Investigation at 1922 Tax Rates*

	Number	Percentage of total estates	Percentages of estates with trade assets
(1) Estates of value exceeding £10,000	1,342	100	—
(2) Estates as in (1) with trade assets exceeding £1,000	373	27·8	100
(3) Cases where gross cash and liquid assets insufficient to meet estate duty payments	24	1·8	6·4
(4) Cases where non-trade assets insufficient to meet estate duty payments, debts proportionally distributed amongst all assets	3	0·2	0·8
(5) Cases as in (4) but all debts charged against non-trade assets	12	0·9	3·2

method of debt allocation was held to be an unduly severe test, but a useful limiting case. The estates were analysed in these three ways in a series of value ranges. The general results covering all ranges of estate are summarized in table 3.5.

The statistics presented a reassuring picture, particularly in view of the wide definition of trade assets taken by the investigators. On the more reasonable assumptions of debt allocation, in only three

[1] 'Gross cash and liquid assets comprised money in the house and bank, life insurance policies, government stock and holdings in public companies, mortgages on real estate, money out on bonds, bills, notes and other securities; the investigators pointed out that the exclusion of realty and leasehold property from liquid assets prejudiced the burden of estate duty vis-a-vis the trade assets in estates including considerable investments in land and buildings.

[2] Assumptions about debt allocation were necessary because in the estate accounts debts were not earmarked to specific assets.

instances (0·2 per cent of estates over £10,000 and less than one per cent of such estates with trade assets) were the non-trade assets insufficient to cover the whole estate duty liability. Even when all debts were charged against the non-trade assets, in only twelve cases, under one per cent of total estates over £10,000 and 3·2 per cent of those with trade assets, did estate duty liability exceed the non-trade assets. It is hard to fault the conclusion of the Colwyn Committee that estate duty did not appear to be a major factor tending towards the disintegration of private businesses.

But this related to 1922 tax rates; since then the maximum rate of estate duty has doubled, and the rates of duty on some ranges of estate have more than trebled. The investigation published in 1951 referred to estates of 1948, but 1951 tax rates (which can be taken as a reasonable approximation to current rates on estates over £10,000)[1] were used in calculating whether or not estate duty could be paid without recourse to trade assets. As in 1922, estates exceeding £10,000 in value with 'trade assets' of over £1,000 were analysed, but on the basis of a stratified sample from all cases arising during 1948, the sampling factor varying from 2 per cent for estates in the range £10,000 to £20,000 up to 100 per cent for those over £250,000. Further, the definition of trade assets used in 1922 was felt to be too wide for the purpose in view since it included 'shares in non-trading companies such as private estate and investment companies, which are often simply a convenient way of holding private assets; minority interests where the death of the deceased cannot lead to the break up of the company; and partnership interests where the partnership deed provides for the remaining partner to buy out the deceased's share and where, therefore, the incidence of the estate duty cannot affect the business as such'. Thus, for the most part, a definition of trade assets was taken which excluded these categories, but one set of calculations was made on the wide definition to provide a basis for comparing the 1922 and 1951 results. A final difference was that the later investigation computed the net value of the individual business (for inclusion within the total of trade assets) instead of the gross value as in 1922, thus reducing the arbitrariness in the allocation of debts.

The later investigation thus analysed estates over £10,000 with trade assets over £1,000 to show the relationship between estate duty payable at 1951 rates and (1) the non-trade assets, 1922 definition, all debts charged against non-trade assets (the one set of calculations to compare with 1922): (2) non-trade assets, with investment companies, etc. excluded from trade assets and all debts charged

[1] See above, pp. 54–7.

against non-trade assets; (3) non-trade assets, investment companies, etc. excluded from trade assets, and debts proportionally distributed amongst all assets. The last two procedures were believed by the authors of the Report to provide the 'true measure of the extent of the problem'.

TABLE 3.6. *Summary of Results of Investigation at 1951 Tax Rates*

	Number	Percentage of total estates	Percentage of estates with trade assets
(1) Estates of value exceeding £10,000 represented by the sample *	12,896	100	—
(2) Estates as in (1) with trade assets exceeding £1,000	3,290	25·5	100
(3) Cases where on 1922 definition non-trade assets insufficient to meet estate duty payments, all debts charged against non-trade assets (cf (5) in previous table)	204	1·6	6·2
(4) Cases where non-trade assets insufficient to meet estate duty payments, excluding investment cos. etc. from trade assets, all debts charged against non-trade assets	86	0·7	2·6
(5) Cases as in (4) but debts proportionally distributed amongst all assets	70	0·5	2·1

* The actual number of cases in the sample was 1,183, but this represented 12,986 estates and in the published statistics the sample is grossed up to cover the whole.

Prima facie, this comparison of 1922 and 1951 suggested that the problem had not been greatly aggravated by the rise in estate duty. The cases where the non-trade assets were insufficient to meet the whole estate duty liability on the definition of trade assets, with all debts charged against non-trade assets had risen from 0·9 to only 1·6 per cent of the total estates over £10,000 and from 3·2 to 6·2 per cent of such estates with trade assets over £1,000. Moreover, these figures were based on a definition of trade assets and a method of debt allocation both of which, according to the investigators, exaggerated the effects of the estate duty. The alternative definition of trade assets resulted in appreciably lower figures. However, a closer examination of the statistical data yields less comforting results. The rise in prices since 1922 meant that 'real' rates of tax had increased more than the money rates: a progressive estate duty assimilates the same real value of estate into constantly higher tax ranges. If, instead of estates over £10,000, we look at estates over £20,000 for 1951 (see table 3.6) then the number of estates where the non-trade assets were insufficient to meet the estate duty payments on 1922 criteria remained unaltered at 204, representing 3·4 per cent of all estates over £20,000 (6,086) and 11·4 per cent of estates over £20,000 with trade assets over £1,000 (1790). If £50,000 is taken as the 1951 minimum, of the 710 estates with trade assets over £1,000 in 134 cases on the 1922 criteria the non-trade assets were insufficient to meet the estate duty liability, representing 7·2 per cent of the total estates over £50,000, and 18·9 per cent of such estates with trade assets. From these figures and table 3.7 showing the estates affected in each value range on the three different criteria used in the 1951 investigation, it is clear that the larger estates (over £50,000) were those where trade assets most frequently appeared and those hardest hit by estate duty, although the two series of calculations using the narrower definition of trade assets show far fewer estates affected than on the 1922 definition with all debts charged against non-trade assets.

It should also be recalled that other taxes, especially income and surtax, were higher in 1951 than in 1922, so that it would be less easy to pay off debts incurred through estate duty liabilities and perhaps more difficult to find friends or relatives able and willing to offer liquid assets on generous terms or to take a share in the enterprise.

The estates where estate duty payments exceeded the non-trade assets, on the modified definition of trade assets with all debts charged against non-trade assets, were the subject of a further investigation in 1951. This revealed that in 51 of the 86 cases (nearly 60 per cent) the proportion of trade assets required to pay the duty was less than 25 per cent; in 15 cases (17 per cent) the duty encroached on more than 50 per cent of the trade assets; in

TABLE 3.7. *Cases where the Non-Trade Assets were insufficient to pay the whole of the Estate Duty (1951 Investigation)*

Range of estate £	Total number of estates	Cases with trade assets over £1,000		Cases where non-trade assets insufficient to pay duty								
				(1) on 1922 criteria debts charged against non-trade assets			(2) As in (1) but investment companies etc. excluded			(3) As in (2) but debts charged proportionally against all assets		
		No.	% of Total	No.	% of Total	% of estates with trade assets	No.	% of Total	% of estates with trade assets	No.	% of Total	% of estates with trade assets
10,000–20,000	6,900	1,500	21·7	—	—	—	—	—	—	—	—	—
20,000–50,000	4,230	1,080	25·5	70	1·7	6·5	30	0·7	2·8	20	0·5	1·9
50,000–100,000	1,245	460	36·9	90	7·2	19·6	40	3·2	8·7	40	3·2	8·7
100,000–250,000	476	180	37·8	30	6·3	16·7	10	2·1	5·6	4	0·8	2·2
over 250,000	135	70	51·9	14	10·4	20·0	6	4·4	8·6	6	4·4	8·6
TOTAL	12,986	3,290	25·3	204	1·6	6·2	86	0·7	2·6	70	0·5	2·1

one case over 75 per cent of the trade assets were required to meet the duty. Fifty-seven (66 per cent) of the businesses affected were private companies; ten (12 per cent) were partnerships, and the remaining nineteen (22 per cent) were individual establishments; sixteen (19 per cent) were engaged in manufacture including building, sixty-three (73 per cent) in distribution, and seven (8 per cent) in services, including hotels.

The Deficiencies of the 1951 Investigation and the Importance of Anticipatory Measures

The 1951 Report on the Statistical Investigation by the Board of Inland Revenue was heavily criticized[1] for misleading presentation, unreasonable assumptions and significant omissions. Its more important limitations are summarized below.

(1) The Report had presented its conclusions of the numbers of estates where estate duty liability exceeded non-trade assets as a percentage of all estates rather than those with trade assets over £1,000, which is the more relevant consideration (and which we have calculated for our presentation of the figures above): it would have been still more valuable had the effect on estates with trade assets in excess of, say, £5,000 and £10,000 been analysed.

(2) The assumption that the whole of the non-trade assets in any estate would be applied to the payment of estate duty before the trade assets were encroached upon was unrealistic; it implied that any dependents of the deceased would sell house and furniture in order to reduce the impact of estate duty on the business.

(3) In applying 1951 estate duty rates to 1948 values of estates no allowance was made for the rise in capital values between 1948 and 1951 which would have brought estates into higher estate duty brackets.

(4) The sample of estates analysed in the investigation necessarily was heavily weighted by trade assets in the hands of older men, and referred predominantly to businesses built up before the heavy rates of war and post-war income tax and profits tax had begun to operate. A representative sample of businesses, including those built up post-war, might have been expected to show a much smaller ratio of non-trade to trade assets.

(5) The Inland Revenue Report contained no recognition that the existence of estate duty could have adverse effects on a business

[1] See especially *Death Duties and the Manufacturing Business*, a report by *The Economist* Intelligence Unit prepared for, and published by, the then National Union of Manufacturers.

before the liability was actually incurred. It ignored, that is to say, the anticipatory effects.

In order, therefore, to make a more realistic assessment of the effect of estate duty on the private business, we must seek evidence on the extent of anticipatory action, the forms it takes, and its likely effects.

One method of trying to obtain a general, if imprecise, picture of the growth in anticipatory action between 1922 and 1948 is to apply 1951 estate duty rates to the 1922 sample of estates used for the Colwyn Committee's investigation and compare the results with the Inland Revenue investigation based on 1948 estates. More specifically, we can compare the relationship between estate duty payable and non-trade assets[1] for the 1922 estates at 1951 tax rates and the 1948 estates at 1951 tax rates. We have already pointed out the effect of inflation between 1922 and 1948 in pushing estates into higher tax brackets and the likely effect of income, surtax and profits tax in reducing liquidity at the later date. Thus, if there had been no tendency for anticipatory action to increase between the two dates, we would expect to find that the application of 1951 tax rates to the 1922 estates would show a *smaller* proportion of estates where estate duty liability was in excess of non-trade assets than is shown by applying 1951 tax rates to 1948 estates. In fact the opposite is true.

There are practical difficulties in trying to make this comparison; in particular, because the 1922 sample of estates is grouped in value ranges wider than estate duty bands and the increases in estate duty between 1922 and 1951 have not been proportional over all estate duty bands, the relationship between estate duty and non-trade assets has had to be calculated on the basis of an average, a minimum and a maximum increase in estate duty. The average represents the most likely single figure of the three, the others represent probable limits.

Appendix D describes the method adopted in more detail. Calculations were made separately for each estate range; the combined figures for all ranges are set out in table 3.8.

The application of 1951 tax rates to the 1922 sample of estates increases threefold the number of cases in which estate duty liability is bigger than the non-trade assets, compared with the 1922 tax rates. But the comparison in which we are particularly interested is that with the 1948 sample of estates. If the 1922 estates had been taxed at the 1951 rates estate duty liability would have exceeded the non-

[1] All debts charged against non-trade assets, the one method of calculation common to the two Inland Revenue investigations.

trade assets for a number of estates between 30 and 41, i.e. between 8 and 11 per cent of the estates over £10,000 with trade assets or between 2·2 and 3·1 per cent of all estates over £10,000. These proportions are distinctly higher than the corresponding figures of 6·2 and 1·6 per cent recorded by the Inland Revenue when 1951 tax rates were applied to 1948 estates.

It would be wrong to place any weight on these *particular* figures. It is possible that there were changes in the size structure of private businesses between 1922 and 1948 which vitiates the comparison. Nevertheless, it is of some significance that the application of 1951 rates to 1922 estates suggests a bigger burden from the effects of estate duty than the application of 1951 rates of tax to the 1948 estates, when we should have expected the opposite result. The probable explanation is that the results for the 1948 sample of estates have been affected by substantial anticipatory action—action which would not have affected the 1922 sample, at any rate not to the same extent, because of the much lighter rates of estate duty then applying.

TABLE 3.8. *Relation of Non Trade Assets to Estate Duty Payments 1922 Sample of Estates over £10,000 with Trade Assets over £1,000*

Multiple of estate duty payable of:	Number of cases Net assets (excluding trade assets)			
	1922 tax rates	1951 tax rates maximum	1951 tax rates miminum	1951 tax rates average
Up to 1	12	41	30	36
1·1–2	11	68	54	59
2·1–3	15	43	37	37
over 3	335	221	252	241
TOTAL	373	373	373	373

This evidence for considerable anticipatory action is confirmed from other sources. *Death Duties and the Manufacturing Business*, the Report of *The Economist* Intelligence Unit, records information from 48 confidential case histories supplied by members of the National Union of Manufacturers. Of these, in 8 cases action had already been taken, or was in the process of being taken, in anticipation of death duties; in 36 cases no action had yet been taken; 4 case histories concerned firms actually caught in the estate duty net. Thus one sixth had taken anticipatory action (or were currently doing so) and such action still remained possible in three quarters of the cases recorded.

Corroboration is provided from other sources. 'Offers for Sale' of shares in family businesses which have 'gone public' have sometimes specifically stated that the purpose has been to avoid the impact of death duties on the business.[1] More recent evidence is provided by the fact that, currently, about 80 per cent of the business of the Estate Duties Investment Trust (see below) is in anticipation of estate duty rather than after liability has been incurred.[2]

Thus, the evidence suggests that anticipatory action may be fairly widespread and of sufficient importance to upset the conclusions of investigations like that of 1951 based on an analysis of estates at death.

What then are the main forms of anticipatory action and what are its effects? The three commonest are probably gift, partial sale or complete sale.

By means of gifts a business may be shared before the death of the proprietor or a large shareholder with those who otherwise would have inherited it later. If the gifts are large and avoid estate duty, business assets may not be encroached on when estate duty ultimately becomes liable. The main drawback for the donor is some loss of control of the business; further, should he die within the 'statutory period' five years in 1951, increased to seven in 1968, estate duty is still payable. The recipients of the gift can insure the life of the donor for the statutory period against the possibility of estate duty liability, but the older the donor the bigger the premium. On the other hand, they ounger the donor the more reluctant he is likely to be to relinguish control. Anticipatory giving clearly has only limited attractions.

Partial sale may take the form of establishing or extending a partnership, introducing outside interests into a private company or converting a private into a public company. The effects are similar to those which might ensue for actual estate duty liability except that action in anticipation instead of under conditions of forced sale may enable the family to obtain better terms; also the proprietor or

[1] *The Times*, January 10, 1949: the Offer for Sale of shares in Teachers, distillers, converting from a private to a public company, stated unambiguously: 'The shareholders' only reason for parting with a portion of their current interest in the business is to create a marketable security thus enabling them to make provision for possible future taxation and death duties without creating financial embarrassment to the business'.

[2] In the two year period to the summer of 1969, of the 37 investments made by EDITH, 30 were in anticipation of death duty liabilities.

shareholder can himself supervise the operation. The main effect is likely to be some loss of control by the family.

Just as a business may be sold in entirety as a result of actual liability to estate duty, so anticipatory action may take the form of sale, merger or takeover. In one of the 48 case histories set out in *Death Duties and the Manufacturing Business* (above) such a sale was recorded. And other evidence suggests that future death duty liability is one of the major reasons for small firms seeking to be taken over.

Anticipation of estate duty liability may create uncertainty of purpose and distract owner-managers from their main business operations. The uncertainty of the value which will be placed on the shares in a private company increases the difficulties of forward planning against estate duty. Attempts on the part of proprietors or major shareholders to accumulate liquid assets against future estate duty liability may be at the expense of new investment.

Developments since 1951

We have so far examined the effect of estate duty on the private industrial or commercial enterprise in the context of the investigations of 1927 and 1951 and considered the limitations of the 1951 Inland Revenue Report. Since 1951 the rates of estate duty have been changed in only minor ways; to the extent that estate duty rates are the crucial factor therefore the analysis remains applicable in 1970. But other factors have changed; and there is an unfortunate and surprising lack of data during the past twenty years on the effective incidence of estate duty on the private business; it is to be hoped that the (Bolton) Committee of Inquiry into the Economic Role and Problems of Small Firms[1] will throw some light on dark places. The best we can do is to indicate some changes of importance which have occurred since 1951, some increasing the burden of estate duty on the private business, others softening its impact, and then to attempt a very tentative summing up.

Inflation and Increased Capitalisation. We have already noted (p. 112) that one of the deficiencies of the Inland Revenue investigation of 1951 was that no allowance was made for the rise in capital values between 1948 and 1951 when 1951 tax rates were applied to a sample of 1948 assets. Since 1951 continuing inflation must have had a very significant effect in pushing estates with private businesses of a particular real value into ever higher tax brackets. We cannot precisely assess the effect of inflation since 1948. Between 1949 and 1967 retail

[1] Set up in July 1969 by the President of the Board of Trade.

prices rose 95 per cent; ordinary quoted shares, which may be a better guide to the rise in capital values of private businesses, rose over 250 per cent.[1] Quoted shares are bound to have had some effect on the value of unquoted, especially where private businesses were large enough to be able to go public; and the price of comparable public shares are a guide-line to the estate duty valuation of shares in private companies. The rise in quoted share prices is both a direct and an indirect effect on inflation. Inflation raises the real value of the assets which the shares reflect; also, in general, inflation may be expected to benefit future profits; and once continuing inflation is recognized, the investing public moves from fixed interest securities and other assets yielding a fixed or relatively fixed money income into equities (and land) as a 'hedge' which accentuates the price rise of ordinary shares.

All this does not enable us to reach any precise answers on the effect on private businesses. We cannot determine whether unquoted ordinary shares rose in value as much as quoted; nor, if we could, would we be able to say how far such a rise represented an increase in real value and how far an increase only in monetary value, for even a particular share is not a homogeneous commodity over time; it is a title to so much real capital (plant, machinery, buildings, land, stock) and goodwill, affected by profit expectation; and the amount of real capital which it reflects may vary over the years. Still less can we assess precisely the effect of inflation on all private businesses, unincorporated as well as incorporated. The best we can do is illustrate the order of magnitude of the problem by some hypothetical examples on the basis of alternative assumptions.

It is convenient to take 1949 as the starting point for the illustrations; in 1949 estate duty rates were increased and then, apart from some raising of the exemption limit and consequential modification of the rates on estates below £10,000, they remained unchanged until 1969, when the basis was altered (see pp. 54–7). We will consider an estate of £100,000 in 1949 of which £50,000 consisted of trade assets in the form of shares in a private company and £50,000 non-trade assets. We will examine the effect of rising prices by considering the position in 1967 on the basis of 3 different assumptions: (1) that all assets (trade and non-trade) rose in price in the same proportion as the index of retail prices over these years (95 per cent); (2) that non-trade assets rose in price in line with the retail price index, but that trade assets rose at the same rate as the index of ordinary shares set out in Appendix A (256 per cent); (3) that non-trade assets did not rise in price at all (i.e. they consisted of items of

[1] See Appendix A, table A1, p. 256.

fixed monetary value, like cash, bank or building society deposits, or of items where, on balance, reductions in monetary value just offset increases)[1] and that trade assets rose in price in line with the index of ordinary shares (i.e. 256 per cent). It is assumed that there are no concessions available to the estate such as the abatement on agricultural land or on business assets where the 'assets' basis of valuation applies.[2]

The results are set out in table 3.9. On each of the assumptions the effect of the price rise is to push the estate into a higher rate

TABLE 3.9. *Estate Duty and the Private Business. Illustrations of Possible Effects of Price Increases*

Estate of £100,000 in 1949 with £50,000 trade and £50,000 non-trade assets	1967 values £	Estate duty rates per cent	Estate duty paid £	Estate duty as percentage of non-trade assets
At 1949 values	—	45	45,000	90
At 1967 values assumption (1)				
Price increases of				
95 per cent trade assets	97,500			
95 per cent non-trade assets	97,500			
total estate	195,000	55	107,250	110
At 1967 values assumption (2)				
Price increases of				
256 per cent trade assets	178,000			
95 per cent non-trade assets	97,500			
total estate	275,500	60	165,300	170
At 1967 values assumption (3)				
Price increases of				
256 per cent trade assets	178,000			
Zero non-trade assets	50,000			
Total estate	228,000	60	136,800	274

[1] See Group A Assets, Appendix A, p. 256.

[2] See above p. 61 and below p. 120.

bracket; on the first assumption the rate of estate duty is raised from 45 per cent to 55 per cent. and on each of the other two assumptions the rate of duty becomes 60 per cent. Perhaps more important is the effect on the relationship between estate duty and the non-trade assets (final column). In the original 1949 situation estate duty liability was less than the value of the non-trade assets. Theoretically, at any rate, it would have been possible for estate duty to be met without impingeing on the trade assets. The effect of the price rise is to make this impossible. On the basis of each assumption estate duty liability exceeds the non-trade assets. As we have seen, there are reasons for believing that in the inflationary conditions of the period 1949–67 trade assets will have risen in value more than the average of assets composing estates. Thus assumptions (2) and (3) may more nearly represent typical situations than assumption (1). And on both those assumptions the excess of estate duty over non-trade assets is very substantial; the duty could not have been paid without either large-scale borrowing or, much more likely, the disposal of a large proportion of the trade assets.

Allied to the effect of inflation has been the need for increased capitalization in real terms associated with technological change. This point has been made for the Swedish situation by D. Helmers, who writes, 'The great increase in capital investment in different trades creates a totally different basis for the discussion of capital taxes. Any comparison with the situation obtaining immediately after the war is unrealistic unless one takes in to account the increased capital necessary for every person employed in industry, agriculture, etc. As an example we may mention that the amount of capital invested per employee in industry has risen from *circa* 24,000 Swedish crowns in 1947 to *circa* 48,000 in 1964 (all in constant 1954 prices).[1]

The same process has undoubtedly been at work in all advanced industrial countries including Britain. It means that, if the size of a firm is measured in terms of the number of employees, a typical firm with ten employees today would have the same capital in real terms as a firm of twenty or more in 1949. This increased need for capital in real terms must have the effect, like inflation, of tending to push businesses into higher estate duty brackets unless the growth in capital has been accompanied by a widening in the circle of ownership.

[1] Extract from 'Capital Taxes—A Few Notes', *Affärsvärlden Finanstidningen*, April 17, 1969. Docent Dag Helmers is Deputy Director of the Association of Swedish Industries.

The Taxation of Capital Gains. Since 1965 the weight of taxation at death has been increased by the long term capital gains tax under which death counts as 'realization' or disposal. Whether the business assets were part of an unincorporated business or shares in an incorporated business, at death the value of the capital appreciation between April 6, 1965 (or acquisition date, if later), and the date of death are liable to gains tax. The first £5,000 of gains (of any chargeable kind) are exempt from tax. But there is a special 'family business' relief provision which may affect this exemption. A man who disposes of a business after the age of 60 (where he has owned the business, or in the case of a trading company has been a full-time working director for the ten years immediately preceding) can claim exemption from gains tax up to a maximum of £10,000 gains; the maximum relief is attainable at age 65 and after, the amount of relief being reduced by £2,000 for each year of age below 65. However, any family business relief taken in excess of £5,000 is off-set against the exemption at death, so that a full £10,000 family business relief leaves no exemption at death.

Gains tax paid on death is a deduction from gross estate for estate duty. The current rate of gains tax is 30 per cent.

We shall be examining gains tax in more detail in chapter 7. But here we should simply note that, in calculating the tax, no allowance is made for changes in the value of money; so that inflation continually increases the nominal gain and hence the amount subject to tax. On the other hand, as the tax is not progressive, inflation does not push the estate into higher rate bands.

Extension of the Gifts Inter Vivos Provision. One way in which the effect of estate duty on the private business has been accentuated since 1949 is by the extension of the gifts-inter-vivos provision to seven years, thus making it more difficult for gifts of shares, or of all, or part, of an unincorporated business, to avoid estate duty.

Estate Duty Concession of 1954. We turn now to ways in which the position of the private business has been improved since 1948. Public discussions on the effect of estate duty on family businesses, stimulated by the Inland Revenue Report of 1951, made its impact on the statute book when the Finance Act of 1954 met the re-iterated demand of the National Union of Manufacturers that the private manufacturer should enjoy similar concessions to those of the agriculturalist. The Act provided that estate duty on industrial hereditaments, machinery and plant should be reduced by 45 per cent where a business was carried on by the deceased alone, or in partnership, or in a private company where the 'assets' basis of valuation applied. This method of valuation, as distinct from an 'open market' value of shares, applies where a company is a 'controlled' company[1] and certain other complex conditions are fulfilled including that there have been no stock exchange dealings in the company's shares in the year prior to the deceased's death and the deceased at some time during the five years previous to his death has had control or may be deemed to have had control.

The concession to the private business resulted from a campaign concerned in part with the valuation procedure for the assets of such a business. The problem arises with a controlled company that a minority shareholding may have a market value which is less than the proportional assets value; hence the 1940 Finance Act had sought to prevent avoidance by defining a controlled company in sweeping terms and requiring an assets valuation for such a company. In these circumstances an assets valuation might considerably exceed an open market valuation of the shares. The application of the provision had led to a widespread conviction that assets were often over-valued—which, if true, would have been inequitable for the heirs of the deceased and have penalized the shareholder of a private company as compared with the holder of quoted shares.

Along with the estate duty abatement in the 1954 Act came also the concession that, if shares and debentures were sold 'at arm's length', otherwise than to relatives, within three years after the death, the sale price (if less) should be substituted for the assets valuation. The cost of the 45 per cent abatement of duty on industrial assets to the Exchequer was £1·7m. in 1968–9.[2]

Estate Duties Investment Trust. Perhaps more important than the 1954 concession by the state have been the developments in the capital market to meet the needs of firms embarrassed by estate duty—most notably the formation of the Estate Duties Investment Trust Ltd, generally known as EDITH.

EDITH was founded in 1952 by a number of insurance companies and investment trusts: it became a public company in 1962 and is managed by ICFC (Industrial and Commercial Finance Corporation Ltd) which was established by the joint stock banks in 1945 to

1 A controlled company is one under the control of not more than five 'persons', but certain groups of persons are treated as a single person for these purposes, e.g. persons who are relatives of one another. Most family businesses are likely to be controlled companies.

2 *Report of the Commissioners of HM Inland Revenue*, No. 112, Cmnd. 4262, January 1970.

provide capital on long term to small and medium-sized businesses.

EDITH was established precisely to assist the private company affected or likely to be affected by the death of a major shareholder. EDITH will supply funds needed to meet estate duty liabilities, if satisfied about the soundness of the management and the prospects of the business. The big attraction for the private company concerned is that EDITH does not seek representation on the Board of Directors—indeed, as a matter of principle will not accept such representation; thus EDITH acts as a minority shareholder of undisputed financial strength without the control or policy of the business being affected.

The exact method by which EDITH invests in the company varies with the circumstances, in particular the amount of capital required, the company's capital structure and the distribution of its shares. It may, for example, recommend the reorganization of the share capital by the creation of a class of share or security which can be issued to the existing ordinary shareholders by way of capitalization of reserves. EDITH can then purchase such bonus issues from the shareholders; that part of the purchase monies received by the executors of the deceased can be used directly towards estate duty liabilities, and the other shareholders can use their funds from the sale to buy up shares from the executors. The bonus issues may be in the form of ordinary shares; they were sometimes in a redeemable form before the 1965 Finance Act provided that all redeemable bonus issues should be treated as distributions for tax purposes.

A possible further advantage for a firm in which EDITH invests is that its purchases count as 'arm's length' sales and may be used as a basis for the valuation of shares even when the business has been valued on an 'assets' basis, provided the sale is within three years of the death. (See above p. 121).

Although its holdings are predominantly in private companies, EDITH also acquires shares in small public companies where the market is restricted and the disposal of large blocks of shares to meet estate duty liabilities could seriously reduce their price.

Since its foundation in 1952, to mid-1969, EDITH had undertaken investments in 205 firms after having carried out relatively detailed investigation of 824 cases. Where no investment results it is not invariably because EDITH has felt unable to offer aid; it may be because the firm decides to accept a takeover bid or a merger offer or indeed to go public. It may be, also, that although some of the shareholders would like to sell shares to EDITH, others do not wish to accept this form of solution and block participation by EDITH.

It is of considerable interest that the large majority of EDITH's investments take place in anticipation of estate duty liabilities. In the two year period to mid-1969, of the 37 companies in which EDITH invested, 30 investments (approximately 80 per cent) were in anticipation of death duty liability.

EDITH is subject to the limitation, applicable to many investment trusts, that not more than 5 per cent of its funds can be invested in any one company. Obviously as the size of EDITH's capital and reserves have increased, the scope for larger investments has also grown. EDITH's individual investments may vary from as little as £20,000 to exceptionally large investments in exceptional companies. Of the 37 investments in the two years to mid-1969, 26 were in companies where the capital employed was under £500,000 of which 18 were in companies with less than £250,000 capital. Five somewhat exceptional cases were in companies with over £1m. capital. Omitting those five, the average investment by EDITH (and other institutions on EDITH's advice) represented about 35 per cent of average capital employed.[1]

EDITH has prospered, despite its almost complete inability to pull out from a bad investment,[2] partly as a result of a policy of spreading investments; more especially because, with the aid of ICFC's specialist staff, it thoroughly investigates any firm seeking its funds.

EDITH is the only trust formed *specifically* and *exclusively* to meet the problem of the effect of estate duty on the private business. Safeguard Industrial Investments Ltd, formed in 1953, offers a service similar to EDITH's as a major sideline to its ordinary business as an investment trust company providing development finance for private and public companies. Also a number of merchant banks and securities houses will take up shares in businesses faced with estate duty problems,[3] but they apply less resources to this particular form of investment than EDITH; they usually require the right to a seat on the board; and are often only interested in a company which is likely to be able to go to the market within a fairly short period of time.

Conclusions

We stressed earlier how little was really known, qualitatively let alone quantitatively, about the consequences of estate duty for the private

[1] I am indebted to Mr J. F. Turner, Manager of EDITH, for kindly providing these statistical details.

[2] If its investment is redeemable, in the course of time (perhaps 18 years) there is a let out; apart from this the only opportunities for pulling out would be if the company had a public issue of shares or was taken over.

[3] Examples are the Charterhouse Group Ltd, Neville Industrial Securities Ltd, Minster Trust Ltd, Birmingham Industrial Trust Ltd, Singer and Friedlander Ltd.

business. The comments and conclusions which follow must therefore be regarded as to some extent speculative. There remains much scope for research on this subject.

First, a conclusion hardly open to doubt. There are many instances in which estate duty at current rates, aggravated by capital gains tax and still more by continuing inflation, is bound to have a significant effect on a private business—on its policy and its ownership. These effects will be most pronounced for businesses in sole ownership; for partnerships where the number of partners is small; and for private companies where shareholding is heavily concentrated in one or a small number of hands. Moreover, the larger the business with these characteristics, the more likely it is to be affected.

The threat of estate duty may divert owners from running the business efficiently to seeking ways of minimizing estate duty. Anticipatory measures may be adopted detrimental to the growth of the business such as the accumulation of liquid assets or their use in insurance schemes against estate duty liability rather than for business development. Partial sale (which might take the form of going public) or a complete sale (which might take the form of merger or takeover) are other possible forms of anticipatory action. Similar actions may follow the actual imposition of estate duty; debts may be incurred which are a charge on the business; and, if at this stage a partial or complete sale is undertaken, bargaining from a position of weakness the family is likely to obtain less satisfactory terms.

A policy of excessive liquidity or incurring debts which hamper development is bad both for the firm and the economy. But where a firm goes public, where shareholders are introduced from outside the family, where a merger or takeover results, whilst this may mean the end of the family firm, at least in its previous form, is this necessarily bad for the economy? Will economic resources be less efficiently used?

The supporters of the private firm and the family business point to the large proportion of British industry which is still in the hands of small firms and claim that they provide a crucial competitive element in the economy; that small firms are often the source of innovation and experiment; that small family businesses are the most economic form of business for a wide range of specialist tasks; and that many small entrepreneurs work better in their own business and many craftsmen work better in firms that they know.[1] These claims may well be true of small firms at their best. In a recently

[1] See *Death Duties and the Manufacturing Business*, pp. 34-6.

published study[1] of a sample of 186 British companies from 1954–1963, the authors found an inverse ratio between profit rates and size of firm; the industrial giants did less well than the smaller companies in the sample, with net assets of £500,000–£1m., which consistently showed the best performance.

On the other hand it is also true that amongst the private firms are many of the most backward in British industry and uneconomic in the use of scarce resources. When therefore, in anticipation of estate duty, or under its impact, a private firm is compelled to partial sale and the introduction of 'outside' interests, the new infusion might be just what was needed. A complete take-over of a business affected by estate duty might mean that new 'scientific' management replaced traditional and less efficient methods. These points may have especial relevance to the situation created by the death of the proprietor or chairman of a firm who has been its main-spring and inspiration and who may not leave anyone within his family circle with comparable abilities and interests.

This raises a point of some significance. In considering the incidence of estate duty on a firm, it is very difficult to separate out the problems which arise because of the necessity of paying death duty from those which result from the fact of the death of an owner, partner, managing director or chairman. This point emerged strongly from an American study of the effects of taxation on corporate mergers.[2] The authors found from their consideration of 104 cases of merger that it was impossible to select companies where tax *only* was the critical motivation; an owner's decision to sell out was always a complex mixture of interacting motives. Helping to account for mergers were a very large number of non-tax pressures for sale including lack of succession; ill-health; wish to retire and to spread investment for increased security in old age; wish to shed the burden of running a firm to concentrate on some aspect of it, such as design; wish to increase size to be more effective at meeting competition; desire for the prestige of being a director on a big company board; family quarrels among the owner-managers; wish to reduce the risks of sudden financial loss or forestall the possibility of bankruptcy. One or more of these factors might be present along with a tax motive for a merger. And, of course, there may be other tax motives for merger as well as a death duty motive.

Let us, therefore, try to pose in a different and more precise form,

[1] J. M. Samuels and D. J. Smith, 'Profits, Variability of Profits and Firm Size', *Economica*, May 1968.

[2] J. Keith Butters, J. Lintner, W. L. Cary, *Effects of Taxation on Corporate Mergers*, Harvard, 1951.

our question on the seriousness for the economy of the effective incidence of estate duty on the private business. Where there is an efficient private firm, with good future prospects and continuity of able managers, will it be possible for prospective owners who wish to continue in independent existence after the death of the present owner or partner or major shareholder, to do so without incurring liabilities that are a serious handicap to the business?

In seeking to answer the question we can distinguish three categories of firm. At one extreme the small private firms of under £50,000 capital. Even if the deceased was the sole proprietor, the business would only be affected by estate duty if trade assets formed the large majority of his estate. At the new (1969) rates, an estate of £60,000 carries a maximum effective estate duty rate of 36·9 per cent and one of £50,000 a rate of 32·2 per cent. The Inland Revenue Report of 1951, for all its deficiencies, was probably not wrong in its implication that few estates under £50,000 with trade assets, would be seriously affected by estate duty (which was fractionally lower at that time); where estate duty encroached on trade assets, in all cases the percentage of trade assets required to meet the duty was under 25. When allowance is made for the 45 per cent reduction of duty available since 1954 on certain industrial assets and to which such a firm would be entitled, it is clear that a firm of this size is unlikely to face serious difficulties.

At the other extreme, the largest of the private companies hold in their own hands the solution to the problem by an approach to the market. For a public issue on the London Stock Exchange profits need to be at least in the £100,000 range—which implies a capital value of the company of not less than £500,000. (Whilst smaller flotations—where pre-tax profits are upwards of £50,000—can be made on provincial exchanges, they are unlikely to achieve the desired degree of marketability for the shares). Conversion to public company form may be distasteful to a family concern, but the essential attributes of a family business need not be lost. The majority of directorships can be kept in the family, which is also likely to be able to retain an effective proportion of shares with voting rights. There is no reason why its change in legal structure must alter the relationship between manager/owners and work people, which is traditionally a merit of the family business. Moreover, disadvantages of conversion will be counterbalanced by advantages, in particular the ease with which future capital can be raised.

The most difficult problem is faced by the private company intermediate between these extremes—large enough to be affected by the higher rates of estate duty if one of its major shareholders dies, but too small for conversion to a public company. It is here that the formation of EDITH and other trusts has been so important, for it is just this intermediate size of company that EDITH was founded to assist. EDITH's judgment may be faulty on occasion, and assistance be refused to a progressive firm; but should this happen there are merchant banks or other investment trusts to whom approaches can be made. Even in this category of firm facing the biggest problems from estate duty, the chances that a really progressive and efficient private business will meet a severe setback must be few.

It is thus possible to be cautiously optimistic in answer to our question, largely because of the provisions which have developed within the private capital market. Moreover, as our evidence suggests, much action is taken in anticipation of death duties—about 80 per cent of EDITH's investments are anticipatory—so that arrangements can be made in more considered fashion. Even so, if these tentative conclusions are valid, whilst the effective incidence of estate duty is less serious to the national economy and the efficient use of resources than might have been feared, there is scope for measures which might bring easement. These we consider in our next chapter on the reform of death duties, along with an examination of the justification for the continuance of the special reduction of duty on certain industrial assets.

(v) THE SUPPLY OF THE FACTORS OF PRODUCTION IN GENERAL

We have examined these particular aspects of the economy where estate duty may be expected to have the most direct effect—namely the private business both agricultural and non-agricultural. We turn now to consider the possible broad 'macro-effects' on the economy—the way in which the effect of estate duty may be diffused through all branches of economic activity. In this section we seek to discover the effective incidence of estate duty in relation to work effort, enterprise and saving in general; to see if it restricts the supply of the factors of production, or alters the form of saving, e.g. by diverting it into less productive channels. In particular we are concerned with its effects on capital formation and by implication the rate of economic growth.

To try to answer these questions we need to distinguish between the effects on the property owner (or accumulator) and on the beneficiary (or inheritor); we also need to distinguish, for both, the effects on the *incentive* (the psychological effects) and on the *capacity* to work, save and take risks.

Incentive Effects

(*a*) *Property Owner*. We shall concentrate, primarily, on the effects of death duties on the incentive to *save*—for estate duty will only affect the incentive of the property owner to work and take risks if he intends to save for heirs at least part of the income derived from work and enterprise.

Let us first examine the situation in the abstract before we turn to the estate duty of the United Kingdom. As a theoretical proposition we can state that the levy of an estate duty, or the addition to an existing duty, may result in more, less, or the same amount of saving by an individual. People who desire to leave their heirs a particular capital sum or annual income, may be impelled by the imposition of a tax to save more, in order to accomplish this object or to come as near as possible to it, despite the tax. Others may be induced to save less, since they now feel that additional saving is less worthwhile—their successors will not benefit to the full extent of their sacrifice. Finally there are those whose saving will be unaffected, either because these two opposing effects just about even out, or because they have little or no interest in saving for heirs, and their saving is for motives quite unconnected with a desire to bequeath. We have here the income and substitution effects, familiar to economists, which work in opposite directions on the supply of a factor of production when its price changes. The analysis is similar to that of the effect of a change in income tax on the supply of work effort or of saving, except that the 'income' effect refers to the income of a third party or parties, the heir(s) rather than the income of the saver.

We can, indeed, demonstrate these propositions very simply on lines similar to Professor (now Lord) Robbins's exposition of the effect of a change in a flat rate income tax on the desire to undertake paid work.[1] Let us consider the effect of an increase in a proportional estate duty on the saving of a fixed income receiver. Robbins's demand curve for income in terms of effort is replaced by a demand to bequeath in terms of economies in consumption—represented by D–D in the diagram below.

The vertical axis represents the 'economy price' per unit bequest. The horizontal axis represents the additions (net of estate duty) to the amount available for bequests. An initial equilibrium is given by point F on D–D where at economy price OE the net addition to bequests is OB. Rectangle OEFB represents the amount of saving.

[1] L. C. Robbins, 'The Elasticity of Demand for Income in Terms of Effort', *Economica*, June 1930.

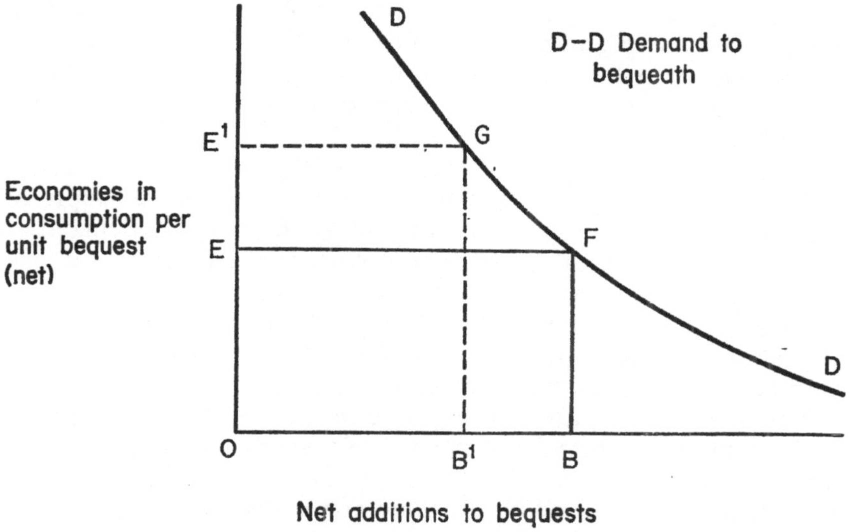

If a proportional estate duty is now imposed (or an existing duty increased) the terms on which bequests can be made are altered. This can be represented by moving E to E^1. The additions to bequests will move to B^1 and saving will be represented by the rectangle $OE^1\ GB^1$. When the price of anything increases, the amount purchased at the new price and change in total outlay depend on the elasticity of demand for the commodity. Similarly, with the rise in the 'price' of bequests in real terms (economies in consumption), the addition to bequests, and the amount of saving at the new terms, will depend on the elasticity of the demand to bequeath. If the elasticity of curve D–D (demand to bequeath in terms of economies in consumption) is less than unity over the relevant range, then more will be saved (the area of rectangle OE^1GB^1 will be greater than that of OEFB). If D–D has an elasticity greater than unity, the amount of saving will fall as a result of the tax (OE^1GB^1 will be less than OEFB). If D–D shows an elasticity of unity, the amount of saving will remain the same (rectangles OE^1GB^1 and OEFB will be equal in area).

The first case ($E_d < 1$) relates to the person determined to maintain, as nearly as possible, the amount of his bequests despite the tax. The second, ($E_d > 1$) relates to the person, who, in view of the tax, finds saving for his heirs less worthwhile. The person whose saving is unaffected because the opposing considerations balance is one for whom the elasticity of curve D–D is unity about the relevant range.

The person with no desire to bequeath, or with a desire to bequeath which plays an insignificant part in determining his saving, is not of course represented in our diagram since has no demand curve D–D. His saving is quite unaffected by changes in the terms on which bequests are made.

This geometrical analysis demonstrates that there is no *a priori* reason for believing that an estate duty *must reduce* the supply of saving. But information as to the likely elasticity of demand to bequeath in real cases can only be obtained by empirical analysis. Unfortunately the available empirical evidence is neither extensive nor really conclusive; much of it consists of little more than a vague appeal to common experience. Some observations can be made with fair confidence; others are very tentative.

The desire to bequeath is only one of a number of motives for saving and an appreciable proportion of saving must be undertaken with no thought of, or reference to, estate duty. Saving by young persons is rarely affected by thoughts of the disposal of their property after their death. If they have family responsibilities a life insurance with a moderate annual premium can cover the possibility of an early death. They save to accumulate a store for future enjoyment and security and the rate of estate duty will not affect this motive. It is unlikely that many childless couples are interested in saving for their successors and a significant proportion of the rich do appear to die childless. Figures compiled by the Department of Inland Revenue from 1924 to 1931[1] show that of those leaving estates of over £100,000 during these years approximately one third (33·1 per cent) died without 'surviving lawful issue'. Even family men who have accumulated large fortunes are not always keen to hand on their wealth to their children. Professor Irving Fisher has written, 'The ordinary normal, self-made millionaire is rather disposed, I believe, to look on the inheritance of his millions by his children with some misgivings';[2] millionaires Leverhulme, Schwab, Read and Carnegie have all written or spoken in these terms and been strong advocates of heavy death duties.[3]

Professor Pigou conveniently summed up many of the motives for saving. 'The desire to build up capital possessions' he wrote, 'is not a simple thing. It is made up of various elements blended in

[1] Available in the Annual Reports of the Commissioners of HM Inland Revenue for these years. Publication of this data ceased after 1931.

[2] Quoted by A. C. Pigou, *Economics of Welfare*, Macmillan, 4th edition, 1932, p. 674.

[3] See W. J. Schultz, *Taxation of Inheritance*, Houghton Mifflin, 1926, espec. ch. XII.

different ways among different men. One element is the desire to be able to exercise the constructive force, which a strong man may find in himself, in conjunction with a large-scale undertaking; another is the desire for that power in society, or, perhaps, in politics which great wealth confers: another is the desire for fame or notoriety: another the desire for a large income accruing without effort in later life: another the desire for posthumous glory in dying very rich: another mere inertia—inability to spend in consumption the whole of a large income. All these motives are concerned only with the life-time of a man who contemplates saving under the stress of them; the fact that after his death the fortune does not also die is, so far as they are concerned, an irrelevant accident. Alongside of them there is the desire to hand on accumulated capital to his children after the accumulator's death'.[1]

Thus, much personal saving is undertaken without reference to the level of death duties by those with no strong desire to bequeath; but for many this desire is present as a motive for saving along with other motives, and for some the desire to bequeath may be all-important. It is significant that the desire to bequeath is a motive likely to grow in potency as the property owner ages, many of the other motives for accumulation having been already realized or perhaps gone by default; and older people are much more likely than younger to have their own accumulations of capital (acquired from a variety of motives in the past) and may be prepared, not only to cease saving from income, but to draw upon their capital, if the state interferes too much in their plans for its disposal after their deaths. We simply do not know how important these considerations are; perhaps not very; as Rolph and Break put it, 'By the time people have reached the age when estate considerations weigh heavily, they have also reached the age when radical departures from previous modes of living are generally unwelcome.'[2]

So far in this section we have considered an estate duty in the abstract, and our geometrical model assumed a proportional tax; the present estate duty in the United Kingdom is highly progressive, with a maximum average rate of 80 per cent and with an average rate of just over 50 per cent on an estate of £100,000. However, high though the rates are even on moderate fortunes, approximately 70 per cent of property assessed to estate duty in GB in 1968–9 (estates over £5,000) fell into estate duty ranges liable at average rates of 40 per cent or less, and about a half was in ranges taxed at a

[1] *Public Finance*, Macmillan, 3rd edition, 1947, p. 143.

[2] E. R. Rolph and G. F. Break, *Public Finance*, the Ronald Press Company, New York, 1961. p. 266.

rate of 18 per cent or less,[1] quite apart from the special reliefs which reduce the average rate of duty actually paid.

Nevertheless, we must expect the high marginal rates, which are implicit in the progression of the present estate duty, to increase the significance of the substitution effects relatively to the income effects, i.e. to increase the liklihood that the effect of the present estate duty in the United Kingdom is to lead people to substitute consumption for saving (or indeed to spend out of capital as an alternative to accumulating or maintaining capital).

In a tentative manner it may be worth while to endeavour to assess the reactions of some of those for whom the desire to bequeath does constitute a significant determinant to action.

One whose demand to bequeath in terms of economies in consumption may be expected to be inelastic is the man who, perhaps having married late in life, is anxious lest his death may leave his wife and children without adequate comfort. Definitions of 'adequate comfort' will vary; but the capital sum required to secure it would not, in general, be large enough to be subject to the higher rates of estate duty and the tax would not exercise a powerful influence. On balance, however, the estate duty might well stimulate rather than reduce saving for this purpose.

Those with large fortunes, ambitious to found a family, or to hand on unimpaired to their children a family inheitance, may conceivably be spurred to greater efforts by the tax or they may be dissuaded by the difficulty of their task. Perhaps the height of estate duty rates, together with the effects of income tax and surtax make the latter alternative more likely. Unless resort is made to some form of avoidance, it is an impossible task at current tax rates for a property owner to save (say by insurance) so as to hand on intact anything other than a very moderate fortune. The ambitions may well go by the board; the property owners may be tempted to treat themselves and families to a trip round the world which all can enjoy before the steps in for its pickings.

Possibly those most generally affected are elderly people with moderate or large fortunes, who would normally live comfortably on the whole or a part of their income, intending that, at their deaths, their capital should pass to their middle-aged children so that life may be easier and more comfortable for them. They feel no urgent necessity to bequeath large sums. Their demand to bequeath in terms of economies in consumption is likely to be elastic, particularly in view of the high marginal rates of duty; the larger the capital accumulated, the more present saving, the smaller the proportion

[1] *Inland Revenue Statistics* 1970, table 111.

which finds its way to the heirs. Such people, especially those with the larger fortunes, must be strongly tempted not only to reduce or stop saving from income, but to draw upon capital. A millionaire, by spending £100, deprives his heirs of only £20, which, less income and surtax, represents an income of but a few coppers per annum to the heir. The incentive to draw upon past accumulations must be particularly great where current taxation makes it difficult to maintain customary living standards out of income. In such circumstances a property owner may be expected to have little compunction in realizing some of his capital to maintain his comforts if, by so doing, it is the Revenue which suffers rather than his heirs.

All this is very speculative and smacks heavily of casual empiricism. Perhaps we are on firmer ground in suggesting, on the basis of our analysis of avoidance earler in this chapter, that people with the most significant demands to bequeath are those most likely to adopt avoidance devices; some will take the extreme solution of residence abroad; others will adopt the easier expedients of gifts inter vivos, establishing trusts or settlements, and reducing estate duty liability by investing in assets which offer some estate duty reliefs. An account of the possible avoidance measures and their consequences was given earlier in the chapter[1] and need not be repeated here. But, in considering the effects of estate duty on the property owner's incentive to save, it is clear that, whatever may be the overall magnitude and direction of its effects, estate duty certainly provides an incentive to save in certain forms—i.e. those that attract less duty—rather than in other forms; and it is probable that the kinds of saving encouraged, e.g. settlements, trusts, pictures, historic collections, are those which often tend to reduce the productivity and mobility of capital.

Let us now briefly examine the incidence of estate duty on work effort and enterprise. As we indicated earlier, it is only in so far as saving for posterity is the purpose behind earning income by work and risk—taking that estate duty would affect them. This emphasizes an essential difference between the effective incidence of an estate duty and of an income tax. Estate duty only influences work and enterprise undertaken from one particular motive. Whatever the motive, the income tax will exert its effects. Put in a different way, estate duty, unlike income tax, does not prevent anybody from enjoying *himself*, the full fruits of additional labour or enterprise.

With the desire to bequeath but one of many motives for work and enterprise—and usually one among many in any individual—the current level of income tax and surtax in the United Kingdom

[1] See pp. 79–90

is likely to act as a deterrent to work and enterprise which is prior as well as additional to, the effects of the estate duty. As long as income taxation remains at its present level the effects of the estate duty on work and enterprise can probably be ignored. Most people, unless imbued with an overwhelmingly strong desire to bequeath (in which case estate duty, unless avoided, might stimulate rather than deter additional paid work and enterprise)[1] will be dissuaded from the additional effort by the income tax before they ever consider the estate duty.

A further related difference between the effects of an estate duty and an income tax is that an income tax, being annually recurrent, cannot be put off like estate duty. Lack of tax consciousness, apathy, procrastination, a sanguine view of one's own life expectation—these tend to push an estate duty into the background. It can easily be forgotten by those who do not wish to remember it.

(*b*) *Inheritor*. The effects of an estate duty on the incentive of the inheritor to work and save raise less conflicting considerations than its effects on the property owner. Both by reducing the expectation of the inheritance and by reducing the amount actually inherited, an estate duty is likely to stimulate the desire to work and save of the inheritor, prospective and actual. These effects will tend to be stronger the heavier the tax. Nevertheless, the advantages are not entirely clear-cut. Stimulation of work and saving amongst the idle rich is all to the good, but prospects of substantial inheritance, and incomes from property actually inherited, have, in the past, enabled industrious and gifted individuals to perform unpaid work of national benefit which would not have been possible had their livelihood not been secure. The more inheritance is taxed, the less leadership we can expect in all fields of voluntary public activity.

Effects on Capacity to Undertake Work, Enterprise and Saving

(*a*) *Property Owner*. The effects of the estate duty on the capacity of property owner to undertake paid work, enterprise or saving are straight-forward. Unless he insures against the estate duty,[2] and

[1] Where there is an incentive effect, its most likely form is the postponement of retirement. A study by Professor G. F. Break of the effects of income and surtax on the incentives to work effort of a group of solicitors and accountants (*British Tax Review*, June 1957) showed that the most common incentive effect was the postponement of retirement. If this is true of income tax it is still more likely to be true of the effect of estate duty on work effort, since it is at ages approaching retirement that estate duty may be expected to impinge on the consciousness.

[2] The insurance has to cover not only the tax on the rest of the estate, but that on estate plus policy. At current rates of income tax, surtax and death duties, this method is only possible for the owners of small estates.

thus, by paying regular premiums turns it in effect into an annual tax, the duty has no effects on his capacity to work, save or take risks. The estate duty does not compel him to work more or less, nor enforce changes in his saving and enterprise. If he insures, then his capacity for saving and enterprise is restricted, since the income available for these activities is diminished.

(*b*) *Inheritor*. The effect of the estate duty is to reduce the amount of the inheritance and so reduce the income from which the heir can save and the capital available for his enterprise. In this, the effects of the estate duty are similar to those of any other tax on the property owner which has reduced the estate he leaves at death. Nevertheless the estate duty is of particular importance in that it is less likely to be met by economies in consumption than income tax. A property owner would probably meet income tax at least partly by economies in consumption, particularly if his intended saving (what he would have saved if there were no tax) was less than his tax liabilities. Estate duty is especially destructive of saving since the deceased need have made no provision for meeting the tax, and the inheritor will probably regard only the post-tax inheritance as his capital, and will also make no attempt to meet the tax, even partly, by reduced consumption. Estate duty, therefore, at current rates, is a tax assessed on capital and almost entirely paid out of capital—particularly for the larger estates, where it would be impossible to meet the tax from income.

The payment of death duties involves the transfer to the goverment of assets which are suitable for debt redemption, but which cannot be used for current expenditure without being inflationary. Increasing an already high estate duty does not significantly reduce the demands of the private sector on current resources. Higher death duties *might* restrict some spending out of capital and might, by reducing the capital of heirs, somewhat diminish the propensity to consume out of income; but, for the community as a whole, higher duties are far more likely to be met by reduced private saving than by reductions in consumption. A chancellor who attempted to fill an 'inflationary gap' by raisng estate duty would be deluding himself. To put the point in a different way, given the desired level of investment, other things being equal, the higher the yield from estate duty the bigger must be the budget surplus to avoid inflation.

Conclusions

In attempting to sum up we must stress again the degree of our ignorance and the lack of quantitative data. It may be ventured with some confidence that at current levels of estate duty, income tax and surtax in the United Kingdom, the effects on incentive, i.e. the psychological effects of the estate duty on the supply of labour and enterprise, are relatively slight and unimportant. On the incentive to save we can speak with less certainty. In some instances estate duty may not only reduce the incentive to save but lead to appreciable spending out of capital. However, the total effect may not be much. The majority of the capital assessed to estate duty is liable only at the lower rates of tax where any effects are likely to be slight. The desire to bequeath is only one of many possible motives for building up and maintaining accumulations of capital, and other motives are not affected by estate duty. Perhaps a third of the rich die childless, and for them the incentive to bequeath can be of little importance. Of those whose desire to bequeath *is* an important motive for thrift, some may be stimulated by estate duty to *increased* saving. Apathy, procrastination, inability to break the habits of a life-time, innate dislike of spending capital, the sanguine view which people take of their own life expectation—these all militate against the disincentive effects of estate duty. The uncertainty of death itself defies a rational calculus of action. Further, any net disincentive effects on the property owner may be offset, in part or whole, by stimulating effects on the inheritor.

With more certainty, it can be stated that the estate duty does have an important restrictive effect on the *capacity* to save. It is a tax largely, if not wholly, paid out of capital.

Chapter 4

Death Duty Reform and Gift Taxes

WHY DEATH DUTIES AT ALL?

In chapter 1 we pointed out the three main arguments for capital taxes in general—equity (or horizontal equity), efficiency (in resource use) and equality.[1] How well does a death duty achieve these objectives?

Merits of Death Duties

It receives some marks on the horizontal equity criterion. A death duty is a form of tax which does something to adjust the inequities which would result by restricting the tax base to income and expenditure. It is a recognition that wealth confers a taxable capacity over and above the income derived from it. It supplements income tax by taxing wealth which has given its owner opportunities and security even though it has yielded little or no income; and a death duty, too, acts as a long-run tax on capital gains.

But capital gains, and accumulated wealth consumed before death, avoid death duties; and also, because they are imposed at irregular intervals, death duties fulfil the equity objective much less well than a regular, annual, wealth tax.[2]

In terms of efficiency in resource use, we have seen that death duties probably have negligible effects on work effort and enterprise in general—although this may not be true of their effect on the private business in agriculture, industry and commerce. Their effect on the incentive to save is problematical; their effect on the capacity for private saving is considerable. If investment opportunities are such that the state wishes to maintain community saving at the level it would have been but for the death duties, it must save itself—i.e. run a budget surplus. In other words it must use the revenue from death duties not for current expenditure but for debt redemption or new investment.

This brings us to the essential characteristic of death duties at current high levels. As we saw in the previous chapter they are paid out of capital; i.e. they are a form of tax concerned with the owner-

[1] See p. 23. [2] See p. 178.

ship of assets—with the distribution of wealth as between the private and public sector and within the private sector. This is a characteristic not necessarily shared by other forms of capital tax, the annual wealth tax and capital gains taxes.

It is for this reason that death duties are so relevant to the third purpose advanced for capital taxation: equality. The distribution of property is, essentially, what death duties at current levels are about. As a means of diminishing inequalities of wealth, death duties have singular advantages over the other forms of capital tax. They are levied at a time when a wealth transfer is inevitable anyway; moreover a capital tax so heavy as necessarily to be paid from capital, in general arouses less hostility and adverse economic reactions levied at death than, say, a capital levy of the same rates, or an annual wealth tax of the same yield, which, with income tax, is too heavy to be met from income.[1] It is an invalid generalization that a death duty bears heavily on no-one, as the deceased, on whose property it is levied, can no longer feel the burdens of taxation, whilst his heirs will not miss what they have never had;[2] but there is some element of truth behind this over-statement, particularly if generous exemptions are accorded to dependents. Taxpayer loss of satisfaction is likely to be less from the payment of death duty than from raising an equal revenue from a levy imposed in the life-time of the taxpayer or an annual wealth tax. Moreover, it is widely accepted that there is a particular ethical justification for taxing inherited property because its acquisition is generally unrelated to the merits and efforts of those who benefit from it. C. Lowell Harriss put what is essentially the same point in a rather different way: death taxes 'fall on a base—transfers from which the recipient makes no corresponding contribution to the community —which seems peculiarly suited to reduction by taxation'.[3] Further, if our object is to reduce inequalities in the distribution of wealth, death taxation strikes directly at the heart of the problem, for inherited wealth is the biggest single cause of large inequalities in

1 See pp. 204–8.

2 'It is much more merciful to avaricious human nature to deprive it of something it has never had than to lop off anything—however superfluous—which has actually been enjoyed . . . on the whole, I can see no better way to diminish the natural pangs attendant upon paying taxes than to collect as much income as possible in the fleeting moments when the property belongs to nobody in particular', Kate Field, *Washington*, 1893, quoted in Max West, *The Inheritance Tax*. Cf. also Jeremy Bentham, *Supply without Burden or Escheat vice Taxation*, 1795.

3 'Sources of Injustice in Death Taxation', *National Tax Journal*, December 1954.

wealth-holding—the more so when heavy income tax and surtax reduce the possibility of new accumulations of wealth from personal saving. Again there are no particular problems about making death duties progressive, as there are with capital gains taxes;[1] thus the tax can be levied at whatever is deemed to be the structure of rates most appropriate to its purpose. Besides these positive merits, death duties have the further advantage over other forms of wealth taxation that the big administrative difficulty of capital taxation, valuation, is reduced in important respects. First, the tax is levied at a time when an inventory, and often a valuation of the property, is required anyway to carry out the will of the testator or implement the law of intestacy. Second, because deaths in any one family occur irregularly, generally at widely spaced intervals, the valuation problem becomes more manageable, for only a fairly small proportion of *total* personal property falls to be valued in any one year. This has the further result (in contrast to a capital levy) that the amount of property coming on to the market, to raise funds to meet death duty liabilities, is insufficiently large at any one time significantly to affect market values in general—though this is not to say that the market in some highly specific properties, e.g. shares in a particular small company, might not be affected.

Injustices in Death Taxation

Having stressed these very real merits of death duties in the abstract, it is necessary to recognize that, as they exist in practice, death duties in some ways like other capital taxes and in some ways more than other capital taxes, suffer from defects which create what C. Lowell Harriss has conveniently, if a little vaguely, called 'injustices'.[2] These injustices partly flow from certain general characteristics of death duties. First, the fact that the circumstance giving rise to death taxation liability is not a market transaction like the sale of a product or factor of production; hence there is no market value which can be taken as an equivalence of worth between buyer and seller. Also, because nothing is received in return for a bequest, there is perhaps both greater freedom and inclination to let tax factors influence the action. Second, the concept of a death duty as levied on 'property passing at death' is far too simple. Gifts have to be taken into account, and also trusts and settlements, where income rights may alter as a result of a death but no wealth changes hands. 'As we reach out to try to include transfers which a generous system of property law

1 See pp. 229.

2 *Ibid;* in the following paragraphs I have drawn heavily on C. Lowell Harriss's penetrating article.

permits to be made at times other than death, the tax loses the objectivity and certainty which death seems to provide'.[1]

Whilst the fact of death is certain, the time is uncertain, and hence the third characteristic leading to injustice—that planning to meet the tax, or to avoid it, becomes something of a gamble.

The significance of these features of death duties can be seen to create injustices in many ways, which can conveniently be grouped under three headings: opportunities for avoidance; valuation and administration; incidence and form.

Opportunities for Avoidance. Some people take advantage of avoidance, others do not. Some may deliberately refuse to adopt methods of avoidance and their heirs suffer accordingly. Others may seek to take advantage of avoidance but are prevented by some misfortune, e.g. under provisions like those of the British estate duty, a property owner may make large gifts to his heirs only to die in an accident shortly after, with the result that no estate duty is avoided. Other people may fail to adopt avoidance devices through ignorance; taxpayers are not equally well situated for dispelling ignorance and it is likely that the consequences are regressive, because the owners of large estates probably get better tax advice than owners of small estates. The type of property affects opportunities for avoidance; the state may discriminate in favour of certain kinds of property (like the favoured treatment of agriculture in the UK); in general inter-vivos gifts and trusts offer the best opportunities for avoidance and some kinds of property are more easily given away or put in trust than others.

Valuation and Administration. A further group of inequities may result from difficulties of valuation and administration. There is uncertainty and an element of arbitrariness about valuing real estate, private businesses and certain personal property such as jewellery or antiques. Moreover, at very high rates of death duty, much depends on a *single* death valuation. The more an estate consists of interests hard to value, the more the chances of inequity. Estates large enough to warrant the expense of expert and persistent challenge will tend to get lower valuations. Fluctuations in property values are a particular source of injustice; because death duties are incurred infrequently and at unpredictable times, differences in burden result which may be largely irrelevant to the underlying conditions affecting people; at one level of share prices death duties

[1] C. Lowell Harriss, *ibid.*, p. 293.

may take a fifth, at another a quarter or a sixth of the shares. Worse still is the situation where, at date of death and valuation, shares stand high, whilst by the time they come to be sold for estate duty liabilities six months later, the market has fallen steeply. 'Economists have long recognized that failure to provide averaging in a progressive income tax can lead to inequities. The same essential argument applies, probably with greater force, to the estate tax. A whole generation's burden, speaking roughly, depends upon the level of property values of a single moment'.[1] Further, perhaps more than any other taxes, death duties depend upon what one or a few revenue agents do and on the quality of taxpayer representatives.

Incidence and Form of Death Duty. Finally, injustices arise because the form often takes little account of the incidence of death duty. The formal incidence, at current rates, is almost entirely on the heir; in principle, it would seem therefore that the rates of tax ought to vary according to the economic circumstances of the heir; but in practice this rarely happens. Again the effective burden on a family falls as the age of the deceased rises; this is partly from the delay in paying the tax; partly because the longer a person lives, the less he need leave to any particular heir, such as an annuity of a given amount for a widow; and generation skipping can be more easily adopted—more can be left to younger persons with less need of an intervening tax. Progression in death duties does not usually make allowance for the ages of dependents and heirs and hence the duty discriminates unequally.

Death taxation has substantial merits; but all these possible sources of injustice point to the urgency of choosing an appropriate form of death duty and applying much thought and care to devise administrative arrangements to minimize the defects. Perhaps, also, they suggest some circumspection about how high rates of duty should be pushed. In the remainder of this chapter we apply ourselves to the question of the reform of the UK estate duty. In the next section we consider aspects of reform applicable whatever basic form the death duty may take—whether it remains an estate duty or is transformed into a form of inheritance tax. Then we consider in detail this vital question of the most appropriate form of death duty—the question which dominated much of the debate in 1894 on Harcourt's new estate duty. In the penultimate section we examine relevant experience in certain other countries. Finally we attempt to draw the conclusions together.

[1] C. Lowell Harriss, *ibid.*, p. 306.

REFORM OF THE UK ESTATE DUTY

International Comparison of the Weight of Death Duties

The British estate duty is seriously marred as a death tax by most of the injustices we have listed. With average rates rising to a maximum of 80 per cent and marginal rates to a maximum of 85 per cent, its exceptional height accentuates the problems.

There are difficulties about making international comparisons of death duties; different exemptions influence effective tax rates; on the basis of the formal rate structure it is difficult to compare death taxes of different forms, e.g. an estate duty with any of the possible forms of inheritance tax; progression according to consanguinity complicates comparison; again, one death duty may have higher *maximum* rates than another but the latter may tax moderate or small fortunes more heavily. But it is not an unfair generalization that, measured in terms of its formal rates, the British estate duty undoubtedly ranks amongst the highest death taxes in the world and might qualify as *the* highest death duty of any advanced country with a mixed economy. Further, the British estate duty is very substantially higher than most other such countries. Some examples will serve to support the generalization. Professor Wheatcroft's comparative study of Great Britain, Australia, Canada and the USA,[1] all of which employed the estate duty form of death tax, showed that in 1964 the British rates were much the heaviest in the middle and upper ranges; compared with the British 80 per cent, the highest rate elsewhere was USA at 65·2 per cent—but this rate applied only to estates left to someone other than a spouse, for whom the rates were much lower. The maximum rates for Canada and Australia were in each case 53 per cent. Comparison with EEC countries is complicated because all employ inheritance taxes as their main form of death duty, not estate duty, so that the proportion of estate paid in tax depends upon its distribution amongs heirs; also all provide for different scales of rates depending on consanguinity. But for only one EEC country in 1967 would it have been *possible* for the proportion of a large estate taken in tax to exceed that in the UK (on the basis of the formal rates); this was Italy, and it could only have happened if all or nearly all the estate had been left to strangers in blood or collateral relatives; the maximum rates for bequests in the direct line were considerably below those for the UK—for example, if an estate was left entirely to one child, the maximum rate of duty would

[1] G. S. A. Wheatcroft, *Estate and Gift Taxation, A Comparative Study*, Sweet and Maxwell, 1965.

have been 52½ per cent.[1] Finally, a comparison with Sweden—reputedly the most heavily taxed country in the world (measured in terms of the proportion of GNP taken in taxes of all kinds); the Swedes have an inheritance tax which is graduated according to consanguinity, and provides special exemptions for a surviving spouse and for dependent children; in addition, comparison is complicated by their legal structure which treats all property of a marriage as jointly owned and therefore equally shared if the marriage breaks up by divorce or death. However, even on the basis of the new and higher rates of succession duty which were proposed to the Swedish parliament in 1970 so that they should come into law in 1971, the maximum rates of duty were appreciably below those of the UK. The maximum *marginal* rate of inheritance tax proposed is 72 per cent; but for spouses, children or grandchildren, 65 per cent. Ignoring specific exemptions which reduce the taxable amount, the maximum *marginal* rate becomes payable at about £80,000 (bequest) for someone outside the immediate family at which point the *average* rate is 60 per cent; and at about £420,000 (bequest) for a spouse, child or grandchild, at which point the *average* rate is about 54 per cent. When the full range of the scale of the Swedish inheritance tax is compared with the British, there are some circumstances in which more might be paid on a Swedish estate than a British of comparable size; this would be true of very small estates, below or just above the (1969) UK £10,000 exemption; it would hold for some slightly larger estates in the direct line if the bequests were concentrated; and for medium-sized estates left wholly or mainly to a stranger in blood or collateral relative. But for all large estates (over about £500,000) the British system *must* be heavier regardless of the dispersion of the estate and the relationship of the beneficiaries; and for all medium-sized estates where bequests were not heavily concentrated, or where the beneficiaries were in the direct line regardless of the concentration, more would be paid under the UK estate duty. Where estates of any size but the very smallest were at all widely dispersed, the payment under the British estate duty could be several times that under the Swedish tax.[2] Moreover, these comparisons make no allowance for the special reliefs for

[1] For EEC rates, see *Taxation in Western Europe* 1967, CBI, 1968. Comparison with Italy is complicated by the existence of both an estate duty *and* an inheritance tax; in the above examples both have been taken into account.

[2] I am indebted to Professor Göran Englund of Lund University for sending me advance details of the 1970 proposals for the Swedish succession duty. An account of Swedish taxes is published in English, with an annual budget statement, by the Swedish Ministry of Finance in Stockholm.

dependent children and the division of property between spouses of the Swedish system.

If the exceptionally high rates of estate duty tend to increase the problems of injustice in applying death taxation in the United Kingdom, they are further accentuated by the ease with which estate duty, as we have seen, can be avoided; most simply by gifts which, if the donor lives for seven years thereafter, are completely free of estate duty and of gift tax; nor are the gifts aggregated with the estate to determine the rate of estate duty, so that the tax paid on the remainder of the estate may be substantially reduced.

It is indeed significant that, of all the countries with which we have compared the British estate duty—Australia, Canada, USA, the six original EEC countries and Sweden—only one, Luxemburg, has *not* got a general gift tax which is more or less integrated with its death duty. Thus Britain has the distinction of the heaviest death duty and the one most avoidable. Little wonder that the British duty is often called the 'voluntary tax'; that it has been referred to as a tax on vice, like that on tobacco and alcohol, the vice of hanging on to one's money until the last possible minute; that it has been called a tax paid by those who love the Revenue more than they love their relatives. Indeed this unhappy combination of maxima—of rates and ease of avoidance—suggest more sinister interpretations; the situation could be regarded as a piece of deliberate deception on the part of those who govern us: the weight of estate duty enables them to claim a concern for the redistribution of wealth, whilst the loopholes can be pointed out to those who complain of the excessive burden of the heavy rates.

With the possible exception of a few avaricious tax lawyers and tax avoiders, no-one can be happy with a capricious duty which falls primarily on the heirs of the unsophisticated or peculiarly unfortunate. Most recent students of estate duty reform in the UK have agreed on the need to reduce the rates of death duties but at the same time to make them effective, by introducing a general gift tax and by other measures to reduce avoidance. The reformers divide on the question of the *form* which a modern death duty should take, and this issue we examine fully in the next section. But in the remainder of this section we concentrate on the kind of reforms needed whether Britain retained the estate duty form of death tax or switched to an inheritance tax.

Measures against Avoidance

Several anti-avoidance measures were included in the 1969 Finance Act; the taxation of trusts was tightened up and the purchase of items of national, historic or artistic interest as an avoidance device was made much less attractive.[1] The detail of this kind of provision is fodder for the tax lawyers, rather than the economist. We shall concentrate our discussion on the closing of the biggest remaining loop-hole, the lack of a general gift tax, and the most important concessions on particular kinds of property, namely the abatement on certain agricultural and industrial assets, which have important economic implications. A general comment is included on trusts and chapter 5 (pp. 215–6) contains a discussion of the basis of treatment of items of art which is applicable to all forms of wealth tax.

A General Gift Tax. Successive measures over a number of years have brought the United Kingdom nearer to a general gift tax. The period within which gifts inter vivos (of over £500 to each donee) become liable to estate duty has been increased by stages to seven years (1968) and tax is levied whether or not the motive was avoidance. The 1965 capital gains tax introduced a new element of taxation of gifts: a gift counts as a 'disposal' or 'realization' under the capital gains tax, subject to a minimum exemption for a donor of £100 per annum. From these two provisions it is a small step to some kind of general gift tax. To integrate it effectively with the structure of death duties is, however, more complex, especially if the estate duty form of tax is retained. It is, indeed, one of the advantages of the inheritance tax form that the integration with a gift tax is easier—and we shall return to this point when we compare the two forms of tax below. A general gift tax has another tax advantage; it reduces the attraction of income tax avoidance by means of 'income-splitting'.

Trusts. The basic problem is that the beneficiary of the income from property in trust does not have control over the assets of the trust; he cannot at will draw on the capital for consumption nor alter his own income by changing the nature of the assets. Because of this the beneficiary of a trust can be regarded as deriving less satisfaction than if he had received an outright transfer. On the other hand, A. A. Tait argues convincingly that 'If we ignore the patina applied to trusts by the accumulation of estate tax avoidance procedures, and return to the original, essential element of the trust, we must consider that it was originally created as a legal means of insuring that an estate would either remain intact and/or would be well managed (i.e. the implication is that the beneficiaries would be minors, wives, or other unreliables who would not be able to conduct

[1] See p. 83

the arrangement of the capital in a responsible or dispassionate manner). That is, the donor reckons that by putting a property in trust he is doing better for his beneficiaries than he would if he transferred the property outright; their welfare is greater than if he had transferred the property outright. . . . If, in fact, the beneficiaries are better off, is there any reason for arguing that settlements are less advantageous than outright transfers.'[1] The principle therefore should be to tax property in trust no less than it would have been taxed had it been transferred outright, with the legislature, if anything, leaning on the side of taxing trusts *more* rather than *less*. The exact interpretation of this principle must depend on the form the reformed death duty takes.[2]

The Treatment of Agricultural and Industrial Assets

We pointed out, above, that one of the injustices in death duties arose from different tax treatment of different kinds of asset. That there was an inequity as between people (or the heirs of people) who possessed wealth in a particular form and those who did not; and that favourable tax treatment of certain kinds of assets created an avenue of tax avoidance. Moreover, where people transfer into a particular asset solely as a media for tax mitigation, some undesirable economic consequences may follow. And preferential treatment for some kinds of assets inevitably creates 'hard cases' on the borderline and demands for the extension of the concession.

In the light of these generalized disadvantages, can the special reliefs of duty on certain agricultural and industrial assets held in unincorporated ownership, or in close companies, be justified? In fact the concessions have had some of the unfortunate consequences predicted. The heirs of an agricultural owner-occupier are favoured as compared with other heirs from a similar size of estate. Thus, consider two men each sole inheritors of an estate of £50,000 value. The estate inherited by A consists entirely of ordinary shares; and that inherited by B is a farm. Because of the agricultural concession, B would have a substantially larger value of inheritance net of tax than A; but there is nothing to prevent him immediately selling his inheritance and investing it in ordinary shares, the value of which would then be considerably larger than A's shareholding. Moreover,

[1] Alan A. Tait, *The Taxation of Personal Wealth*, University of Illinois Press, 1967, p. 164.

[2] A detailed set of proposals for taxing trusts with an estate duty are given in G. S. A. Wheatcroft, *Estate and Gift Taxation, a Comparative Study*, Sweet and Maxwell, 1965, pp. 132–6. They have been partly superseded by the measures taken in 1969.

the benefit is not confined to farmers' sons. People with no interest in agriculture are known to buy land to take advantage of the abatement of duty. Indeed there is no legal bar to a death-bed purchase of land. Whilst the heirs of some who buy land in this way may put it back on the market, others may cling to it so that their heirs in turn may benefit from the estate duty concession. Thus agricultural land passes into the ownership of those who may lack the knowledge to manage it well. Moreover, the concession has resulted in some net addition to the demand for land and it must be counted one of the factors which has helped to create the boom in land prices which we documented in Appendix A. In this way, not only has it been made more difficult for genuine new farmers to purchase a farm, but it has paradoxically added to the estate duty problems of the owner occupier.[1] There can be no doubt that also the concession to agriculture stimulated a similar demand for concessions to the family concern in industry on grounds of parity of treatment. That granted, the commercial concern feels itself left out in the cold.

In view of these manifest inequities, combined with some economic disadvantages, are there any counter arguments with which to justify the concession? We saw in chapter 3 that the private industrial businesses might face difficulties as a result of estate duty; that some anticipatory measures might be detrimental to the business; but that, although we presented the conclusion as tentative, there were grounds for believing that a really efficient business with continuity of able management could get through the difficulties either by going public or by taking advantage of the facilities developed by the capital market, most notably EDITH. The owner-occupier in agriculture is less well-placed with access to suitable credit institutions. It is possible that as a result of inflation combined with estate duty and capital gains taxation, even with the agricultural concession, an owner-occupier may find it impossible to pass on his farm to his son. Does this provide a sufficient justification for the concession?

Agriculture is a way of life as well as an occupation, and one can appreciate the human problem posed to an owner-occupier by estate duty and inflation. Yet wealth is wealth; if inflation has posed problems by bringing his estate into higher tax brackets, it is also inflation, with its *particular* effect in raising land prices, which has made him rich. He is the beneficiary as well as the victim of the land boom. And why should the sons of present farmers be favourably placed as against men who wish to enter farming and whose position is made worse by a concession which raises land prices? There is, indeed, an economic argument for seeing that land

[1] See below p. 102.

comes onto the market frequently. As Glenn E. Hoover puts it: 'Through the ordinary competitive processes, inefficient owners of property are eliminated; they sell their property voluntarily or lose it by forced sale. It is bought by those who fix the highest value on its ownership and are willing to back their convictions with their money. Property acquired by purchase tends normally to drift into the hands of those who can use it most productively. On the other hand there is nothing in the process of acquiring capital by inheritance which gives any assurance that its new owners are the best qualified to use it. A good economic argument exists, therefore, in favour of an inheritance tax sufficiently high to force inherited property back into the competitive arena where its ownership may be determined in the normal fashion.'[1]

Whilst there is much in this argument applicable to both the family business in industry and in agriculture, there is one considerable problem which applies especially to agriculture. If the effect of death duty is to be put the whole business in the market, be it agricultural or industrial, then this may not be a bad result. What is likely to be economically detrimental, and what is much more likely to happen in agriculture than industry, is that part of the business goes onto the market. In other words, heavy death duties carry the danger of diminished efficiency through a reduction in the scale of production. A keen farmer, inheriting a farm, may meet the death duty liability by selling part of it. Such fragmentation may be detrimental to agricultural efficiency. It is for this reason that the effect of estate duty on the owner-occupier may be more serious than the effects of the duty in diminishing the estates of the large private landowners. Although reducing the size of an agricultural estate below a certain optimum might make administration less economic in that a full-time agent, or specialist labour for maintenance, might not be as efficiently used, the sale of a complete farm from a landed estate to meet death duties would not fragment the key unit of agricultural production in the same way as the sale of part of his farm by an owner-occupier.

It can be seen that the economic arguments for the concession, in particular the agricultural concession, are not all on one side. The equity arguments are. It is submitted that the concessions should go, and easement for the private business in agriculture and industry be sought not by special concessions confined to certain assets used in these forms of productive activity, but rather from the general reduction we have proposed in the rates of death duty,

1 Glenn E. Hoover. 'The Economic Effect of Inheritance Taxes', *American Economic Review*, March 1927.

the development of credit facilities to assist farmers affected by death duty (which we discussed in chapter 3), some modifications to capital gains tax, which we discuss in chapter 7 and some changes in administration, to which we now turn.

Improvements in Administration

The 1969 Finance Act effected an important improvement in removing the necessity for so-called 'marginal relief' (which led to the injustice of the 100 per cent marginal rate of tax) by the substitution of progression by brackets (or slices) for a scale of duty progressive by totality (or slabs). But there would seem to be further ways of administering death duties which might remove or reduce sources of injustice, possibly with economic benefits as well as gains in equity. The following are suggestions presented with this hope.

The Extension of Payment in Kind. Currently the UK estate duty provisions contain very limited opportunities for payment in kind. Under certain conditions 4 per cent Funding Loan 1960–90 and 4 per cent Victory Bonds may be accepted at stipulated prices in settlement of estate duty; and each year a small amount of land and 'chattels' are so received; the equivalent value of duty is paid to the Exchequer from the National Land Fund[1] and the properties are transferred to bodies of a public nature, the principal beneficiary being the National Trust.[2]

This procedure might be extended both along its present lines and in entirely new ways. First, the present exemption (unless sold) for items of national, artistic and historic interest could be entirely abolished, but such items accepted in lieu of death duties and made readily accessible to the public; occasionally they might even remain in the same location if it were suitable and appropriate access could be provided; but they would have become the property of the nation. This could be administered, as at present, through the National Land Fund—though it might be appropriate to change its name. More significant, however, would be the extension of payment in kind to items when there was no question of special collectors' pieces or of land suitable for the National Trust. A special commission could be set up to administer the property and executors, acting on behalf of heirs, would have the right to pass to the

[1] See p. 62.

[2] In the year ended March 31, 1969, eight items of land or chattels were accepted, at a total value of £194,000. All were handed over to the National Trust except for one painting which went to the National Museum of Wales, and Drake's Drum, lent to Plymouth Corporation.

commission towards settlement of death duty, any kind of property at its *agreed estate duty valuation*. This would have a number of advantages:

(i) Readily marketable items, such as government securities or quoted shares, would not need to be sold; heirs would benefit through the reduction in transfer and administration costs.

(ii) The purchase by the commission of items of limited marketability would confer a bigger benefit on heirs; the commission might subsequently sell the items, but unlike heirs or executors, it could choose its time and would not be forced to a hurried realization.

(iii) The heirs would be insured against the misfortune of a fall in the value of property, especially stocks and shares, between the date of death, which determined the death duty valuation, and the date of disposal. Admittedly the commission would be in danger of receiving all the items which fell in value and none of those which rose, but this is not a serious objection; the state is better able to withstand temporary fluctuations in value, or even to stand the occasional permanent loss, than the heirs; and if necessary some safeguards could be provided e.g. the executors might be required to specify, within a defined period of the death, which items they proposed to hand over.

(iv) Some estates could be wound up more quickly.

(v) There is scope, within the scheme, for the development of special facilities to deal with the problems of the private business, more particularly in agriculture. For example, an owner-occupier, faced with death duty problems, might be permitted to pass over part of his land to the commission, at its market value, which could then lease it back to him at an economic rent, with perhaps an option to purchase in the future at current prices. This would be some safeguard against fragmentation of farms, discussed earlier.

The commission would be run as a kind of giant investment trust, covering the whole range of property, with its own specialists in the various types of property. It could sell holdings, in the interests of maximizing its income or capital, and it might even be given some general and limited buying rights outside the property received in lieu of death duties. There are doubtless those who will attack the proposal as 'back door nationalization'; but, apart from the possibility of some limited purchasing rights to provide its management with some flexibility, it would only receive what private individuals handed over to it, at strictly market values, at the time of death. Whilst it would have the rights of any institutional shareholder, as a general principle it would not be concerned to become involved in the management of a business; some restrictions on the size of its holding in any one company might be desirable. In general terms there would seem to be much good sense in the state having a share in the general prosperity of the country and being able to derive income for financing the public sector from sources other than taxation. Such a commission could serve this purpose and its income could become, in the course of time, a significant and valuable addition to government revenue.[1]

Payment by Instalments. Another, less revolutionary, proposal is that provisions for paying duty by instalments might be extended; at present applying only to real property, there is an argument for extension to other forms of property which have the characteristics of limited divisibility and marketability. The provision might, for example, cover the private unincorporated business. We have set our face, on grounds of equity, against concessions to particular kinds of property; but if the relief were granted to all forms of property with these particular characteristics, it would be correcting an inequity rather than creating a new one. The concession would need to be applied with care, and interest charged on the outstanding duty at a rate nearer to market rates than the present provisions.[2]

Cost of Administering the Estate. Some countries, e.g. USA and Canada, permit an allowance to be made against the costs of administering the net estate liable for duty. The costs of administering a complex estate can significantly reduce the after-tax residue if no

[1] Cf Harry G. Johnson, 'The Social Policy of an Opulent Society' in *Money, Trade and Economic Growth*, George Allen & Unwin, 1962, p. 194: '. . . the dilemma that more extensive social measures require more taxation is fundamentally a consequence of our antiquated way of financing governmental activity. Though government plays an important role in creating and maintaining the conditions under which wealth is created and income is earned, we allow the wealth and income to accrue as private property, and finance the government by taxing back the money after it has passed into private hands. I suggest that a more sensible way of conducting public finance in an opulent society would be to give the government a direct participation in the income of the economy, rather then a tax claim on it. One way of moving in this direction would be to accumulate the proceeds of inheritance taxes in the form of a government portfolio of ordinary shares and industrial bonds, instead of spending them as current income.'

[2] The rate of interest on unpaid estate duty was raised from 2 to 3 per cent by the 1970 Finance Act.

allowance is made and there is a good case in equity for a carefully controlled allowance.

ESTATE DUTY OR INHERITANCE TAX

We now turn to the major question in death duty reform—the form the duty should take; we link this with the question of varying the rates according to consanguinity—differing rates for differing relationships—and the treatment of spouses and dependent children.

As we saw in chapter 2, when, in 1894, Harcourt introduced the estate duty as the major death duty in the UK, a central issue of debate was the relative merits of an estate duty, levied on the corpus of the estate regardless of its distribution amongst heirs, as compared with an inheritance tax, levied on what is received by heirs regardless of the size of estate from which it came.[1] This controversy continues; modern would-be reformers of UK death duty are divided on whether the estate duty form should be retained or a switch made to the inheritance tax form.[2] We shall review the main arguments in this controversy, noting particularly how the basis has changed and developed since the Commons debated the issue over seventy years ago.

The Incidence and Equity Argument

Sir William, in presenting his new estate duty, supported it with three arguments all of which seemed to imply that the incidence of the tax was on the deceased. First, the spurious legal argument, which need not detain us long, that because the property owner could only exert some control over the disposal of property after his death by virtue of rights conferred by law, then the state, as guardian of the law, had the *prior* claim to a share in the property; it should take its pickings *first*, and this implied the estate duty form. Worthy of more serious consideration were two arguments that estate duty was a 'back tax' in lieu of income tax on the deceased. At the time it was considered administratively impracticable to tax

1 See pp. 45–8.

2 G. S. A. Wheatcroft, *Estate and Gift Taxation, A Comparative Study*, Sweet and Maxwell, 1965, favours the retention of estate duty and is supported by A. R. Prest (chapter 15, *Public Finance*, Weidenfeld & Nicolson, 3rd edition, 1967). Reformers who wish to switch to an inheritance basis (with various modifications) include J. E. Meade, *Efficiency, Equality and the Ownership of Property*, Allen & Unwin, 1964, *The Economist*, 'Taxing Britain's Wealth', January 15 and 22, 1966, and Oliver Stutchbury, *The Case for Capital Taxes*, Fabian Tract 388, December 1968.

income progressively although many considered it desirable; it was also held to be impracticable to tax income from property more heavily than income from work, although such discrimination was widely held to be justified mainly because of the more permanent nature of income from property which was not dependent on the health of an individual and which did not terminate with his working life. A progressive estate duty, Harcourt argued, compensated for these deficiencies of the income tax. But since Harcourt's day we have introduced and developed the progressive taxation of income and differentiated income tax according to the source of the income, so those two arguments are no longer applicable. More fundamentally Harcourt, in his own day, was attacked by the Opposition for the inequity of relating the weight of the tax to the property of the deceased rather than to the benefit of heirs; for taxing a man according to his father's wealth rather than according to his own; for graduating the tax in proportion to the amount left by those who could no longer enjoy it, rather than in proportion to the amount enjoyed. Whatever may have been the case in Harcourt's day, the weight of estate duty has increased so much since 1894, that there is now little likelihood of a property owner, by insurance or other means, attempting to save against the duty. Whilst, as we have seen, the effective incidence of estate duty is not simple to analyse, and may affect both property accumulator and heir and have its implications for the whole economy, the formal incidence of the duty is almost entirely on the heir. If the tax is to accord with modern conceptions of 'ability to pay', vague though these may be, it surely must be related to the economic circumstances of heirs.

To quote Lowell Harriss on the incidence of death duties and its implications: 'The dominant and I believe correct view is that the tax falls primarily on the heir, depriving him of property he would otherwise have. The *potential* for discrimination to approach equity is therefore high, for tax can be presumably be varied according to significant features of the economic position of the heirs.' Under estate duty, however, the death tax burden is 'determined in amount by the total left by one person. The tax, then, takes little or no regard for the absolute or relative economic positions of the persons who suffer because of it.'[1] The point has been succinctly put by Professor Nicholas Kaldor: 'Death duty is a periodic levy on property falling on the person or persons who inherit a man's estate. The legal notion that the estate duty is a tax on the deceased is really nonsensical—though it may have had rather more justification in the old days when people saved specially during their lifetime to cover death duty

[1] *Ibid.*, pp. 294–5.

liabilities on their decease. If the incidence of estate duty is really on the legatee and not the testator, the sensible thing is to recognize this and to impose a tax on the recipient.'[1]

The first argument in support of the inheritance tax therefore, as against estate duty, is that it is more logical, sensible and in accordance with the true incidence of a heavy death duty to tax in relation to the amount received rather than the amount left; and only some form of inheritance tax enables the economic circumstances of the beneficiaries to be taken into account.

The Equality Argument

In the debates of 1894 the argument that death duties should be used to diminish inequalities of wealth played a minor part. Although the tax constituted a fiscal landmark because of the explicit adoption of the principle of progression, at the rates at which it was introduced, the estate duty was rightly thought of as a revenue yielder which *could* be met from economies in consumption and could be spent by the government like revenue from any other tax; indeed it made the substantial contribution to tax revenue of upwards of 12 per cent per annum from 1894 to 1914. Since 1894 the rates of duty have risen so much that there is no question of the tax being met by reductions in consumption; we also have come to understand more about the workings of the economy and appreciate that revenue from heavy death duties does not serve to cut consumption in the private sector, and so release resources for public sector needs, in the way that other taxation does to a large extent. In short, death duties at current levels are essentially concerned with the distribution of assets or of wealth—between the private and the public sector and within the private sector. Also, with the twentieth century has come an increased concern about the inequality in the distribution of income and of wealth; and the author would submit that the death duties have become a tax the main purpose of which is to reduce inequalities in the distribution of wealth.

If heavy death duties by their very nature are concerned with the distribution of wealth; and if their prime purpose is to promote a more even distribution; then we should choose that form of death duty which is likely to do this most effectively, subject only to certain constraints such as a humane concern for widows and dependent children and the need to guard against adverse economic effects. Of the two forms of death duty, estate or inheritance tax, in some, at least, of its forms, the inheritance tax would be the more effective in

[1] Nicholas Kaldor, 'The Reform of Personal Taxation', *Essays on Economic Policy*, vol. I. Duckworth, 1964, pp. 212–13.

achieving this purpose. It is large inheritances rather than large estates as such that *perpetuate* inequality. An estate worth £250,000 and left to one heir results in bigger inequalities than an estate of £1 million equally divided amongst twenty heirs. A tax graduated according to the size of inheritance thus strikes at the heart of the problem. Moreover a graduated inheritance tax provides some positive inducement to the diffusion of wealth; the more widely a property owner spreads his bequests, the less the total duty paid on the estate. We have little or no evidence on which to determine how important this effect might be; where, as in most instances, testators leave the largest legacies to their spouses or to be equally divided amongst their children, the dispositions resulting from their natural inclinations may be unaffected by the form of duty. But in some instances the incentive to disperse may prove effective.

The Revenue Argument

This brings us naturally to an argument, used by Harcourt and by others since, to support estate duty: that it is a better revenue yielder than inheritance tax. This is obviously true if taxation is progressive and identical rates are applied to an estate and a legacy of the same size: then, only if an estate were left to a single heir, would the inheritance tax yield the same revenue as estate duty; in all other cases the yield would be less. For example, ignoring special concessions, in round terms the present (1970) rates of estate duty are 80 per cent (average) on an estate of £1 million, 50 per cent (average) on an estate of £100,000. Let us assume the same rates for an inheritance tax, and compare the effects for an estate of £1 million. Under estate duty £800,000 (80 per cent) is taken in tax. Under inheritance tax, the yield depends on the disposition of the property. If the estate was all left to one heir then his pre-tax inheritance would be £1 million, the 80 per cent rate would apply and the yield to the Exchequer would be £800,000 as under estate duty. If, however, the estate was left in parcels of £100,000 each to ten people, then under inheritance tax the rate on each bequest would be 50 per cent, giving a total tax yield of only £500,000, i.e. £300,000 less than under estate duty.

But there is no *need* for the rates to be the same. Inheritance tax rates could be calculated which would realize the same aggregate yield as any particular estate duty; the total burden on taxpayers would be the same, but the distribution of the burden would have changed: sole inheritors would pay more than under estate duty, whilst beneficiaries from an estate widely dispersed would pay less.

However, the response to the revenue argument is really more fundamental than this. Once it is recognized that high death duties affect the ownership of assets and do little to reduce the demand of the private sector on current output; and once it is accepted that their purpose is to reduce inequalities in the distribution of wealth; then the amount of revenue raised by them is incidental. There is even a sense in which the less revenue they raise, the more effectively they are achieving their purpose: to take an extreme example, assuming that all loopholes to avoidance had been closed, if an inheritance tax raised no revenue at all, it would mean that all estates were being dispersed at death in such small parcels that no-one was receiving more than the exemption limit of the tax (at present £10,000 under the estate duty). If it seems odd to find that the purpose of a tax is achieved with zero revenue, readers might like to reflect that this is precisely the situation with a protective tariff.

The argument that the lower the yield of an inheritance tax the more effectively it is serving its purpose, must however be treated with care. There are two components to the way in which an inheritance tax may reduce inequality; one is by the heavy taxation of large inheritances—the larger the proportion of the big legacies to be taken in tax, the bigger the contribution towards equality in wealth ownership. The second is by encouraging dispersion of legacies; the more widely an estate is dispersed in small parcels, the lower the tax yield and the more equality is promoted. To ensure that it was more effective in reducing inequality, an inheritance tax substituted for estate duty should be given a rate structure which, on the basis of the same distribution of estates at death as under estate duty, would yield the same revenue. The hope must then be that, subsequently, the yield of the tax diminishes because it leads to a wider dispersion of estates.

The Administrative Argument and the Form of Inheritance Tax

A more powerful argument in favour of estate duty is that it is administratively easier than inheritance tax.[1] If one is comparing a simple estate duty (without a supporting general gift tax) with the simplest form of inheritance tax—in which tax is graduated simply in relation to the size of each individual bequest—then this is undoubtedly true. Quite apart from particular complications which may arise from the treatment of settlements of various kinds, it is obvious that the estate duty is less cumbersome and expensive

[1] In this chapter we are concerned to compare the administrative merits and defects of estate and inheritance taxes *per se*, ignoring the additional transitional problems which arise in changing from one form to another. These transitional difficulties of substituting inheritance tax for estate duty are considered on page 246.

to administer: there is only one tax account and only one rate of duty for each estate; with inheritance tax, whenever an estate was left to more than one beneficiary, there would be more than one account and usually more than one rate of tax; and there could be particular complications if, for example, the testator required that duty should be paid from the undivided estate, which then proved insufficient for the purpose. But the comparison between the two forms of tax is not as simple as this. We have already established the necessity for a death duty, whatever form it takes, to be integrated with a general gift tax if it is to be effective. It is time now to introduce a further complication; an inheritance tax can itself take one of several forms. If our comparison is to be realistic we must now select the species of inheritance tax to be adopted and compare that with estate duty, each with integrated gift taxes.

Apart from special possibilities, such as graduation according to consanguinity or according to the age of the beneficiary, which we briefly consider below, an inheritance tax may take one of three main forms: it may be progressive according to the size of each individual bequest from each estate; it may be graduated according to the total received in bequests over a period of years, preferably throughout a lifetime; or it may be progressive not only according to the size of the individual bequest, but also according to the prior wealth of the beneficiary, so that a rich man pays inheritance tax at a higher rate than a poor man who inherits a legacy of the same size. In each case gifts can be treated exactly on a par with legacies and, in considering the relative merits of the three forms of inheritance tax, it will be assumed that this is done.

In assessing the merits and defects of these various forms of inheritance tax, it is clear from our earlier analysis of the 'injustices' associated with death duties that we need to consider equity in its broadest sense and in the more specific sense of 'horizontal equity'—the equal treatment of persons of similar taxable capacity; ease of avoidance is therefore a major factor in the comparison. Further, we must obviously consider each form of inheritance tax in the light of the main purpose of death duties—diminishing inequalities of wealth holding.

To graduate simply in relation to the size of the individual legacy or gift is the least satisfactory of the three forms. The progression is imperfectly related to the ability to pay of the recipient who may receive a number of legacies or gifts from the same or different sources. Clearly, other things being equal, A who receives four legacies or gifts in a year of £25,000[1] each, has the same taxable capacity on

[1] This example ignores minor differences in the timing of the legacies.

them as B who receives £100,000 in a single legacy or gift; yet under the first form of inheritance tax A would pay substantially *less* duty on the four legacies combined than B would pay on his single legacy. This characteristic would open up various means of avoidance. The division of a person's property between a gift and a legacy to the same person, or 'gift splitting'—a series of small gifts to a person rather than one large gift—would attract lower rates of duty and a smaller total tax. Avoidance, too, could be pursued by an arrangement between relatives or friends each to leave legacies of a certain size to the children of the others, so that these children each received a series of smaller legacies instead of one large legacy from their parent.

The second form of inheritance tax, the taxation of gifts and legacies on a cumulative basis throughout a lifetime, would be free from these objections. Each person, receiving a legacy or gift, would be taxed at the rate appropriate to the aggregate received by legacy and gift, less the amount of inheritance and gift tax already paid. For example suppose the (average) rate of tax on an inheritance of £100,000 was 50 per cent and that on an inheritance of £50,000 was 30 per cent. Then anyone receiving two legacies (or gifts) at different times would pay exactly the same as someone receiving one legacy of £100,000—as follows:

	Legacies/ gifts received	Cumulative total of legacies and gifts	Tax rate	Tax paid	Cumulative total tax paid
	£	£	per cent	£	£
1st.	50,000	50,000	30	15,000	15,000
2nd.	50,000	100,000	50	35,000*	50,000

*Made up as follows:

£100,000 at 50 per cent	=	£50,000
less tax already paid	=	£15,000
tax paid on receipt of 2nd legacy	=	£35,000

This second form of inheritance tax would be free from the inequities of the first and also would be more effective in reducing inequalities. It would necessarily be somewhat more difficult and expensive to administer: a record would have to be kept of all legacies and gifts (above a minimum exemption limit) received throughout the lifetime of each taxpayer.

To graduate an inheritance tax not only in relation to the size of legacy, but also in relation to the wealth of the beneficiary, is attractive as perhaps the most effective method of the three to reduce inequalities of wealth holding. Yet it has its disadvantages too. Unless there were an annual wealth tax (which would automatically supply the valuation of the wealth of the beneficiary) this form of inheritance tax would be much the most expensive to administer, since it would be, in effect, a combination of inheritance tax and wealth tax—although the annual valuations would not need to be as extensive as for a wealth tax for only the wealth of legatees would need to be assessed, not the wealth of all, and the accuracy would only need to be sufficient to establish the broad band of wealth into which the legatee fell for purposes of inheritance tax. If there were already an annual wealth tax, the necessity, and even the desirability and wisdom, of also taking existing wealth into account in determining the rate of inheritance tax, can be questioned. There is a case for taxing inheritance wealth on a separate basis from wealth acquired by personal saving and enterprise; it can be argued that receipts by gifts and inheritances are in a special category of windfall additions to wealth. Moreover apart from this moral argument, there is the practical economic argument that, to tax inheritances and gifts in relation to the prior wealth of the beneficiary might be a particular disincentive to saving and lead to spending out of capital. For example, in anticipation of a large legacy, an heir might spend some of his present wealth if by so doing he substantially reduced the rate of tax on the legacy when it came; in these circumstances much of this spending from capital would have been at the Revenue's expense, not his own.

Whilst, admittedly, the choice between the second and third forms of inheritance tax must necessarily be to some extent a matter of value judgment, the arguments against the third form have convinced the author of the desirability of adopting the second—an integrated gift and inheritance tax, with the rate of duty progressive according to receipts throughout a lifetime; the proposal is not a new one, and, as we shall see, it has been discussed in American literature during the past 15 or 20 years under the name of an accessions tax: and, to make it clear what form of inheritance tax we are referring to, it will be convenient to use this term henceforward.

Let us return, now to the issue which led to this consideration of the various forms of inheritance tax. In terms of administrative complications and cost, how does the estate duty with integrated gift tax compare with the cumulative inheritance and gift tax, or accessions tax. One difference is immediately apparent. Whereas a gift tax integrates easily and perfectly with the inheritance tax, gifts and inheritances being treated precisely the same, with the legatee or donee paying the tax, the integration of a gift tax with an estate duty is far less easy. Where such integration is attempted, the donor pays the tax; but there is a basic problem; until he dies and the size of his estate becomes known, the appropriate rate of gift tax cannot be determined. For the full integration of an estate duty and a gift tax it would be necessary (1) to determine a scale of gift taxation; (2) to apply this scale to the cumulative total of gifts by a donor throughout his lifetime; (3) to add the aggregate life-time's gifts to the estate at death to determine the appropriate rate of estate duty; and then to calculate death duty at this rate, deducting the amount of gift tax already paid. The scale of gift taxation could be made identical with the estate duty rates, but this would not reduce the necessity for the other requirements; aggregation would be essential to prevent avoidance, for, during the life of the donor, gift tax would only be paid in relation to the total of gifts, not the total estate; hence, unless a man gave away the whole of his estate and died leaving nothing (or at least, a sum below any exemption limit), the amount paid in gift tax would be less than would have been paid on the same property at death.[1] In practice gift taxes linked with estate duty have rarely achieved this degree of integration. For example, the gift tax of the USA provides for the life-time cumulation of gifts in determining the rate of gift tax, but the rate schedule for gifts is at three-quarters of that for estates at death and there is no aggregation of life-time gifts with estate; thus there is a substantial gain from avoidance by gifts.[2]

Professor Wheatcroft has argued in favour of deliberately setting lower rates of gift tax to encourage the old to part with their property sooner. Such a policy lessens the effectiveness of death duties as a means of reducing inequalities in the distribution of wealth and has the disadvantage that it still further complicates the integration of estate duty and gift tax. Under Professor Wheatcroft's proposals there is still the need to aggregate gifts over a life-time (to prevent a series of

1 There is one exception to this generalization which arises because the marginal rates of a progressive tax are levied in discrete units on wide estate 'bands' the combined cumulative total of gifts and estate at death might not raise the estate into a higher bracket but simply increase its size within a bracket; then the *same* rates of tax would apply.

2 For example, a 40 per cent gift from an estate of $280,000 reduces the effective rate of gift plus estate tax from 20·3 to 11·1 per cent; a 40 per cent gift from an estate of $2,800,000 reduces the effective rate from 40·2 to 26·3 per cent. See G. S. A. Wheatcroft, *ibid.*, p. 115.

gifts eroding the basis of the tax); gifts are still aggregated with the estate to determine the rate of estate duty on the remainder of the estate (but not on the gift); however, since there is now a tax advantage from giving rather than bequeathing, it is necessary to have some further provision to cover gifts 'in contemplation of death', for example, gifts in the two years prior to death, on which duty must be paid at the same rates as if the gifts had remained part of the estate.[1]

Whether the taxation of settlements and trusts is more complex under accessions tax than under estate duty is disputable. A switch to an accessions tax from estate duty provides a completely new basis of approach; tax could be paid in relation to trust *distributions* rather than trust *creations*. There are several possible bases of taxation; one of the fairest and simplest would appear to be that proposed by Professor Rudick.[2] 'The tax on the principal of the trust would not be payable until termination of the trust. To make up for this delay in the payment of tax on the principal, there would be paid by the trustee, as accessions tax on the income beneficiary's right to receive the income, that proportion of the annual trust income which the tax that would be payable were the property left outright to the income beneficiary bears to the principal of the trust. This would have the effect of making the government a partial income beneficiary of the trust.' An example will help to make the procedure clear. Suppose a trust of £100,000 is created and that the accessions tax payable on an outright gift or inheritance of that amount by the first income beneficiary (B) were £50,000. Then half of the annual income of the trust would be retained by the trustee and paid over to the government as tax on the beneficiary's right to receive the income. The beneficiary would, of course, have to pay income tax on his share of the income. Thus, if the annual income of the trust were £8,000, £4,000 would be paid over annually as accesssions tax, the remaining £4,000 being B's income liable to income tax at the appropriate rate.

The remainderman (C) of the trust would pay tax when the trust terminated, the amount being dependent on the value of the trust property and his accessions tax bracket (determined by the cumulative total received by gift and inheritance) at that time. Under this method a transfer in trust fares similarly to an outright transfer. Thus, in our example, if B had received an outright bequest or gift of £100,000, he would at once have paid £50,000 accessions tax so that only the income from £50,000 would have been available

[1] See G. S. A. Wheatcroft, *ibid.*, pp. 126–32.

[2] Harry J. Rudick, 'What Alternative to the Estate and Gift Taxes?', *California Law Review* vol. 38, 1950, pp. 169–75.

to him. There has, however, been some tax advantage in the trust arrangement in that, had outright transfer been undertaken at each stage, C would only have inherited £50,000 from B instead of the £100,000 which he receives under the trust arrangement; but it can be argued that as B only had the benefit of the income and had no access to capital under the trust, it is equitable that payment at that stage should take the form of the appropriate proportion of income.[1]

A discretionary trust, as always, poses bigger difficulties—but the same general principle could be applied—i.e. that an appropriate proportion of the income could be paid periodically to the Exchequer in lieu of accessions tax. For example, suppose the beneficiaries consisted of A B and C and that, of the total income accruing to the trust in a particular year, A received 10 per cent, B 30 per cent and C 40 per cent. Then the amount of tax paid on behalf of A would be that proportion of the income equal to the proportion of capital which A would have paid in accessions tax if he had received 1/10th of the capital as an outright gift or bequest. Thus, suppose the principal of the trust was £100,000; if A had received a 1/10th share, i.e. £10,000, he would have paid, say, £3,000 in accessions tax. Then, under the trust, as A's right to 1/10th, of the income, 3 per cent of the trust income is paid in lieu of accessions tax. Similarly with B and C. Any payments of capital from a discretionary trust would be treated for accession tax purposes in the same way as outright gifts and bequests.

Settlements and trusts raise problems which are difficult to solve satisfactorily both under the estate duty with integrated gift tax and under the accessions tax. Many of the niceties are the province of lawyers and accountants rather than economists. But it is certainly not clear that these problems are more difficult under the accessions tax than under estate duty. Indeed, some American lawyers have argued that they are less and that herein lies one of the distinct advantages of accessions tax over estate duty. Rudick's view that 'An accessions tax reduces to a significant degree the discrimination which will be present under all the other methods except the inheritance tax in favour of property settled in trust'[2] is endorsed by Professor W. D. Andrews. After a detailed and comprehensive

[1] We have previously put an argument that trusts should be taxed as heavily as outright gifts; and that at any rate, the state should lean in the direction of severity rather than leniency in its tax treatment of trusts to check their use as avoidance devices. Such tougher treatment could be implemented by a simple flat rate settlement estate duty which would apply to all settlements including discretionary trusts and be paid from the principal of the trust when it was established. Admittedly this is an additional administrative complication.

[2] *Ibid.*, p. 169.

consideration of methods which could be used to deal with trusts under the accessions tax proposal, Andrews concludes: 'The simplification that results under the accessions tax proposal from taxing trust distributions instead of contributions, whilst not what was originally sought, is one of its chief attractions.'[1]

To sum up the argument of this section. In considering the administrative aspects of estate duty and inheritance tax we need to compare an estate duty and integrated gift tax with an accessions tax (i.e. an integrated inheritance and gift tax in which tax is levied on the cumulations of a life-time). To operate an accessions tax it is necessary to maintain, for each beneficiary, a record of gifts and legacies received and this necessarily imposes a bigger administrative load than the operation of an estate duty on its own. But the necessary integration of a gift tax with estate duty raises administrative complications and requires records of the life-time gifts of donors. In dealing with settlements and trusts the balance of administrative advantage may lie with the accessions tax. It would be absurdly presumptuous for one mere economist to pontificate on where, overall, the balance of administrative advantage lies between these two forms of death duty-cum-gifts tax; experienced administrators and tax lawyers would need to be brought into the debate, and even then, perhaps the answer would only emerge from actually trying out both—which is hardly possible. It is clear, however, that unlike the comparison between the simplest form of estate duty and inheritance tax, the administrative arguments are not overwhelmingly on the side of estate duty once the need for an integrated gift tax is recognized and its implications realized.

Graduation by Consanguinity and Age of Beneficiary

If we replace estate duty by inheritance tax, it becomes possible to follow the practice of many countries, and indeed that of the old UK legacy and succession duties, and introduce a series of scales to vary the rate of tax according to the relationship of the beneficiary to the deceased. Should we do this? A number of reasons have been adduced to support a consanguinity discrimination. It is argued that to strangers and distant relatives a legacy is more in the nature of a windfall; this may or may not be true in any particular case and the inevitable arbitrariness of state rules cannot adequately take account of complex personal relationships; as Lord Randolph Churchill maintained,[2] it is for the testator to take account of the closeness of

[1] William D. Andrews, 'The Accession Tax Proposal', *Tax Law Review*, vol. 22, May 1967.

[2] See above, p. 48.

personal relationships in framing his will. Again, it has been argued that the biggest burden of death duties is borne by the immediate family whose expectations of inheriting are partially frustrated by the tax and whose customary living standards may be threatened. But expectations should relate to the net of tax inheritance rather than the pre-tax inheritance—in other words expectation should include the tax. And if the taxing authorities took notice of 'customary living standards' the whole basis of taxing the rich more than the poor would be undermined. One argument for limited recognition of consanguinity is much weightier, i.e. preferential treatment for widows and dependent children; but this can be dealt with by special provisions rather than a consanguinity scale. That apart, the arguments are of doubtful validity.[1] Much better to relate the rate of tax to the relevant economic circumstances of the beneficiaries. Moreover, any general application of the principle of different rates according to consanguinity would cut right across the main purpose of the death duties—to even out the distribution of wealth; and the attempt to apply it with the accessions form of inheritance tax, in which gifts and legacies from different sources are cumulated, would add serious administrative complications.

If we reject the general application of the consanguinity principle, we must give more sympathetic consideration to the position of spouses and dependent children. The British estate duty is almost unique in according virtually no concession to transfer between spouses.[2] Indeed there is a marked dichotomy in the treatment of spouses under income taxation and death taxation. For purposes of taxing income, husband and wife are treated as one unit, with the result that under present (1970) tax provisions, married couples in the surtax range jointly pay more tax than if they had been single. Under estate duty husband and wife are treated separately and hence more tax is paid than if they were treated as one unit. Moreover, inequities arise as between married couples with similar amounts of wealth according to the (often arbitrary) way in which wealth is divided between the partners. There are several possible ways of meeting this situation; much to be commended is the Swedish

[1] For a fuller consideration of this matter see Alan A. Tait, 'A Comment of Rates of Taxation Varied According to Consanguinity', *Finanzarchiz*, NF, July 1966. Tait concludes: 'Overall there appears every reason to question rates varied according to consanguinity and little reason to recommend them'.

[2] The only relief is that settled property which bore estate duty on the death of one spouse, or which would have done had the estate been above the minimum dutiable limit (£10,000 in 1970) is exempt from duty on the death of the survivor unless the survivor was competent to dispose of it.

solution, dependent on the ordinary laws of marriage and succession. When a Swedish marriage breaks up, whether by divorce or death, unless the partners have made specific provision to the contrary, the property is deemed to be in common ownership (although the husband will normally have managed it) and is therefore divided equally. At the death of a husband, a widow's entitlement to half the common property means that this part is entirely excluded from death duties. It is significant that Britain is moving towards this position in the breakdown of a marriage by divorce; proposals for better financial protection for divorced spouses are contained in the Matrimonial Proceedings and Property Act 1970 to coincide with new divorce law; by this Act the courts have wide powers in the determination of property rights on the breakdown of a marriage and, in exercising their powers, they should, for example, take into account the contribution of the wife in looking after the home. A further move towards common ownership, on the Swedish pattern, would be a welcome milestone towards equal treatment of the sexes and would largely meet this particular death duty problem.

In addition the Swedish fiscal provisions for a spouse and dependent children might also be adopted. Under Swedish succession duty there is a larger tax exemption limit for surviving spouses than for other beneficiaries and also a special tax free provision for each dependent child, the amount of which varies inversely with age.[1] A special rate should also be introduced into our accessions tax for gifts and bequests received by charities, which should either be completely exempt or subject to a low flat rate duty. But it would be necessary to define charities with care and perhaps impose restrictions about the control of their properties. As E. Gordon Keith has pointed out, to the extent that the charitable trust permits the control over vast accumulations of property to be retained within a family group from one generation to the next, it would seem to be thwarting the intention of a highly progressive death duty. Although the income from such properties may not be used for other than charitable purposes, the loss of income may be considered more than a fair price to pay for the retention of control over the properties themselves. A strong case can therefore be made for limiting the

[1] These features have long characterized the Swedish succession duty, but their detail is currently being revised. In 1970 the Finance Minister has made the following proposals which are expected to come into effect in 1971. For a surviving spouse the first £2,500 (approx.) of inheritance is to be exempt, compared with about £1,250 for children and other close relatives; besides this £1,250, under-aged children (or children of a deceased child) are to receive a £250 deduction for every year or part of a year below the age of 20.

concession to charities to situations where control as well as benefits are surrendered.[1]

We have earlier pointed to the uneven burden of death duties resulting from the differing ages at which people die and the avoidance device of 'generation skipping.'[2] W. Vickrey[3] propounded the idea that the rate of death duty might be related to the age of the deceased and the life expectancy of the beneficiary. Although ingenious and designed to cope with a real problem, his solution must be rejected. The administrative complications of seeking to incorporate this provision within an accessions tax rule it out. But it must be accepted that this inequity remains; and, indeed an accessions tax may accentuate it. As 'children' (the first generation) may be expected to have received more by gift and bequests than 'grandchildren' (the second generation), the lower rate of accessions tax on grandchildren will be an incentive to pass property on to them. At least the practice will tend to diffuse property more widely within the family; and the merit or economic advantage (if there is any) in people receiving property whilst young, will be realized.

SOME INTERNATIONAL CONSIDERATIONS

In concluding our examination of the reform of estate duty and, in particular of the relative merits of the estate duty and inheritance tax forms of death duty, let us examine some relevant international experience. First, a look at three countries, including Britain, which since the second World War have experienced *both* estate duty and inheritance tax and have then chosen one in preference to the other. Then an examination of the practice and policy within the countries of the European Economic Community, which Britain is currently seeking to join and with which some tax harmonization will be necessary if her application is successful.

Why Britain Abandoned the Legacy and Succession Duties, 1949

In 1949, Britain, which had hitherto had a dual structure of estate duty and inheritance tax, decided to drop the inheritance tax.[4] It might be argued: 'If the inheritance tax is a form of death duty superior to estate duty, why was it that estate duty survived and the

1 E. Gordon Keith, 'How Should Wealth Transfers be Taxed?', *American Economic Review*, vol. XL, May 1950.

2 See p. 83.

3 W. Vickrey, *Agenda for Progressive Taxation*, New York, Ronald Press, 1947.

4 See p. 52.

legacy and succession duties were abolished? Why not the other way round?' An examination of the details of the taxes and of the statements of the Chancellor, Sir Stafford Cripps, provide a very clear answer. Whatever the respective merits of estate duty and inheritance tax, as they stood in Britain in 1949, the legacy and succession duties were a complicated anomaly. At the time of their abolition they yielded less than a tenth of the revenue from estate duty. Sir Stafford maintained: 'This method of imposing three separate taxes on death causes a great deal of unnecessary work, both to the Inland Revenue and to executors. Judged by modern standards of taxation, the legacy and succession duties are most unsatisfactory in their present form. The rates are unrelated to taxable capacity, but are flat rates depending on the degree of consanguinity . . . the legacy and succession duties also have the drawback that they impose a proportionately heavier burden on the small than on the large estate.'[1] Thus the duties went, in what Sir Stafford rightly called a 'major simplification'. What was sought by the abolition of the British legacy and succession duties was an immediate administrative gain. No attempt was made to weigh up the respective merits of a modern inheritance tax and a modern estate duty.

Why Canada Abandoned Succession Duty, 1958

In 1958 Mr Fleming, Canadian Finance Minister, proposed the resolution: 'That it is expedient to introduce a measure to replace the present Dominion Succession Duty Act to provide that the tax on property passing or deemed to pass, on death, be computed by reference to the property comprising the estate of the deceased rather than the property contained in the bequests from the estate to the beneficiaries; and also to consolidate, revise and simplify those provisions of the present act that continue to be appropriate.'[2] The Act which followed the resolution brought to an end a succession duty which had been introduced in 1941.

In fact the Canadian succession duty was a rather peculiar combination of estate duty and inheritance tax. The tax consisted of an initial duty and an additional duty. The former was a tax on the estate varying with its size; the additional duty was determined by the amount received by the individual legatee and was also affected, to a lesser extent, by the relationship of the beneficiary to the deceased. No consideration was taken of other legacies received. Professor A. R. Prest, who remains unconvinced of the superiority of inheri-

1 *Hansard*, April 6, 1949. Cols. 2088–90.

2 *Canadian Hansard, House of Commons Debates*, January 28, 1958, p. 3944.

tance tax over estate duty, has written 'It is surely significant that the Dominion Government of Canada tried out such a system [a mixture of estate and inheritance taxes] for some sixteen years in the 1940s and 1950s but then decided, essentially because of administrative complications, to switch to a straight estate duty system'.[1]

The decision was indeed significant, but perhaps not in precisely the way which Professor Prest inferred. A search through the Canadian Hansard reveals no great debate on the principles of death taxation and the merits of alternative forms, like that in the British parliament in 1894. Rather the position is comparable to that of Britain in 1949. A complex and somewhat anomalous structure of death duties existed and the Canadian finance minister, like Chancellor Stafford Cripps, sought to simplify in the most obvious and direct way. But the decision reveals little or nothing of the relative merits of an inheritance tax or an estate duty, with integrated gift taxes, to meet the requirements of the second half of the twentieth century. Of the Canadian succession duty Professor Rudick wrote in 1950: 'This variation of the inheritance tax, which is in essence a compromise between the estate tax and the inheritance tax, suffers in part from the defects of both these. Besides, its attempt to reach greater equity as between the distributees [by progression according to consanguinity] is purchased at the cost of considerable complexity.'[2]

It is of some interest that, when the Canadians commissioned a complete review of their system of taxation, the (Carter) Report[3] recommended the taxation of gifts and inheritances as income and the repeal of the federal estate tax and gift taxes. Whilst this proposal is more radical than that for an accessions tax, they have much in common; both require that the rate of tax should be determined by the size of the gift or legacy received by the beneficiary, taking into account other receipts considered relevant.

Why the Swedes Abandoned Estate Duty, 1958

The final example of a country which, having experienced both estate and inheritance tax, opted for one form only, is Sweden; here the choice went the other way from the United Kingdom and Canada. The Swedes had long operated an inheritance tax known

1 A. R. Prest, *Public Finance in Theory and Practice*, Weidenfeld & Nicolson. 3rd edition, 1967, p. 313.

2 Harry J. Rudick, 'What Alternative to the Estate and Gift Taxes?', *California Law Review*, vol. 38, 1950. p. 165.

3 *The Royal Commission on Taxation* (*Canada 1966*)—the Carter Commission.

as a succession duty. Between 1948 and 1958 they also levied an estate duty. The estate duty was abolished on the advice of a specialist committee. To have the two forms of tax was felt to be unnecessarily complicated both for those liable to tax and for the authorities. In favour of abolishing estate duty rather than the inheritance tax it was argued that the inheritance tax was more firmly rooted in the traditions of Swedish taxation; that the succession duty made possible a more realistic distribution of the burden; and that it could be better adapted to the taxable capacity of the individual recipients. To quote from the Committee's findings:

> 'In accordance with the principles of Swedish tax law it is important that death duties should as far as feasible take account of the tax capacity of the inheritor or beneficiary concerned. On this point the inheritance tax may be regarded as being on the whole suitably adjusted. It is graded both as regards the extent of the inheritance or legacy, and—by means of different tax classes—as regards the nearness or distance of relationship to the deceased. Legacies of equal size are thus equally taxed—irrespective of the size of the total residual estate—if they are left to persons in the same tax class. By virtue of the division into tax classes according to relationship the deceased person's surviving spouse and direct heirs are more lightly taxed than other heirs or legatees. This favours those who to a greater extent than any others may consider themselves to have a justifiable and to some extent legally protected interest in being allowed to take over the deceased person's property. Inheritance tax is not however able to take into account a recipient's tax capacity inasmuch as practical reasons make it impossible to match capacity to the recipient's general economic situation. By calculating estate duty on the estate in its entirety, inheritances of equal size are taxed more heavily the greater the total residual estate is. This is unfavourable above all to families with several children. Three children who inherit altogether 300,000 crowns thus suffer a heavier reduction than one child that inherits 100,000 crowns.'[1]

In deciding to retain inheritance tax and abolish estate duty the Swedes, more than Britain in 1949 or Canada in 1958, tried seriously to examine the relative merits of the two forms of duty. The Swedish choice is therefore perhaps the most significant of these national precedents. Yet it would be wrong to press the point too

[1] A translation of extracts from pp. 32–7 of the Report of the Swedish Capital Tax Committee (*Arvsbeskattning, Betänkande av Arvsskattesakkunniga*), Stockholm, 1957.

far, for the Swedish tax is not the accessions tax that we have advocated, although the Swedes go some way towards it by having identical rates for gifts and bequests, and by cumulating gifts and any bequest *from the same person* over a period of ten years in determining rates of gift and inheritance tax. The Swedes, too, retain the principle of progression according to consanguinity, which we have rejected; although it is of interest that their 1970 proposals for modifying succession duty reduce the number of 'classes' under which tax is levied to three, one of which consists of bodies of a charitable nature.

The European Economic Community

All six original members of the EEC have inheritance taxes as the main form of death duties, although Italy also operates an estate duty. All EEC members, except Luxembourg, have gift taxes closely integrated with the inheritance tax. None levy duty on the cumulative basis we have recommended and all have some form of graduation according to consanguinity.

In any programme of tax integration in the Community, death duties are far down on the list; if Britain's current application to join the EEC is successful, she would certainly be able to influence the form of harmonization of death duties, if harmonization should be deemed necessary. The Neumark Committee did have this to say:

> 'For the taxes on inheritance, their fiscal importance measured as the proportion they represent in the over-all product, is today everywhere restricted. It is however often—at least for large inheritances or estates—so high that gross inequalities between countries can lead to transferences of domicile and to movements of capital for tax reasons. Certainly this argument concerns the nature and the types of tax on inheritance less than their level. But if 'tax transparency' is desired to be as great as possible, a certain formal harmonization of the system of taxes on inheritances (tax affecting either devolvement of part of the inherited estate or the estate as such, or a certain combination of the two) would also be desirable.'[1]

CONCLUSIONS AND POLICY RECOMMENDATIONS

In this final section we attempt to draw together the main conclusions

[1] *The EEC Reports on Tax Harmonisation: Report of the Fiscal and Financial Committee* (The Neumark Report), Amsterdam, 1963, p. 128. The term 'inheritance tax' is used in this quotation in its wide rather than its specific sense.

and policy recommendations of the chapter and clothe them, if somewhat tentatively, with quantitative flesh.

A. We characterized death duties as a form of tax with very real merits but inherently liable to create 'injustices'. The conclusion to be drawn was that a system of death taxation should be the kernel of any tax policy to reduce inequalities of wealth; but that death taxes must be devised with careful regard both to detail and form.

B. Applying these principles to the reform of death duties in the United Kingdom, *whether or not the estate duty form of death duty was retained*, the following changes should be made:

(1) The rates of death duty should be reduced. (Say, to a maximum *marginal* rate of estate duty of 65 per cent.)
(2) *At the same time* the duty must be made effective, in particular by being fully integrated with a general gift tax.
(3) The law of property should be amended so that the property of a marriage should normally be regarded as held in common by the partners. When one spouse dies, only half the property of the partners then falls liable to death duty.
(4) The special concessions on agricultural and industrial property should go.
(5) The payment of duty in kind should be extended and a special commission created to receive and administer property handed over in settlement of death duties.
(6) Payment by instalments should be extended to all assets characterized by limited divisibility and marketability.
(7) A carefully controlled allowance should be permitted against those costs of administering the estate which result from death duties.

C. The form of death duty most to be commended is an inheritance tax with integrated gift tax in which the rate of duty depends on the cumulative receipts of legacies and gifts throughout a lifetime, sometimes called an accessions tax. It is superior to estate duty because it is more in accordance with the incidence of heavy death duties, more closely adjusted to the ability to pay of the beneficiary and likely to be more effective in reducing inequalities of wealth; and to put the point at its lowest, the administrative inferiority of inheritance tax to estate duty is not as pronounced as has been thought when allowance is made for the need to integrate a gift tax with death duties.

D. To ensure that the accessions tax is more effective than estate duty in diminishing inequalities of wealth, the rates of tax need to be set at a level such that, if the pattern of estate dispersion at death remained the same, an equal revenue would be raised. If, subsequently, estates became more widely dispersed as a result of the tax, revenue would fall; but this would be cause for rejoicing not sorrow; the tax would be achieving its purpose.

In fact because of the cumulative nature of the tax which could not be made retrospective, some small initial revenue reduction might have to be accepted; but this effect would be gradually offset by the cumulative provisions.

E. It would not be difficult to estimate the reduction in estate duty yield as a result of the lower rates proposed for a reformed estate duty; the various other minor changes would affect the yield somewhat—the abolition of the special concessions on agricultural and industrial property would save some £10 million or so (the figure for 1967–8 at the old estate duty rates) whilst the proposed change in the law of property would reduce yield. The big question mark lies over the amount of additional revenue from the general gift tax. At this we can only guess, but our evidence on the amount of avoidance suggests that this and other measures to make the death duty effective, would have a very substantial revenue effect. The total yield could be as much, or more than, that of the unreformed estate duty.

Estimating the accessions tax rates necessary to raise revenue equivalent to a reformed estate duty adds further complications. We need to take account of the manner in which property is distributed from each estate, by gift and bequest, and also how many gifts and bequests are received by the same person. We have some evidence that testators have tended to leave a large proportion of their estate to one or a small group of beneficiaries (for example, an equal division amongst children) and that the proportion left to a single main beneficiary has been in inverse proportion to estate size.[1] But we have no evidence of the extent to which people benefit from more than one bequest or gift.

The following table, therefore, is no more than a guess at rates which might achieve the objectives desired. It gives, for purposes of comparison, the unreformed (1970) estate duty rates; suggested rates for a reformed estate duty combined with gift tax; and suggested rates for an accessions tax. Apart from the addition of tax paying 'brackets' at the lower and upper end for the accessions tax, the property bands of the unreformed estate duty have been retained. The degree of guesswork in the exercise did not justify elaboration

[1] G. F. Fijalkowski—Bereday, 'The Equalising Effects of the Death Duties', *Oxford Economic Papers*, June 1950, see especially table III, p. 182.

at this stage; but, if the accessions tax were adopted, a sub-division of the bands to give a smoother progression would be desirable. The figures should be taken, simply, as broadly illustrative of the alternative approaches to reform.

TABLE 4.1

Slice of net capital value over £	not over £	Estate duty rates introduced April 15, 1969 per cent	Suggested rates for a reformed estate duty and gift tax per cent	Suggested rate for an accessions tax per cent
2,000	5,000	Nil	Nil	10
5,000	10,000	Nil	Nil	15
10,000	17,500	25	15	20
17,500	30,000	30	20	25
30,000	40,000	45	30	35
40,000	80,000	60	40	45
80,000	150,000	65	45	50
150,000	300,000	70	50	55
300,000	500,000	75	55	60
500,000	750,000	80	60	65
750,000	1,000,000	85*	65	70
1,000,000	1,500,000	85*	65	75
1,500,000	2,000,000	85*	65	80
2,000,000	—	85*	65	80

*With a ceiling of 80 per cent of the total estate.

Additional provisions under the accessions tax might be that:

(1) Legacies from spouses would benefit from an additional £3,000 exemption limit.
(2) Under-age children receiving legacies from parents should have an additional £250 of the legacy exempted from tax for every year by which their age was less than eighteen.
(3) Gifts or legacies of less than £200 in any one year would be disregarded.

Part III

ANNUAL NET WEALTH TAXES

Chapter 5

The Annual Net Wealth Tax in Theory and Practice

INTRODUCTION

Britain has no annual tax on personal net wealth, but in the past decade proposals for a wealth tax have emerged from varied sources and the possibility of introducing an annual wealth tax in the United Kingdom must be seriously considered. We first examine the general arguments advanced in favour of an annual tax on net wealth, then the problems to which it gives rise and its likely economic effects. Argument on the theoretical plane is followed by a look at wealth taxes in other countries, in particular the Swedish wealth tax, one of the oldest in existence; after a detailed consideration of the Swedish tax, we seek to assess how far it achieves the advantages claimed for wealth taxes and at what cost. In the light of this analysis we turn, in Chapter 6, to the possibilities for the UK; we examine various proposals, consider the problems a wealth tax would pose in Britain and finally attempt to assess its desirability and practicability.

THE ATTRACTIONS OF AN ANNUAL WEALTH TAX

A wealth tax is usually envisaged in principle as a tax levied annually on personal net assets (total assets minus liabilities) above a specified exemption limit. It would cover all assets not specifically exempted whether or not they yielded a money income and would include: stocks and shares; real property of all kinds; the assets of unincorporated businesses; personal chattels such as furniture, jewellery, cars and yachts; and money balances. We discuss below whether the capitalized value of future earnings should be included, but no wealth tax has yet, in practice, attempted to include this asset.

The arguments in favour of an annual wealth tax are those outlined in the first chapter, which apply to wealth taxes in general; we here examine them in their detailed application to an annual wealth tax.

Equity

Possession of wealth confers on its owner a 'taxable capacity' which is different from and additional to the taxable capacity of the income (if any) from the wealth. Income can be accepted as the best single criterion of 'ability to pay' and it is also convenient to keep income as the main personal tax because, by its nature, it constitutes a flow from which payment can be made. But equity is best served if the income tax is complemented by a wealth tax, in particular an annual wealth tax.

The argument can be seen at its most extreme form by comparing a beggar with no wealth and no income with a maharajah, who does not work but has vast wealth in the form of gold and diamonds. If income tax were the only personal tax they would be treated the same; neither would pay anything. But the maharajah is clearly 'better off' than the beggar, with a much higher 'taxable capacity'. Equity, as between taxpayers, is served by a wealth tax which supplements the income tax and takes account of these differences in taxable capacity. An annual wealth tax does this better than other forms of wealth tax; a capital gains tax would not trap the maharajah unless his wealth appreciated (and then he would be taxed only on the *additional* taxable capacity conferred by the appreciation.) A death duty might ultimately encroach on his assets, but the death duty is irregular in time and the maharajah might avoid the duty in whole or in part by a series of spending sprees. Only a regular and frequent wealth tax really satisfies the equity argument.

It is not only in order to tax wealth with no income that equity demands a wealth tax as a supplement to income tax. A wealth tax allows for differences in taxable capacity resulting from the differing yield of capital assets. Consider two taxpayers A and B; each receives the same sum in income from property, but A's property has a higher value than B's. If in all other relevant respects their circumstances are identical they will pay the same income tax. But it is inequitable to tax them the same. The owner of the capital with the higher value (and lower yield) A, has opportunities open to him which are not available to B. (To put it at its simplest, he could sell a proportion of his capital and enjoy a spending spree and then maintain his income by switching into the kind of asset held by B).

An annual wealth tax is a partial substitute for a capital gains tax. In so far as a capital gain adds to taxable wealth at assessment dates, it is subject to wealth tax in the same way as other additions to wealth; and where a wealth tax is progressive the gain may have the effect of pushing the taxpayer into a higher bracket. An annual capital tax thus acts as a kind of accruals gains tax. But it does not remove altogether the case for a realization gains tax; it does not tax the gain *as such*, and it is arguable that additions to wealth from capital gains ought to pay tax at a higher rate than, say, additions to wealth from saving; nor does it catch gains spent between assessment dates.

The equity arguments so far used to support an annual wealth tax are unrelated to any communal or governmental wish to tax *income* from property ('unearned income') more heavily than income from work ('earned'). The case for this differentiation as presented originally, rested not on any alleged moral inferiority of unearned over earned but on the argument that unearned income was more certain; unearned income continued when earned might be interrupted by the sickness or unemployment of the worker and would terminate on his retirement. This argument has lost much of its force with the various state social security provisions; but if it is still wished to impose a higher tax on income from property than on income from work, then a wealth tax is a method of achieving this objective which removes the need for complicated differential provisions in an income tax.

Thus an annual wealth tax supplements and complements income tax by taking into the reckoning taxable capacity missed or inadequately allowed for by income tax—wealth which yields no income and wealth of differing values yielding the same income. Further, a wealth tax offers some regular taxation of accrued capital gains. Also it is a method, alternative to income tax differentiation, of taxing income from property more heavily than income from work. These are the equity arguments for an annual net wealth tax.

Efficiency in Resource Use

The efficiency arguments rest on the premise that the annual wealth tax is a partial substitute for income tax; that, in assessing its effects, we can compare the consequences of raising £x by wealth tax with those of raising £x by an addition to income tax. (Thus, if £y is the revenue raised from an income tax complemented by a wealth tax which raises £x, the alternative is an income tax of £z, where $x + y = z$.) Efficiency in this context has both a negative and a positive aspect: negative in that a wealth tax, as an alternative to an additional increment of income tax, restricts the supply of the factors of production less; positive in that a wealth tax may provide an inducement to employ resources in ways which generate the highest return.

The partial substitution of a wealth tax for income tax redistributes the formal incidence of tax. Assuming the same income and wealth as before the substitution, affected tax payers will fall into three classes:

(1) Those who benefit from the income tax deductions more than they lose from the imposition of the wealth tax.
(2) Taxpayers at the opposite end of the scale, who are liable to pay more in wealth tax than they save from reduced income tax.
(3) Taxpayers whose increased payments under wealth tax just balance their reduced income tax.

The effect of income tax on work effort is generally analysed in terms of income and substitution effects working through the demand for leisure. The income effect of an *increase* in income tax is a tendency to work more; since the tax has made the payer worse off, he can afford less of most things, including leisure and, as there is no reason for believing that leisure is an 'inferior' good, the income effect favours an increase in work effort. The substitution effect concerns the 'price' of leisure, the terms on which leisure can be acquired. If income tax is increased, the 'cost' of an extra hour of leisure has correspondingly fallen; the substitution of an extra hour of leisure for an hour's work involves a smaller sacrifice of income (and hence of the things which income will buy) than before. Thus the substitution effect of an increase in income taxation is to increase the demand for leisure, i.e. reduce the taxpayer's willingness to work.

Theory provides no conclusive answer on which of these two effects will be the stronger; but it offers some pointers. The income effect works through the change in aggregate income, whilst the substitution effect works through the change in the terms on which income can be acquired at the margin. Thus the more the effect on marginal income relatively to aggregate, the more an income tax increase is likely to reduce the amount of work done and conversely. An individual taxpayer, for the same payment to the Revenue, is likely to reduce his work effort more if faced by a progressive rather than a proportional tax. At the opposite extreme a lump sum income tax, which was irrespective of amount earned, would have an incentive effect, for it would generate an income but no substitution effect.

Let us apply this analysis to the three taxpayer situations postulated by a partial substitution of a wealth tax for income tax. The effect will depend in part on the precise form of the substitution;

but let us concentrate on the most likely case, i.e. that the income tax reduction has taken the form of a lowering of income tax rates at the top of the scale, allowances remaining unchanged.

The taxpayer of situation (1), who faces wealth tax payments less than his income tax payments, has had a net increase in his income (after income tax and wealth tax) and also a reduction in his marginal rate of income tax. The income effect, by which he can now afford more leisure, will tend to induce him to work less; the substitution effect, to induce him to work more. There is no clear-cut answer but possibly a presumption in favour of increased work as the reduction in income taxation has been concentrated on the top marginal rates.

The taxpayer of situation (2), who faces more total tax, will clearly be encouraged to increased work effort where the motive is increased consumption. On the one hand his disposable income (income net of income tax and wealth tax) has fallen, and the income effect will be to stimulate work effort; on the other hand the marginal rates of income tax have also fallen, so that the substitution effect will work in the same direction as the income effect. Thus, work effort which has consumption as its objective should clearly be stimulated.

The taxpayer of situation (3), whose total tax liabilities remain unchanged, will experience no income effect, but the reduced income tax rates should provide a positive substitution effect in favour of work effort where consumption is the objective.

The stimulus of a wealth tax to work effort rests fundamentally on the fact that it has effects rather like that of the lump sum income tax; the tax base is not related to present effort. But whilst a wealth tax is clearly favourable to work effort for consumption purposes, its effect on saving is more disputable; the saving argument we examine below under the problems of a wealth tax.

Turning to the positive arguments, advocates claim that a wealth tax should lead to the more efficient utilization of capital resources. Because the tax has to be paid whether an asset yields any income or none and regardless of how much it yields, the wealth tax acts as an incentive to hold wealth in a form which yields a high income; it encourages wealth owners to transfer wealth from nil-yielding assets to earning assets and from low-earning assets to high-earning assets. The income tax reduction consequent upon the substitution of a wealth tax further encourages this move.

Let us illustrate this tendency. A wealth tax may be expected to discourage the holding of idle money balances; money balances attract wealth tax and yield little or no income with which to pay it.

Similarly, a comprehensive wealth tax would discourage 'investment in jewellery, pictures, stamp collections and the like, which yield no money income but incur liability to wealth tax. A wealth tax is an additional incentive to the owner of an unincorporated business to minimize stockholding and adopt an efficient policy of stock control —to reduce his level of stocks to the necessary minimum and employ the capital in income-yielding form. Again, a landowner pays no income tax on a piece of land which he leaves uncultivated and undeveloped; but he must pay a wealth tax whether his land yields a monetary return or not, and the tax may induce him to cultivate or develop the land so that at least it yields a return sufficient to pay the tax; alternatively the wealth tax may induce him to sell the land, so that it passes into the hands of someone prepared to put it to use.

Thus, it is argued that a wealth tax does not have the deterrent effect on earnings associated with income tax and would reinforce the profit motive to secure an efficient allocation of capital resources.

Equality

An annual wealth tax offers a method of reducing inequalities of wealth in the community; to tax wealth is a more direct and comprehensive method of attacking the problem of wealth inequality than to tax income (even differentially) and a wealth tax is more regular in its incidence than death duty.

Administrative Efficiency

An annual wealth tax is a useful administrative adjunct to income tax; returns of wealth provide a cross check on returns of unearned income. Similarly, wealth tax returns can be linked with returns for death duty and gift taxation to provide a comprehensive network to foil the tax evaders. Valuations of property for wealth tax purposes can serve for gift and death duty purposes, which can speed the winding-up of estates and provide a guide to the valuations of unquoted shares and other business assets which removes an uncertainty damaging to business development.[1]

PROBLEMS OF A WEALTH TAX

Saving

If an annual wealth tax would encourage effort and enterprise, what would be its effect on saving? The answer is not clear cut and might depend very much on the weight of the tax. If the tax were so heavy as of necessity to be paid from capital (i.e. income tax and wealth tax

[1] See above, chapter 3, p. 116,

combined exceeded 100 per cent of aggregate income) then private saving would necessarily be reduced; the effect on community saving would depend on how the government used the revenue.

Let us consider the effect on the incentive to save from a wealth tax which was a substitute or partial substitute for surtax. There are opposing considerations. On the one hand the tax base is accumulated savings; the more income saved the more wealth tax paid. The compensating reduction in income tax leaves more disposable income for consumption or saving, but as that part saved now adds to wealth tax liability, substitution of consumption for saving might be expected, including a tendency for consumers to buy non-durable instead of durable goods. On the other hand, the stimulus which the tax is expected to give to enterprise and equity investment may be an encouragement to saving; and a wealth tax with lower rates spread over the entire accumulation of wealth may have a less deterrent effect than an income tax with more highly progressive rates concentrated on earnings from additional savings. We cannot predict with any certainty the net effect on the quantity of personal saving.

What could be predicted with more certainty is that if there are particular forms of saving which avoid the wealth tax, in whole or in part (because some kinds of property are exempt or undervalued), then these forms of saving will be substituted for others which attract the full weight of the tax.

Administration

The main administrative problems are two-fold—discovery (i.e. preventing evasion) and valuation. To secure the advantages we have listed a wealth tax must be comprehensive; it must cover all or a very wide range of assets. Yet the concealment of personal, non-income yielding assets, such as jewellery, is easy.

But more serious is the problem of valuation. In principle valuation should accord with the price the asset would fetch if sold in the market at the time of assessment. There is no valuation problem for bank balances, nor for stocks and shares quoted on the stock exchange; the problems arise for real estate, where it is usual to take cadastral values (i.e. an assessed value from a periodical valuation), for unquoted shares and the business assets of sole proprietors and partnerships, and for personal effects—cars, boats, jewellery, pictures and the like. There is a direct relationship between the cost of administration and the equity of the tax; attempts at short-cuts in valuation procedure reduce the equity. Thus, any attempt to value assets by capitalizing yields would cut right across the equity argument for the tax, which rests on the need to complement, not duplicate, the income tax base; and attempts to ease the administrative problems by exempting certain kinds of assets would likewise undermine the whole basis of the tax, since it is assets yielding no money income, like owner-occupied real estate and personal chattels like jewellery, which create the biggest valuation problems.

Not only valuation of assets but valuation of debts, to obtain the value of net assets, can also create problems; the Swedes not infrequently find that, for tax purposes, the lender values his asset at a lower figure than the borrower his debt. Given returns from both, such discrepancies can be discovered and removed, but the necessity for such cross-checking illustrates the administrative complexity of the tax.

Human Capital

One of the most interesting and potentially useful and unifying recent developments in economics has been the concept of investment in human beings (apart from slavery!) which has demonstrated the similarities between investment in formal education and on-the-job training on the one hand and investment in a piece of capital equipment on the other,[1] e.g. both involve the sacrifice of current resources for the sake of future earnings and both may be used as a security for loans. The question therefore arises, should a wealth tax be assessed not only on physical but on human capital?

The two *main* determinants of future earning power are education (already referred to) and innate ability. The desirability of taxing human capital therefore depends primarily on whether taxing the capitalized value of future potential earnings, resulting mainly from investment in education and from natural abilities, would promote equity, equality and efficiency.

Natural abilities are akin to wealth in the form of 'land', the free gifts provided by nature. In *principle*, equity and especially equality would be furthered by taxing the capitalized value of potential earning power from differences in innate abilities; indeed this should particularly please egalitarians because, like differences in inherited wealth, differences in innate abilities are unrelated to individual merit. A wealth tax on human capital counteracts some basic inequalities of nature. If we could devise a measure of 'potential

[1] T. W. Schultz (ed.), 'Investment in Human Beings', *Journal of Political Economy*, vol. LXX, No. 5, Pt. 2 Supplement, October 1962.

G. S. Becker, *Human Capital: a Theoretical and Empirical Analysis with special reference to Education*, New York, National Bureau of Economic Research, 1964.

Harry G. Johnson, 'The Economic Approach to Social Questions', *Economica*, vol. XXXV, No. 137, February 1968.

future earning power' unrelated to actual earnings, then we could also hope to gain an incentive benefit from substituting wealth tax for income tax because the wealth tax base was not directly related to present effort. But it seems unlikely that we can find a method of valuing human capital other than expected future earnings, and likely that such a base will be closely linked to *actual* earnings. Then the danger is that we duplicate the income tax base, and that the individual may be inclined to apply his innate abilities to more leisure and less work.

Taxing the capitalized value of potential future earnings from education raises still more complex issues. Education provides a consumption benefit (comparable to that of a durable consumer good) throughout a life-time, e.g. the capacity for fuller enjoyment of leisure; and an investment benefit of higher life-time earnings. In addition, over and above individual benefits there may be social benefits (e.g. the growth of new knowledge). Capitalizing future potential earnings simply abstracts the investment-type benefit of education to the individual.

If we compare two persons of similar ability, of whom one has invested in a physical asset from which he obtains an (unearned) income and the other has invested in education, gaining an incremental addition of (earned) income, equity requires that both types of investment should be liable to wealth tax provided that the persons are treated on a comparable basis in matters of depreciation and maintenance (e.g. that tax allowances are available against expenditure to maintain skills); and that the tax on human capital is assessed on less than the full capitalized value of expected future earnings. With human capital there is no asset separable from the owner; hence the capital value of future earning power is not a readily negotiable asset; further, the value of human capital is subject to particular uncertainties like the taxpayer's health and length of working life. For these reasons people cannot normally borrow to the full capitalized value of their earning power, which thus represents a more limited stock of spending power than an equivalent value of physical capital. Provided these differences are recognized, such a tax would not only promote equity, but it would reduce the inequalities between the educational 'haves' and 'have nots'.

Many objections may be made to this proposal. Some might argue that the life-time consumption benefit of education should also be capitalized and taxed, just as a (physical) wealth tax includes the value of consumer durables yielding no money income; but how can we measure this benefit? A very different argument is that it is folly to tax the fruits of education when, because of its social benefits, governments heavily subsidize it. But there is no necessary contradiction; this is precisely how we treat investment in physical assets, which we stimulate by allowance or grants whilst taxing the profits. Indeed, state subsidization strengthens the equality argument for taxing the capitalized value of potential earning power from education, as the expenditure has been largely undertaken by the general taxpayer rather than the prime beneficiary. A more serious objection is the effect on efficiency; taxing human capital would risk discouraging the pursuit of formal education, and hence restricting investment in education and reducing the supply of skilled labour.

Including the value of human capital within a wealth tax base clearly raises complex and controversial issues. But whether or not it is desirable in principle, with our present state of knowledge, understanding and capacity for measuring the value of human capital, any attempt to include it would be inadvisable.[1] It is difficult to conceive it as being administratively or politically practical at this moment of time. In fact none of the countries currently operating a wealth tax attempts to include human capital and our further consideration of a wealth tax will assume that the tax is confined to non-human assets.

NET WEALTH TAXES IN PRACTICE

The theoretical arguments in favour of a wealth tax are attractive. But there is always a danger that in assessing a new tax we consider a blue-print, an ideal which never exists in practice. Hence we now examine actual wealth taxes. For a general perspective we survey, briefly, the range of wealth taxes as a whole; we then concentrate on a much more detailed analysis of the Swedish wealth tax.

Fourteen countries have a net wealth tax (all small countries except West Germany and Pakistan);[2] five impose the tax on companies as well as individuals. In all cases the wealth taxes are regarded as a supplement to income tax and rates are low enough for income tax and wealth tax combined to be payable out of income. Exemption limits vary from as low as about £800 or slightly more (in Luxembourg, Columbia and Switzerland) to about £35,000 (in Pakistan).

[1] For a contrary view see G. F. Break and R. Turvey, *Studies in Greek Taxation*, ch. 6, pp. 176–7.

[2] This survey of net wealth taxes abroad is based on 'The Taxation of Net Wealth' by Nobornu Tanabe, *International Monetary Fund Staff Papers*, vol. XIV, No. 1, March 1967, which, besides an analysis and commentary on wealth taxes in general, includes a summary of the main features of net wealth taxes in the various countries. The summary above refers to the position at the time Noboru Tanabe's article was written; no attempt has been made to allow for changes which may have taken place since, except in the Swedish wealth tax (below).

Rates are generally progressive and basic nominal rates vary from a low of 0·2 per cent to a maximum of 3 per cent; some countries provide a 'ceiling' provision, e.g. a maximum percentage of income which can be taken in tax by income and wealth taxes combined. In general 'fair market value' is adopted as the principle for valuation, but specific and often elaborate rules are applied to certain classes of assets. The range of exempt assets varies. Administration of the wealth tax is usually integrated with that of the income tax.

In most countries the yield from the wealth tax is between 1·5 and 2·6 per cent of national tax revenue; only in one, Columbia, was it 4·4 per cent; in several it was below 1 per cent. These figures may somewhat under-estimate the effective contribution of the wealth tax to revenue because the tax may indirectly increase the yield of other taxes. Thus, if in accordance with the theory considered earlier, the wealth tax leads to a reduction in idle cash balances and an increase in the income yield from assets, then income tax revenue benefits therefrom; thus a wealth tax may add more to the revenue than its nominal yield. But this qualification is highly unlikely to overturn the generalization that all existing wealth taxes make only minor contributions to tax revenue.

THE SWEDISH NET WEALTH TAX

Origin and Scope

The Swedish annual net wealth tax is perhaps the example most often cited by those who advocate a wealth tax for the United Kingdom.[1] The Swedes have a long tradition of wealth taxation. Their first regular annual tax on wealth dates from 1910 when under a combined national income and wealth tax a proportion of the value of personal net wealth (originally 1/60th) had to be added to income for income tax assessment. The wealth tax in its present form dates from 1947 and is separate from income tax except for the 'ceiling' provisions (see below) which relate income and wealth tax and the administrative arrangements by which wealth and income are returned on the same form.

The Swedish tax is basically a personal tax, applying to Swedish residents on net assets (wherever situated). It does not tax corporations as such, but non-resident individuals and foreign legal entities are subject to net wealth tax on their capital invested in Sweden. Swedish family trusts and individual estates are also subject to tax

[1] For example, M. Stewart, 'The Wealth Tax', *Bankers' Magazine*, 1963; NEDC *Conditions Favourable to Faster Growth*, p. 42, HMSO, 1963.

and non-family trusts and similar organizations pay at a very low rate.

For purposes of net wealth taxation the assets of husband and wife are combined and the assets of children under 21 with no taxable income and living at home are added to those of their parents.[1]

The Swedish tax is probably more comprehensive than most other wealth taxes. The assets covered include quoted and unquoted stocks and shares, real property including houses and the capital value of rights in real property, bank balances (except house-keeping balances), the business assets of individuals and partnerships and personal chattels (cars, horses, motor-cycles, yachts, boats and jewellery being specifically listed). The main exemptions are the capital value of insurance or pension rights, furniture for personal use, works of art and collections of books and paintings and similar collections held for personal and not commercial use.

Yield and Rates of Wealth Tax

In the fiscal year 1968–9 the wealth tax yielded 380m. Swedish kroner (about £30m.),[2] 1·2 per cent of central government revenue from taxation. Wealth tax in that year was paid by just over 200,000 taxpayers (often representing two persons, husband and wife) from a total population approaching 8,000,000.

The tax is progressive. The first £8,000 of wealth is exempt,[3] the first £4,000 over £8,000 carries a rate of 0·8 per cent rising as shown in table 5·1 by four steps to a maximum of 1·8 per cent on property over £80,000.

The significance of these rates can perhaps best be appreciated if expressed as income tax equivalents on capital with various yields. Consider the marginal rates. An additional £1,000 of wealth to a person (A . . . E) at the minimum of each tax step would attract tax as set out in table 5.2.

In table 5.3 the marginal tax payment is expressed as a percentage

[1] By an amendment in 1969 the age was reduced to 20; it was also provided that, where children living at home had an income large enough to render them liable to state income tax, there would be an assessment of the combined wealth of parents and children which would make it less profitable to split fortunes. After the combined tax was fixed it would be divided between man, wife and children in proportion to their fortunes.

[2] All figures relating to the Swedish taxes have been converted from Swedish kroner to pounds sterling at the exchange rate of £1 = 12·5 Kr.

[3] These rates of tax and the provisions which follow were in force at the time of writing (Spring 1970). Proposals for changes, which, if accepted, would mainly come into force on January 1, 1971, and be used for the 1972 assessment, are described in a postscript at the end of this chapter.

of the income from the marginal increment of wealth (taken as £1,000) at various assumed yields. Allowance should be made for capital gains in considering the implications of the wealth tax, not just the nominal 'income' yield. Thus, if an asset with an 'income' yield of 5 per cent benefits from a 3 per cent per annum capital gain it should be treated as an investment yielding 8 per cent.

TABLE 5.1. *Rates of Swedish Wealth Tax, 1970*

	£ sterling	Rate per cent
first	8,000	Nil
next	4,000	0·8
next	4,000	1·0
next	16,000	1·3
next	48,000	1·6
over	80,000	1·8

A 'person' with wealth of £100,000 would thus pay £1,408 (average 1·408 per cent). A 'person' with wealth of £1,000,000 would thus pay £17,808 (average 1·78 per cent).

TABLE 5.2. *Wealth Tax Payments and Rates*

Person	Wealth	Tax	Average tax rates	Marginal tax rates	Tax on £1,000
	£	£	%	%	£
A	9,000	8	0·09	0·8	8
B	13,000	42	0·32	1·0	10
C	17,000	53	0·31	1·3	13
D	33,000	224	0·68	1·6	16
E	81,000	786	0·97	1·8	18

To assess the significance of these rates it must be remembered that they are on top of local and national income tax rates. Local income tax varies between localities but is a proportional rate currently averaging just under 20 per cent.[1] It is allowed as a deduction against national income tax which rises to a maximum marginal rate of 65 per cent on taxable incomes, from earnings and investment

[1] Strictly 19·35 per cent; *The Swedish Budget 1968/9*. A Summary published by the Ministry of Finance, p. 114, Stockholm, 1968.

TABLE 5.3. *Wealth Tax as percentage of Marginal Income*

	Yield per cent (on additional £1,000)												
	Nil	1	2	3	4	5	6	7	8	9	10	15	20
Income from marginal £1,000	—	*10*	*20*	*30*	*40*	*50*	*60*	*70*	*80*	*90*	*100*	*150*	*200*
Wealth tax as percentage of income at 0·8 per cent rate (Income level A)	∝	80	40	26·67	20	16	13·33	11·43	10	8·89	8	5·33	4
Wealth tax as percentage of income at 1·0 per cent rate (Income level B)	∝	100	50	33·33	25	20	16·67	14·28	12·5	11·11	10	6·67	5
Wealth tax as percentage of income at 1·3 per cent rate	∝	130	65	43·33	32·5	26	21·67	18·57	16·25	14·44	13	8·67	6·5
Wealth tax as percentage of income at 1·6 per cent rate (Income level D)	∝	160	80	53·33	40	32	26·67	22·86	20	17·78	16	10·67	8
Wealth tax as percentage of income at 1·8 per cent rate (Income level E)	∝	180	90	60	45	36	30	25·7	22·5	20	18	12	9

combined, above £12,000.[1] Thus if a person with a taxable income of £12,000 received an additional £1,000 of property which yielded 5 per cent, the combined local and national income tax would amount to 72 per cent of income (assuming local income tax at 20 per cent) and wealth tax would take a further 16 per cent at the minimum rate and 36 per cent at the maximum rate. Thus an owner of £80,000 wealth, whose taxable income was over £12,000 would suffer a reduction of income (of £4 a year) by receiving an additional £1,000 yielding 5 per cent.

Special Provisions

There are two special provisions designed to mitigate the burden of the combined income taxes and wealth tax. The 'thirty-times-income' rule, to help the owner of low yielding property, states that the value of total net wealth for purposes of the wealth tax shall not exceed 30 times the taxpayer's income (from all sources) except that this provision shall not reduce the value of net wealth by more than 50 per cent.

Thus consider a man with the following income and wealth:

Earned income	£2,000
Investment income	£1,000
	£3,000
Wealth	£100,000

Then, the thirty-times-income rule would reduce the value of his property for wealth tax purposes to £90,000.

Suppose, however, that he had no earned income so that his total income was £1,000. In that case, because the maximum permitted reduction is 50 per cent, the value of his property for wealth tax purposes would be reduced to £50,000 (not £30,000).

The thirty-times-income provision applies automatically. The other provision, the 'eighty per cent' rule only applies at the request

[1] There are certain 'standard deductions' before taxable incomes are calculated, e.g. (in 1968–9) single person's allowance (£180) or married couple's allowance (£360), local income tax paid during the preceding year and a maximum of £240 for a wife's earned income. On the other hand capital gains liable to tax are treated as income. Also a basic pension fee is levied at a flat rate of 5 per cent on the same taxable income as for State income tax purposes, up to £2,400. The average rate of income tax (including local tax and pension fee) reaches 52 per cent for a single man and 48 per cent for a married couple with £8,500 gross income.

of the taxpayer. This rule provides that the total sum taken in local and national income tax and wealth tax combined shall not exceed 80 per cent of a taxpayer's total income (except that in no case must the tax on net wealth be reduced below the amount which would have been due on 50 per cent of the taxpayer's wealth).

Valuation Procedures

In principle the valuation sought after is a 'fair market value', but the method of arriving at the appropriate valuation varies. Let us concentrate on the valuation procedures for the following types of property—real property, quoted stocks and shares, unquoted stocks and shares and other business assets, and personal chattels liable to wealth tax—e.g. boats, jewellery.

Real property is valued for wealth tax purposes on the basis of an assessment undertaken every five years (with modifications between assessment dates to allow for development or destruction). This assessment is used also for calculating an assumed income for income tax purposes, where no money income arises; and it is the valuation used for gift tax and succession duty.

Quoted stocks and shares are valued at the stock exchange valuation on December 30th of the preceding year.

Unquoted stocks and shares provide a much more difficult problem. A firm's balance sheets are submitted to the taxing authorities each year for income tax purposes, and the authorities suggest a valuation of shares (against which the taxpayers can appeal). This valuation is published in a catalogue available to wealth tax assessment boards. Either of two methods is used in arriving at the valuation. Where the numbers of shareholders is large the method used is to take the dividends of the firm, compare them with the dividends of quoted companies in the same industry, and capitalize dividends on the basis of the average yield of the listed firms in the industry; a very small reduction is made to allow for the lower price at which unlisted shares normally sell compared with listed. Alternatively, for a close company with a small number of shareholders, valuation is based on the individual assets with no attempt to include goodwill. This is likewise the basis of valuation also for business assets held in personal possession.

Personal chattels are taken at the taxpayer's valuation which is rarely challenged by the authorities.

Evaluating the Swedish Wealth Tax

Having outlined the main features of the Swedish wealth tax in some detail, we are now equipped to assess the tax against the criteria set out earlier. How far does the Swedish wealth tax achieve the advantages of equity, efficiency in resource use, equality and administrative efficiency and with what effect on saving and at what administrative cost?

Undoubtedly the Swedish wealth tax achieves something under the heading of equity; it taxes capital over and above the income from it; it taxes also some non-income yielding capital which would have been completely exempt under a differentiated income tax. But the achievement is partial. The wealth tax is itself riddled with inequities, which is a particularly damaging criticism of a tax recommended primarily on grounds of equity.

First, by its nature, a capital tax must be levied on the value of capital at a *point* of time; it cannot like an income tax be levied over a period of time.[1] This necessity for a single date for valuation (the end of the taxpayers' year under the Swedish tax) means that there is always some inequity between those whose wealth has increased before assessment date as compared with those who receive additional wealth just after assessment date. It is indeed possible to avoid wealth tax by a general spending spree just before the assessment date and for people to transfer from assets which carry high wealth tax to assets with a lower tax liability just before assessment dates, subsequently switching back to the original assets; but this risk is probably slight because of a transfer tax of 1 per cent on real estate and 0·3 per cent on shares.

The exemptions to the Swedish tax also make for inequity; the exempted collections of various kinds, such as art and book collections, can be held not so much for purposes of personal pleasure but as an investment.

More serious discrepancies arise through the valuation procedure. The cadastral valuation of real property is invariably below market value. The assessment board's valuation is deliberately and properly 'cautious', because prices *may* fall between assessment dates and indeed in certain areas of depopulation this has happened; but for most properties inflation has widened the gap between the assessed and the real market value throughout the five years from one assessment date to the next. Thus, close observers suggest that the assessment value of a particular property may be anything between 40 and 90 per cent of its market value. It is also recognized that the personal chattels subject to wealth tax (when returned at all) are generally included on the taxpayer's return at a nominal rather than

[1] It would, of course, be possible to have a series of valuation dates within a year and take the average; but this would be impossibly complicated and expensive.

true value. Inevitably, also, the valuation procedure for unquoted shares has uneven results. The valuation of business assets, excluding the value of goodwill, is somewhat arbitrary in its results; valuation by reference to average dividends in the same sector of industry in quoted shares is perhaps even more unsatisfactory. Firms with quoted shares in one industry may differ considerably from each other in the dividends earned; and firms with unquoted shares in the same line of production may similarly show large differences; averages are thus the roughest justice. One study[1] showed that when the valuations carried out in accordance with the guiding principles of the national tax board were compared with sales at 'arm's length' of (mainly small) businesses which took place within a short period of the valuation, in general the sales value was substantially more than the assessed value; in extreme cases it was seven to ten times more; it was not unusual for it to be four to six times more; but in a few cases sales value was less than assessed value.

Thus it is clear that the tax is unequal in its incidence between owners of different kinds of wealth. While some forms of wealth, notably quoted stocks and shares and bank balances, pay on the full market value, others are exempt or valued very much below market value, whilst unlisted shares may exceptionally be valued above market value. Moreover, the procedure by which the valuation of personal chattels is taken on trust from the taxpayer, with no evidence required in support of the valuation, penalizes the more honest members of the community.

If we return to the example used earlier to illustrate the equity purpose of a wealth tax, namely the difference in taxable capacity between the Maharajah and the beggar, each with no income, but the Maharajah possessing many jewels, it can be argued that had the latter gentleman been a Swedish citizen he might not have declared his jewels at all; if he had they would have been valued only at nominal value; and perhaps he might even have been able to hold his jewels in a form which would have secured their exemption as a collection.

The result of exemptions and the under-valuation of many assets is to raise the effective starting point of the tax and reduce the real burden of its rates.

Turning to the second criterion, *efficiency in resource use*, there is no direct evidence, but it is a reasonable inference that, in

[1] G. Englund, 'Tillförlitligheten av de enligt riksskattenämndens anvisningar framräknade aktievärdena'. (The reliability of the values on shares that are reckoned according to the guiding principles from the national tax board) in the review, *Skattenytt*, 1966, pp. 99–108.

general, incentive to effort under the wealth tax plus income tax will be greater (or the disincentive less) than if the wealth tax were abolished and the difference raised by additional income tax. But even so odd things happen. As indicated earlier the maximum marginal rate of local and national income tax combined is about 72 per cent. But the operation of the 80 per cent rule can have the effect of raising the effective marginal rate of income tax to 80 per cent. Supposing, for example, that a taxpayer has income (from earnings and investment combined) of £100,000 on which combined income tax and wealth tax liability was £90,000; the 80 per cent rule would reduce this liability to £80,000. If he should then *earn* an extra £1,000, this would be taxed at 80 per cent.[1]

The Swedish tax may also have the hoped-for effect, at some levels of wealth and income, of encouraging the transfer of wealth from low income earning assets and idle balances into high income earning assets. Table 5.3 above demonstrates the incentive to seek a high yield. To take the extreme example, if a taxpayer at top income and wealth tax rates wishes to add *at all* to his disposable income from a marginal £1,000 of additional wealth, he must invest it to yield over 6 per cent; at 6 per cent or less the combined income tax and wealth tax exceeds the income. A taxpayer on maximum income tax rates, but liable only to the minimum rate of wealth tax, would need a return of almost 3 per cent not to be worse off in terms of income from his marginal £1,000 of wealth and at a 5 per cent return to capital he would only retain 12 per cent of the income.

But the provisions of the Swedish wealth tax may also lead to quite other consequences than the search for high yield investments—indeed, the very opposite may be result. Thus the tax provides a strong incentive to transfer wealth into forms of assets which are exempt, notably collections, which are nil-yielding assets but which

[1] The following fuller statement clarifies the point:

	Income	Income and wealth tax liability (if no 80% rule)	Income and wealth tax liability under 80% rule
	£	£	£
Initial position	100,000	90,000	80,000
After earning additional £1,000	101,000	90,720	80,800

Tax on marginal £1,000 earned	800
Effective marginal rate of tax on earned income	80%

may be held as an investment for capital gain. Moreover the exemption makes insurance an attractive form of investment.[1] But the application of insurance funds will not generally be of a kind associated with risk-taking and enterprise, which is what the wealth tax is supposed to promote. Swedish insurance companies are restricted in the range of their investments and are required by law to keep 90 per cent of their policy funds in investments of a gilt-edged nature[2] at nominal value. Even the remaining 10 per cent cannot be invested in ordinary shares, although surplus funds may be so invested provided that the total amount of shares held by an insurance company does not exceed 1/20th of the shares of one industrial company.

Investment in low-yielding capital is also encouraged by the thirty-times-income rule. If the yield from wealth is low, income tax is low and the value of wealth for wealth tax purposes can be reduced. However, it would be wrong to assume that this result is necessarily detrimental to risk taking and enterprise. Investment to minimize tax could take the form of a close company which retains profits for capital gains, which are taxed relatively lightly in Sweden where the gain has accrued over a period of more than five years; this form of investment may or may not be of a risky nature.

It is perhaps the possibility of minimizing wealth tax and income tax in this way by taking advantage of the thirty-times-income rule which has prevented the wealth tax being more effective in promoting *equality* in the distribution of wealth. Wholly reliable statistical evidence on the distribution of wealth in Sweden is lacking, but if it were available, we would not be able to sift out how far the wealth tax, as such, was responsible for any reduction in inequality that may have taken place; but a widely held view in Sweden is that the richest have become richer whilst the rich have become poorer.[3] The richest are best able to buy expert advice on tax avoidance and to put their wealth into a family business which provides owners with the income they need by way of directors' fees and managerial

1 Perhaps there is a symbolic significance in the fact that the tallest building in Stockholm is the Skattehuset, the tax building, whilst an insurance building is a close runner-up!

2 Swedish government and local authority, loans to state credit institutions, bank holdings, mortgages up to 66⅔ per cent of the assessed value, other equivalent securities and policy loans and advances.

3 As an eminent Swedish economist said to the author in private conversation: 'Our finance minister is the enemy of the millionaire and the friend of the multi-millionaire,' His measure of 'a million' was Swedish crowns, not pounds sterling; so that a sterling paraphrase might be that the provisions favoured the millionaire but not the man with £100,000.

salaries, but pays low dividends; thus advantage can be taken of the thirty-times income rule to minimize wealth tax whilst wealth is augmented by capital gains.

The annual wealth tax carries such a small yield and is so open to avoidance as a result of exemptions, under-valuation and the use of the ceiling provisions, that its effectiveness, on its own, in promoting equality, must be doubtful.

Finally, the criterion of *administrative efficiency*. Wealth tax and income tax are administratively integrated; returns of income and wealth are made on the same form and there is an immediate cross-check between wealth and investment income. Also a check is to some extent kept on earned income through the net wealth return. Everybody is obliged to state his net wealth (even when only debts) and if the assessment board considers that a man has increased his net wealth during a year more than seems possible in view of his total income, he is asked to explain.

There is, however, less direct link-up between the wealth tax and other capital taxes, the gift tax and succession duty. There are partial valuation links; the assessed values for real property apply to wealth tax, gift tax and succession duty and the suggested values for unquoted shares, used for the wealth tax are taken as a guide to the value for gift tax and succession duty. In other respects the link is weak. Three different authorities are respectively responsible for the three taxes and although the officers may occasionally correspond for purposes of cross-checking in exceptional cases (for example, when a big decline in net wealth suggests large gifts) there is no automatic tie-up. Thus, under succession duty, the value submitted for jewellery has to be authenticated by a valuer's certificate; yet there is no automatic check to see that the beneficiaries of the succession record the jewellery at the authenticated value in their next wealth tax returns. Similarly, there is no automatic notification sent to the wealth tax authorities of property passing by gift. Thus, whilst the administrative advantage of the cross-check for income is obtained, other potential gains of administrative efficiency in the structure of wealth taxes (annual net wealth tax, gift tax, and succession duty) are only imperfectly realized.

How does the Swedish wealth tax appear in the context of the traditional problems of wealth taxation? Does it have a detrimental effect on saving? Is it difficult and costly to administer?

Most of the available evidence about *saving* we have already reviewed in considering investment. It is hard to resist the view that, at any rate for taxpayers at or near the top rates of income and wealth tax, the combination of the two must be detrimental to saving via the ordinary media; such as stocks and shares, bank or building society balances. As we have already seen, a taxpayer on the top rates who saves £1,000 has to obtain a yield in excess of 6 per cent if he is not to suffer an actual diminution of income for his pains. But saving in other forms may be encouraged where the asset is treated favourably for wealth tax purposes; thus saving by means of insurance and through art collections is encouraged; saving applied to the purchase of under-valued real property is favoured; and saving through the retention of profits in close companies is encouraged. Whether, in total, private saving is encouraged or diminished it is hardly possible to judge; but the wealth tax undoubtedly affects the *form* which saving takes.

Finally, the administrative problems and costs of a wealth tax. These problems, it will be recalled, were principally 'discovery' and valuation. It is probable that there is evasion of tax in the failure to return certain personal chattels, particularly jewellery which can be easily concealed; but how much cannot be assessed; beyond that, it is unlikely that much evasion takes place. What of the administrative difficulties associated with valuation? Surprisingly, in view of the generally held view of the difficulty of administering a wealth tax, the officers immediately responsible for the Swedish tax did not consider that it was difficult to administer. The solution of this paradox was not hard to find. In the areas where valuation might have been expected to be difficult, valuations for wealth tax were either supplied for other purposes or taken on trust. Thus the structure of real property valuation was used for purposes of national and local income tax (to determine a notional income from property not yielding a money income) for gift tax and succession duty as well as for wealth tax. The valuation of unquoted shares and business assets was derived from balances submitted for income tax purposes and was used as a guide for gift tax and succession duty as well as wealth tax. The valuation of personal chattels was largely taken on trust from the taxpayers. The fact that, apart from indisputable exceptions such as the value of bank balances and quoted stocks and shares, valuations were generally too low, must also help to minimize the number of appeals and problems of administering the tax.

Because the structure of valuation existed independently of the wealth tax, it is not possible to establish any meaningful cost of administering the tax.

It is not the purpose of this extensive analysis of the Swedish wealth tax to praise or to condemn; the Swedes themselves are conscious of short-comings within their whole system of wealth taxes and a

Capital Tax Committee is currently sitting.[1] Our purpose is to gain a realistic appreciation of the problems of wealth taxes by a close examination of a working example, not just a blue-print. From this examination we can hope for guidance whether or not Britain should adopt an annual wealth tax; and if so what form it should take and perhaps what pitfalls we should take care to avoid. To this we turn in our next chapter.

POSTSCRIPT: PROPOSED MODIFICATIONS TO THE SWEDISH WEALTH TAX

In December 1969 the Swedish Capital Tax Committee (referred to above) in its first report to the minister of finance, proposed sweeping changes in the annual net wealth tax: a higher exemption limit; increases in rates to a maximum of 3 per cent; and big modifications in the ceiling provisions. When, in accordance with normal Swedish procedure, the proposals were sent to interested organizations for comment, the committee was particularly criticized for ignoring economic considerations. In the light of the comments, the minister of finance presented a bill to parliament in March 1970 which proposed rather less severe changes than the committee had recommended and also included some interesting new provisions designed to soften the effect of the tax on family businesses (including agriculture). The main proposals are summarized below.

Rates. The exemption limit to be increased from £8,000 to £12,000 and tax rates to be raised to a maximum of 2½ per cent. Table 5.4 compares the proposals with the 1969 rates and the recommendations of the capital tax committee.

Ceiling provisions. The thirty-times-income rule to be abolished and the 80 per cent rule to be replaced by a new 80 and 85 per cent rule: by the new rule if the total amount of net wealth tax, state income and local income tax combined, exceeds 80 per cent of the first £16,000 of taxable income and 85 per cent of the remainder of taxable income, the excess is to be (automatically) refunded to the taxpayer, with the proviso that the amount of tax must not fall below the sum of the local income tax and the tax on 50 per cent of the net wealth of the tax-payer.

[1] Spring 1970. The modifications arising from the proposals of the first report of the Capital Tax Committee are described in the following postscript.

TABLE 5.4. *Swedish Wealth Tax*

Size of net wealth	1969 rates	Rates proposed by capital tax committee	Rates proposed by Minister of Finance
£ sterling		per cent	
first 8,000	Nil	Nil	Nil
next 4,000	0·8	Nil	Nil
next 4,000	1·0	1·0	1·0
next 4,000	1·3	1·0	1·0
next 12,000	1·3	1·5	1·5
next 20,000	1·6	2·0	2·0
next 28,000	1·6	2·5	2·0
next 52,000	1·8	2·5	2·5
over 132,000	1·8	3·0	2·5

Concessions for family businesses. A series of provisional rules are proposed to prevent family enterprises being placed in a worse position by the new wealth tax provisions than by the old. 'Enterprises', in this context, means activity in agriculture, forestry, industry or commerce carried on by the taxpayer alone or with other persons by means of a joint stock company or partnership. The concession is to apply only where the total net value of the enterprise (or the sum of all the shares) does not exceed £160,000; where the enterprise is owned by the tax-payer alone or together with at most nine other (natural) persons to the extent of at least 75 per cent; where the taxpayer has at least 75 per cent of his net wealth placed in the enterprise; and where he depends on the enterprise for his living. If these conditions are fulfilled then, for wealth tax purposes, the value of the taxpayer's net wealth (the whole of his net wealth, not just the part in the enterprise) is reduced by 25 per cent on that part of the net wealth exceeding £40,000. (This limit is introduced because below £40,000 there has been no significant increase of wealth tax.)

It is proposed that, with one exception, these amendments should come into force on January 1, 1971, which means that they would be used for the first time at the assessment which takes place in 1972. The exception is the increase in the exemption limit. The finance minister is proposing that this should be introduced at once (so that it would be used for the first time at the assessment which takes place in 1971) to coincide with the application of the new assessed values for real estate property.

No changes have been proposed in valuation or administrative procedures, but the Capital Tax Committee has indicated that, in a later report, it intends, to recommend the application of wealth taxation to the larger private collections of works of art and the like.

Chapter 6

An Annual Net Wealth Tax for the United Kingdom?

THE DEBATE

The 1960s have been a period of considerable discussion on the possibility and desirability of an annual net wealth tax for Britain. Of the politicians, Mr Callaghan started the debate when, in a Party Political Broadcast before the 1964 General Election, he suggested the possibility of a wealth tax levied on the owners of wealth above £20,000 or £25,000. But on attaining the Chancellorship he shelved the proposal in favour of other tax changes. His successor, Mr Jenkins, soon indicated his interest in 'the further exploration of the ways in which the taxable capacity of those who possess wealth should be differentiated from that of those who depend primarily on wages and salaries.[1] But in 1968 the congestion in the Inland Revenue from Mr Callaghan's measures was such that the Chancellor could only say of a wealth tax 'I will not spend time on a discussion on the merits of such a tax since it would be quite impracticable at present because of the problems of valuation which would be involved.[1] In 1968 Mr Jenkins had to content himself with a 'once and for all' special charge on investment incomes.

Perhaps the most important words in Mr Jenkins' wealth tax statement were 'at present'. The Labour Party's mid-sessional report of 1968 included vague references to additional taxation of wealth; but when Chancellor Jenkins presented his budget in April 1969 the same practical objections still applied; the Revenue was still far too overloaded for a new major tax to be introduced, let alone one with the administrative complications of a wealth tax.[2] Labour's interest in an annual wealth tax continued; *Agenda for*

1 Extracts from the Budget speech, March 19, 1968.

2 'I must continue to give great attention to the overstrain which persists in the Inland Revenue. The two major and worthwhile changes of 1965 were a heavy meal to digest and the process is still not complete. I could not in these circumstances justify measures, possibly desirable in themselves, which would involve great administrative tasks, particularly of valuation for little revenue, as in the case of a gifts tax, or, even if the revenue were greater as in the case of a wealth tax, for little demand effect.' Extract from the Chancellor's Budget speech, April 15, 1969.

a Generation, a statement by the NEC to the Party's annual conference at Brighton in 1969 proclaimed that 'Serious consideration must be given to an annual wealth tax' and indicated that studies were being 'carried out in depth' for a report to a subsequent conference on this and other ways of reducing inequality. *Labour's Economic Strategy*, published in August 1969, indicated rather more fully the kind of wealth tax envisaged: 'With a starting point of £50,000, and with progressive rates of 1 per cent through to 5 per cent on wealth above £400,000, the yield could be in the region of £250m. A tax of this kind has already been successfully levied in a large number of countries, including the whole of Scandinavia, Germany, Luxembourg, Holland and Switzerland, and should present little difficulty here once the nettle has been grasped.' It is clear, from what we have already written that the accuracy of the second half of the statement is very doubtful. The wealth tax proposed (without any reduction in income tax and surtax) was so much heavier than that of the other countries listed that it amounted to a difference in kind as well as degree. Nor would an analysis of the Swedish tax suggest that an annual wealth tax of any kind, let alone of the level proposed in *Labour's Economic Strategy*, would 'present little difficulty'. In fact, although the Labour Party Manifesto for the 1970 General Election referred to the need to reduce inequalities of wealth by taxation, an explicit commitment to a wealth tax was avoided.

A strong supporter of a wealth tax has been the TUC. In its first major economic review, published in 1968, a wealth tax to raise £1,000m. was advocated; the review of the following year contained a more modest proposal for a wealth tax yielding £500m.

It would be wrong to conclude that the leanings towards a wealth tax have come from only the political left and the unions. About the time that Mr Callaghan first raised the issue the National Economic Development Council expressed the view that 'the introduction of a wealth tax here would be a controversial step but it may have a useful role in any major review of taxation related to a programme for growth'.[1] At least one eminent industrialist, Mr Joe Hyman, has given his support to a wealth tax; in a letter to *The Times* he wrote: 'A shift in taxation by substituted charges on capital for income tax would do wonders for the better utilization of resources'.[2]

The debate has also been carried on in professional journals.[3]

1 *Conditions Favourable to Faster Growth*, HMSO, 1963.

2 September 18, 1968.

3 Particularly in 'Symposium on a Wealth Tax' (by Professors A. T. Peacock R. C. Tress and G. S. A. Wheatcroft), *British Tax Review*, November/December 1963.

the press and pamphlets. Proposals for a wealth tax as part of a reform in the whole structure of capital taxation was made by *The Economist* newspaper which recommended a combined wealth and windfall tax;[1] whilst Oliver Stutchbury in a Fabian tract [2] proposed a 'modest' wealth tax in the context of a major reduction in income tax and the substitution of a Gratuitous Enrichment Tax (GET) for the present estate duty. Not all pamphleteers have been enthusiastic over a wealth tax and the often radical Bow Group published *The Case Against the Wealth Tax.*[3]

A CONFISCATORY WEALTH TAX

A distinction needs to be made between proposals for a tax which must *necessarily* be paid largely from capital and those for a wealth tax as a substitute or partial substitute for surtax, which it would be *possible* to meet from income.

Let us take as our example of the confiscatory wealth tax the proposals of the TUC (although those continued in *Labour's Economic Strategy* would do equally well). Its 1968 recommendation was for a tax to be levied on property over £20,000 at a rate 'of the order of 3 per cent on average' which would 'probably yield £1,000m. a year'. This was to be imposed on top of income tax and surtax currently at a maximum marginal rate of 18s 3d in the £ or 91¼ per cent. A wealth tax of 3 per cent is the revenue equivalent of 100 per cent income tax on capital yielding 3 per cent, a 50 per cent tax on capital yielding 6 per cent, and a 25 per cent tax on capital yielding 12 per cent. Thus, on capital earning 6 per cent a taxpayer on maximum surtax rates with property over £20,000 would pay a marginal rate equal to 141¼ per cent of income in wealth tax, income tax and surtax combined. Only if the yield on capital was greater than 34·3 per cent would the maximum rate surtax payer be left with a positive net of tax income on his marginal investments.

Indeed, this example under-estimates the severity of the TUC's proposals for the very rich. The TUC recommended a tax of 3 per cent '*on average*'; this should, presumably, be interpreted to mean a progressive tax varying from, say, 1 per cent to 5 per cent. A taxpayer at maximum surtax rates and paying wealth tax of 5 per cent would need a return on capital of over 57 per cent simply to 'break

1 'The Case for a Capital Tax,' January 22, 1966.

2 *The Case for Capital Taxes*, Fabian Tract 388, December 1968.

3 A Bow Group Memorandum by Theo Wallace and John Wakeham, March 1968

even'—i.e. to be able to pay income tax, surtax and wealth tax from income.

Even if we take a surtax payer about half way up the scale, with unearned income of £7,000, paying combined income tax and surtax at a marginal rate of 14s 9d (73·75 per cent), and wealth tax at 3 per cent, his combined income and wealth tax payments would exceed income on a return on capital of less than 11·4 per cent.

Table 6.1. shows income tax, surtax and wealth tax payments combined for various amounts of net wealth held by single taxpayers whose income was all investment income. The average and marginal gross return to investment is assumed to be 5 per cent and the wealth tax is a flat 3 per cent. A return of 5 per cent may be regarded as low, but it should be recalled that the wealth tax applies to all net assets, not only those yielding a monetary return; this necessarily brings down the average return of income which can be expected from wealth holding. Marginal and average returns are assumed to be the same to keep the mathematics simple; it might be reasonable to expect the marginal rate of return to be higher than the average because of certain 'overheads' of non-income yielding wealth, such as an owner-occupied house, car and furniture. On the other hand, wealth holding in the form of jewels and art or other collections (which does not yield a money income) may well form an increasing proportion of marginal increments of wealth.

On balance it is probable that the rate of return assumed is high for the smaller wealth holders in the table and low for the larger wealth holders, especially when we allow for capital gains, partly because of the 'overheads', partly because of the opportunity of the really rich to spread investments and to afford the best professional advice. Also, as mentioned earlier, the TUC's proposal of 1968 implied a progressive scale with a 3 per cent *average*. The smaller wealth holder in our example is hit more heavily and the larger less heavily than under a progressive tax averaging 3 per cent. But the example serves well enough to demonstrate clearly that a wealth tax of the order of that proposed by the TUC, imposed on top of current rates of income tax and surtax, would *necessarily* be largely paid from capital. Even if prepared to take a big drop in living standards, taxpayers would be able to meet their new wealth tax liabilities only by drawing on accumulated savings, i.e. parting with capital assets.

This being so, it was economic nonsense for the TUC to imply that the £1,000m. of revenue from its proposed wealth tax would 'make possible not only necessary improvements in public expenditure but also such modifications in the structure of existing taxes as are

TABLE 6.1. *Combined Effect of Income, Surtax and Wealth Tax at various levels of Wealth and Investment Income*

Net wealth	Income from wealth p.a. (at 5 percent gross return)	I.T. and S.T. at 1967/8 rates	Marginal rate of I.T. and S.T.	Average rate of I.T. and S.T.	W.T. at 3 per cent	Combined I.T., S.T. and W.T.	Income after I.T., S.T. and W.T.	Combined I.T., S.T. and W.T	
								As per cent of marginal income	As per cent of total income
£	£	£	per cent	per cent	£	£	£	per cent	per cent
25,000	1,250	381	41·25	30·4	750	1,031	219	101·25	82·5
50,000	2,500	947	51·25	37·9	1,500	2,447	53	111·25	97·9
100,000	5,000	2,440	63·75	48·7	3,000	5,440	−440	123·75	108·8
200,000	10,000	6,178	78·75	61·8	6,000	12,178	−2,178	138·75	121·8
300,000	15,000	10,515	88·75	70·0	9,000	19,515	−4,515	148·75	130·1
400,000	20,000	15,078	91·25	75·2	12,000	27,078	−7,078	151·25	135·4
500,000	25,000	19,640	91·25	78·5	15,000	34,640	−9,640	151·25	138·6
1,000,000	50,000	42,453	91·25	85·0	30,000	72,453	−22,453	151·25	144·9

Notes to table: W.T. = Wealth tax; S.T. = Surtax; I.T. = Income tax.
Assumptions: Single taxpayer with minimum allowances and all unearned income; average and marginal gross rate of return to investment is assumed the same.

judged to be desirable on social or economic grounds.[1] As the report had already ruled out tax concessions to the higher managerial groups, these somewhat enigmatic propositions presumably meant using the revenue from the wealth tax for ordinary current expenditure and for reducing taxes on the lower paid. A more certain formula for inflation could hardly have been devised.

The 1969 TUC *Economic Review* represented a welcome advance in realism. A wealth tax was considered in the context of capital taxes as a whole. The Report indicated the need for a gift tax to limit avoidance (both of estate duty and the proposed new wealth tax) and a readiness to accept a 'review' (which presumably meant a reduction) of estate duty rates if a gift tax were introduced. Further, the yield proposed from a wealth tax was reduced from the £1,000m. of 1968 to a more modest £500m. and the Council clearly recognised that the revenue could not be treated as ordinary receipts. 'It is not likely that the fall in consumption expenditure by those who were subject to the tax would be a high proportion of the additional taxation. Thus, substantial increased expenditure by the state out of the proceeds of such a tax might lead to a net increase in total demand in the economy which would be undesirable (unless the economy was less than fully employed). The General Council therefore assume that a substantial proportion of the revenue from a wealth tax would normally be devoted to increasing the budget surplus, thus making possible some net reduction in the burden of the national debt.'[1] The TUC then went on to suggest some possible ways in which work people might benefit from the tax without the immediate pressure on demand being increased.

The 1969 Review made no specific proposals on the starting point or rate of wealth tax, except that the tax should be progressive. Since the yield proposed, at any rate as the initial objective, was to be only half that of a 3 per cent wealth tax on fortunes over £20,000, then a higher starting level or a much lower average rate of tax, or a combination of the two, would suffice. But even this lower tax, as the TUC clearly acknowledged in 1969, would necessarily be largely paid from capital.

The 1969 proposals offer a consistent step in a programme for diminishing inequalities in the distribution of wealth: a wealth tax imposed on top of existing income tax and surtax, largely paid from wealth and largely used for capital purposes. It can hardly be doubted however, that an annual tax of this nature would drastically diminish the incentive to save, except in forms which might avoid the tax by

[1] TUC *Economic Review*, 1968 p. 81.
[2] *Ibid.*, 1969 p. 61.

taking advantage of loopholes; it would lead to a depression of asset prices as wealth owners sought to unload property on to the market to raise the means to pay the tax, with possibly depressing effects on business confidence; it would inevitably stimulate a flight of capital from the country and with the capital a flight of enterprise. This could hardly fail to be the result of any *regular* tax which *had* to be met largely from wealth. Such would be the cost of the reduction in inequality.

It is for these reasons that, whatever its merits in evening out the distribution of wealth, a wealth tax imposed on top of current income tax and surtax is unlikely to be considered practicable. We have had two levies since the second World War which were necessarily paid largely from capital, the 'Special Contribution' imposed by Chancellor Cripps in 1948 and the 'Special Charge' of Chancellor Jenkins twenty years later. Both Chancellors kept the yield reasonably low and stressed that the impositions were of a 'once and for all' nature. To quote Chancellor Jenkins: 'This charge is imposed for one year only. It obviously should not and indeed could not be repeated in its present form except at long intervals. It would otherwise militate against the employment of capital so as to produce investment income.'[1] It was at this point in his budget speech, 1968, that Mr Jenkins went on to state the desirability of seeking further ways of taxing the owners of wealth and added: 'This might make it both possible and desirable to reduce the highest rates of tax on earned income.'

Whilst Mr Jenkins' statements are not wholly free from ambiguity, the general tenor of the Chancellor's remarks suggest that an annual wealth tax as a substitute or partial substitute for surtax accords more with his intentions or inclinations than a confiscatory wealth tax.

Before we consider this second possibility, it is worth a brief digression to examine the details of the 1968 special charge, which has sometimes been loosely called a wealth tax. The charge was payable on investment incomes over £3,000 at rates rising from 2s in the £ to 9s in the £ (on investment incomes over £8,000). It had hardly any of the merits claimed for a wealth tax. The tax base was investment income, so it duplicated, not complemented, the income base and it failed to touch wealth yielding no income. Similarly, it offered no advantage in terms of our efficiency criteria; idle balances escaped, whilst high yielding assets attracted the highest tax. It must have had some effect in diminishing inequalities in the distribution of wealth but in a haphazard and inequitable way.

[1] Extracts from Budget Speech, March 19, 1968.

This comparison of a tax on investment income with a wealth tax both emphasises the advantages of the latter and also provides a warning. Because of the administrative problems of a wealth tax there is a natural tendency to seek short cuts in valuation procedures; one such short cut would be the capitalization of incomes. But to adopt it would be to cut right across the whole purpose of the tax.

A WEALTH TAX FOR SURTAX

Most advocates of a wealth tax in the United Kingdom have seen it as a substitute or partial substitute for surtax—as a 'package deal' by which the highest rates of tax on incomes, especially earned incomes, can be reduced in exchange for a tax levied on a capital base.

The general arguments in favour of a wealth tax which partially replaces a tax on income—equity, efficiency of resource use, equality and administrative efficiency—we have already analysed in the previous chapter and need not repeat. But two particular aspects of the advantages have a special relevance to the British tax scene and deserve mention.

First and most important, a wealth tax, at an appropriate level, would enable us to sweep away the distinction in our income tax between so-called 'earned' and 'unearned' income. This would have two signal advantages. It would remove the administrative complications for Revenue, taxpayers and their advisers, to which the present distinction gives rise. Second, it would eliminate a source of confusion which leads many wage earners to believe that they are taxed at a higher rate than in fact they are. Researches have demonstrated the ignorance of taxpayers about the workings of the tax system and in particular the failure of taxpayers to understand the principle of the earned income allowance.[1] From a group of 179 workers and 53 managers in the Glasgow area, all of whom were in the standard rate bracket, not one worker and only 6 per cent of the managers gave the correct answer to the question 'If you were to earn an extra pound a week, how much of it would be taken off in tax?' Moreover, nearly three-fifths of the workers and nearly four-fifths of the managers thought they would pay more tax than

[1] On the general ignorance on taxation, see for example, A. Seldon, *Taxation and Welfare*, chapter 3, Research Monograph 14, Institute of Economic Affairs, 1967. On the specific point of the earned income allowance and the standard rate of income tax, the figures are from C. V. Brown, 'Misconceptions about Income Tax and Incentives', *Scottish Journal of Political Economy*, vol. XV, February 1968.

they would have paid. If a wealth tax were introduced the need for the distinction between earned and unearned income would go and, to take the 1969–70 rates, the 'standard rate' of income tax could be called 6s 5d (instead of 8s 3d with a two-ninths earned income relief). *If* it is true that income tax at this level is a net disincentive to effort, then the disincentive results from what people *think* they pay rather than from what they *actually* pay; to those who had failed to appreciate the benefit of the earned income allowance, the simplification would have as much incentive effect as an actual reduction of income tax by two-ninths. Even if there were no incentive effect, the change would still be worthwhile, for surely, in a democracy, citizens ought to know what they pay in taxes. Only then can they make rational decisions about public expenditure.

On this issue the comments of Chancellor Jenkins in his 1969 budget speech are of interest. 'I would greatly have liked to separate off the effective earned income rate, that is to show the actual percentage of tax paid on earned income. This would be a good deal easier to understand than the present system under which the effect of the standard and reduced rate is substantially lessened by the earned income relief. Unfortunately, despite intensive effort, this proved to be quite impossible without imposing a very considerable administrative burden on the Inland Revenue. This is because of the complicated impact upon allowances—of which there are many—of incomes which are partly earned and partly—perhaps only in very small part—unearned.[1]'

Another less significant advantage, would result from the administration of the wealth tax. We saw in chapter 3 that one of the problems of the private company, with unquoted shares, facing potential death duty difficulties, was the uncertainty surrounding the valuation of its shares.[2] Given an annual wealth tax, the valuations for wealth tax purposes would also apply (or at least be a reliable guide-line) to valuation for death duty purposes. This would remove, or at least alleviate, this uncertainty.

THE YIELD OF A WEALTH TAX

The gross yield of a wealth tax depends very much on the classes of property exempt (if any), the starting level of the tax, the rate or rates at which it is levied and the steepness of the progression (if any). The net yield to the Revenue depends very much on the extent to which it replaces other taxes, in particular taxes on in-

1 Extract from the Chancellor's Budget speech, April 15, 1969.

2 See above, p. 116.

come. The number of permutations and combinations is almost infinite.

We have already looked at the TUC's proposal for a wealth tax averaging 3 per cent from which was expected a yield of about £1,000 million. This is a very rough and ready estimate derived from taking a straight three per cent of all the wealth of those with £20,000 or over (not the amount by which their wealth exceeds £20,000) and can be taken as a slightly optimistic estimate of yield from the kind of heavy wealth tax which would impinge very severely on capital.

Let us examine in more detail possible wealth tax rates and yields to meet three situations. Each situation is of interest but none of the proposals should be regarded as recommendations.

First the gross yield from a wealth tax similar in starting point, rates and steepness of progression to the Swedish tax in 1970. Second, an illustration of a wealth tax which would replace the revenue from a reduction in all surtax rates by approximately 25 per cent so that the maximum tax rate on income was 70 per cent. Third, an illustration of a wealth tax to replace the revenue lost by abolishing the distinction between earned and unearned income, charging all income at earned income rates and completely abolishing surtax.

Several *caveats* must be entered. We have used the Inland Revenue statistics of the distribution of personal property.[1] The deficiencies of these figures are indicated in chapter 1; in particular they almost certainly under-estimate the total of personal wealth, so that, correspondingly, estimates of yield are likely to be on the low side. Further, the Inland Revenue statistics exclude some settled property and discretionary trusts; if a wealth tax were adopted in Britain, it would be sensible to include within it, as in Sweden, property in undivided estates and trusts on which tax could be levied at a flat rate; no credit for this is taken in the calculations of yield.

It is also necessary to remember that the estimates of the yield of the wealth tax are based on the unreal assumption that the distribution of wealth remains the same after the wealth tax as before (and similarly for income tax changes, where appropriate); also, no allowance is made for any changes in income tax or capital gains tax arising from changes in asset holding resulting from the wealth tax.

A Wealth Tax Like the Swedish

The point of this example is to give an idea of the yield of a wealth tax on lines similar to a tax actually in operation elsewhere. Allowance is not specifically made either for the exemptions of the Swedish

[1] Report No. 111, Cmnd. 3879, January 1969.

tax, or for the marked degree of undervaluation; but, to fit in more conveniently with the wealth categories of the Inland Revenue Report, the starting level for the tax is taken to be £10,000 (instead of £8,000 as in 1970 in Sweden) and the bands are somewhat wider, making the progression slightly less steep. As in the Swedish tax the rates are marginal rates, applying to the different 'slices' of wealth, not to the whole estate.

The calculation suggests that a yield of around £400 million or a little less might be expected from about 1½ million taxpayers; somewhat larger than the yield of death duties in 1967–8[1] at £330 million and about 3½ per cent of central government revenue from taxation in that year. If the exemption limit were raised to £20,000 and the same rates of tax retained for wealth bands above that figure, the yield would drop by about £94 million to just under £300 million; two wealth bands would have dropped out of assessment altogether and those in the higher wealth bands would have exemption for a larger proportion of their wealth. The number of taxpayers would have dropped by 890,000 to about 600,000.

TABLE 6.2. *Gross Yield of a Wealth Tax approximating to the Swedish based on Net Personal Wealth, GB 1967*

Range of net wealth	Rate of wealth tax	No. of cases (thousands)	Amount of net wealth* £000m.	Revenue £m.
under 10,000	Nil			
10,000– 15,000	0·8	620	7·6	11·2
15,000– 20,000	1·0	270	4·8	18·3
20,000– 50,000	1·3	436	13·3	98·8
50,000–100,000	1·6	109	7·5	85·1
Over 100,000	1·8	51	10·9	166·6
	Taxpayers	1,486	Total yield	380·0

*The *total* wealth of persons in the respective ranges; *not* the amount by which their wealth exceeds the minimum of the range.

A Small Wealth Tax as a Partial Substitute for Surtax

Surtax is currently yielding £200–£250 million. Thus a 25 per cent reduction in surtax rates bringing the maximum rate down to just

1 Comparison has been made with 1967–8 because the figures of the distribution of wealth refer to 1967.

below 70 per cent (strictly 68·4 per cent) would cost the Exchequer, gross, some £50–£60m. One simple way of raising this sum would be a tax on wealth holders of over £100,000, at 1 per cent of the amount of wealth above £100,000, as in table 6·3.

TABLE 6.3. *A Wealth Tax to raise £50–£60 million to replace top Surtax Rates*

Range of net wealth £	Rate of wealth tax %	No. of cases (thousands)	Amount of net wealth £000m.	Revenue £m.
over 100,000	1·0	51	10·9	58

A Wealth Tax as a Substitute for Surtax and the Unearned Income Tax Differential

The exact sum required to abolish surtax and the unearned income differential cannot be precisely ascertained from the published statistics. If we take the figures for 1966–7, which is the latest year for which a detailed breakdown of income tax receipts is available and which matches fairly well with the year of the data on which our wealth tax estimates are based, surtax yielded £244m. and income tax £3,236m. The income tax yield cannot be precisely divided between 'earned' and 'unearned', but the £2,507m. collected by PAYE under schedule E was all earned, leaving £729m. collected under the remaining schedules. On the basis of the schedule D income tax yield from individuals and partnerships (table 36, Report No. 111) taken in conjunction with the schedule D 'net true income' figures for the trading profits of individuals and partnerships (table 37), it is clear that at least £300m. of the schedule D income tax yield was earned income; thus a *maximum* yield for income tax on unearned income would be £429m. If the differentially higher rate of tax on unearned income were abolished the yield would drop by a maximum of £95m. Thus the complete abolition of surtax and the unearned income tax differential would mean a revenue reduction (in 1966–67) of something *under* £339m. This could be made good in various ways, e.g. a wealth tax using Swedish rates (table 6.2) but starting at £20,000 (estimated yield £286m.) might not quite compensate, but one commencing at £15,000 (estimated yield £334m.) certainly would. Alternatively, a straight 1·5 per cent on all wealth over £20,000 (estimated yield £297m.) might be enough; 1·7 per cent (estimated yield £336 m.) would certainly be. There is an almost infinite number of variants depending on starting point and progressiveness; but these examples serve to indicate the order of magnitude.

THE PROBLEMS OF A WEALTH TAX FOR THE UNITED KINGDOM

We have examined the particular advantages a wealth tax might have for Britain. Let us now see if there are any ways in which the problems associated with a wealth tax—connected with saving and administration—may have special relevance to the British situation and also, in the light of our examination of the Swedish tax, see if methods adopted by the Swedes might be helpful to us and what pitfalls their experience reveals which we should seek to avoid. Finally, let us attempt some general conclusions about the desirability and feasibility of a wealth tax.

Saving

The only specific point relevant to Britain additional to the general considerations on saving outlined in the previous chapter, is that the proportion of GNP being saved and invested by the British is below that of our major rivals. This is undoubtedly one of the factors of our comparatively low rate of growth. Chancellors have recognized the need by offering special incentives to personal saving, such as the premium bond and the Save As You Earn (SAYE) scheme outlined in the 1969 budget, a contractual saving scheme at favourable tax free interest rates for those who leave their savings intact for at least five years. In these circumstances, to make tax changes which significantly reduce incentives to save would seem illogical not to say foolish.

Administration and Detailed Application

First, what should be *the coverage of a wealth tax*? In principle, to satisfy our three main criteria, equity, equality and efficiency, all forms of property should be included. To omit any item favours the owners of the exempt items as against owners of taxed items, provides a means of avoidance likely to be detrimental to the efficient use of capital and reduces the effectiveness of a wealth tax for mitigating inequality.

But are there any special grounds on which it may be necessary or desirable to exempt particular kinds of assets? Let us consider two of the main exemptions under the Swedish system, both of which might be regarded as candidates for exemption here. Art and other collections are exempt in Sweden; the treatment of pictures and other items of artistic and historical importance under estate duty in Britain (see above, p. 62) suggests that our taxing authorities might similarly treat art leniently under an annual wealth tax. What are the grounds for exemption? The exemption may reflect a desire on the part of the authorities to encourage art—both the collecting of art and the creation of art. But how clearly thought out is this desire and how effective is the means? Under the Swedish tax, works of art, collections of books and paintings, etc., are exempt provided that their owner does not make them available to the public on a commercial basis. Thus what is encouraged is private collections, the enjoyment of which is likely to be restricted to a few; presumably if a private individual opens his gallery to the public at a small charge he is using the works of art for a commercial purpose and the exemption no longer applies. But ought not government policy be concerned to make art widely available to the general public rather than encourage the growth of private collections?

It might, alternatively, be argued that the government seeks to encourage people of modest means to have their own few pieces of art—culture in every cottage, a Picasso in every parlour. If so, the policy is doubtful in its effect. With a progressive tax, the exemption is worth more to the richest at the top of the scale then to the modest wealth holder at the bottom. Moreover, rich people without a genuine interest in art are encouraged to collect to avoid income and wealth tax and benefit from capital gains. Thus the exemption adds the demand of the tax avoider and the speculator to that of the genuine collectors, inevitably raising prices—which makes it more difficult for the modest wealth holders to buy works of art and also more difficult for the state or other public museums and galleries working with strictly limited budgets to develop their collections.

What of the effect on artists? Here again, benefit is doubtful. The concession may marginally help living artists, but the main effect is to benefit, by immense capital gains, those fortunate enough to possess or discover the works of a master long since dead, who may often have sold his pictures for a song in his life-time. Those who need help are not the well-established artists, dead or alive, but the artist struggling to make a name whose work does not attract the attention of those who buy art as an investment. Whilst the concession *may* have some beneficial effect for him, if this is the purpose of the state there would seem to be other much more effective ways, without the detrimental effects, of encouraging art and artists, e.g. by using the revenue gained from abandoning the tax concession to provide more funds for public galleries and museums and endowing fellowships, with minimal teaching duties, to be held at universities and colleges by promising artists, poets and authors.

A completely different ground for exempting works of art is the practical one of expediency; i.e. the administrative problem that works of art can be concealed and hence lend themselves to evasion, and are also difficult to value. This is undoubtedly a major problem about which more will be said below under methods of valuation; but if this is the reason for exemption in Sweden, there is an illogicality here, for jewellery, which is easer to hide and equally difficult to value, is included in the Swedish tax. However, its inclusion demonstrates the conflict between the principle of equity and of simplicity (interpreted in this context to mean ease and cheapness of administration) for in Sweden it is widely accepted that much jewellery never figures in returns and when it does it is generally undervalued. This situation, of evasion and under-valuation, is the worst of both worlds, creating inequities between the wholly honest, the wholly dishonest, and the majority, the more or less honest, who inhabit a large grey area in between; moreover this particular kind of inequity has a generally debilitating influence on tax morality: the honest, smarting under a sense of inequity, tend to move into the grey areas, the more or less honest become less rather than more, and the successful dishonest look around for other tax fiddles. If it is impossible or disproportionately costly to prevent widespread complete or partial evasion, it is better to omit a class of property altogether.

Whether insurance should be exempt raises more difficult problems; few would query the exemption that the Swedes accord to the capitalized value of pension rights acquired by employment. But if these are excluded and the capitalized value of insurance included, then the self-employed person who seeks to provide for his retirement by insurance, is penalized. But to exempt insurance wholly offers a fruitful method of wealth tax avoidance. Perhaps the answer is to allow an insurance exemption but strictly limit its amount. Moreover, surrender values, which are the appropriate valuation as being the nearest to a market valuation, always tend to be low—and this would prevent the inclusion of insurance from being too harsh in its effect.

Other exceptions under the Swedish tax, like furniture and housekeeping balances, are acceptable in principle as being, in general, of comparatively small value, not justifying the trouble of valuation and inclusion in the return. But, as a form of property like furniture could be used as large scale investment to avoid tax, it would be better to exempt all such household chattels up to a specified *sum*, rather than to exempt *classes* of goods. Works of art which were not of great value could come under this blanket exemption.

The second issue after coverage is the desirability of *ceiling provisions*. We saw that under the Swedish tax the eighty per cent rule, as it stood, could lead to an effective rate of tax on earned income in excess of the nominal maximum rate of income tax; whilst the thirty-times-income rule provided a loop-hole for avoidance. Would any special ceiling provisions be necessary for the United Kingdom, or could they happily be dispensed with?

The overall ceiling provision, like the eighty per cent rule, carries the justification that there should be *some* proportion of income on which a person should be able to rely after the tax authorities have had their slice; e.g. that disposable income should be at least one fifth of total income. Yet (even with the qualification in the Swedish tax by which the value of wealth for wealth tax purposes shall not be reduced by more than 50 per cent) one wonders about the wisdom of the provision because it can so plainly cut across the purposes of the tax, in particular the encouragement to productive investment. There is a particular reason for the Swedish provision which does not apply in the United Kingdom; the eighty per cent rule refers to local income tax, national income tax and wealth tax. Although local income tax is deducted from income to obtain assessable income for national purposes, clearly local income tax is one part of the total income tax–wealth tax complex which is not under the control of the central government.

But even if Britain dispensed with an 80 per cent rule or its equivalent, providing instead any safeguards considered necessary or desirable through a 'reasonable' structure of income tax and wealth tax combined, this would not wholly meet the type of problem for which the Swedish thirty-times-income rule was designed.

There are at least three main contingencies when to have a wealth tax without a rule such as this might cause hardship or economic difficulties:

(i) The first relates to the position of the person such as an aged widow with a small amount of capital mainly in the form of an inherited house and land yielding no money return and with some investment income from gilt-edged securities or similar low yielding investment. Hardship for a person so situated, however, only occurs when the exemption limit of the wealth tax is low.[1] The problem can best be met by setting the limit higher than at present in Sweden.

(ii) A newly established company, not yet earning much profit, but with potential. The shareholders of such a company have to pay wealth tax on their shares which are not yet generating the income to meet the tax. Moreover, if the company is a family business which has monopolized the family resources, there may be real difficulties in meeting wealth tax liabilities from income derived from other sources. Granted that companies, however promising, cannot be expected to be profitable immediately they are set up, a wealth tax without a thirty-times-income rule or its equivalent may be detrimental to the very kind of enterprise that in general it is expected to encourage. Another example of the same kind of problem arises with growing timber in a newly established plantation which has not yet existed sufficiently long to be able to establish a regular pattern of planting, felling and selling.

(iii) The third example has a particular relevance to the United Kingdom, i.e. the effect of a wealth tax on the owner-occupier in agriculture. We saw in chapter 3 the death duty and capital gains tax difficulties faced by a farmer wishing to hand on his farm to his son. For a variety of reasons, the capital value of land has become disproportionately high in relation to the yield from agriculture. A sizable wealth tax without some ceiling provision such as a thirty-times-income rule would bear hardly on the agricultural owner-occupier who, to pay the tax, would almost certainly need to make periodic sales of part of his land (or go heavily into debt). This result would cut right across government policy which has been concerned with stimulating the efficiency of agriculture by building up larger farms. The rise in the price of land has been such, as our figures in chapter 3 demonstrate, that the exemption limit for a wealth tax would have to be set very high if the difficulty was to be met in this way.

In some of the countries which operate a wealth tax—e.g. Germany and Denmark—a different approach to a ceiling provision is adopted, by which the amounts paid in wealth tax can be deducted from in-

[1] Docent Dag Helmers in 'Kapitalskatterna—några anteckningar,' *Affärsvärlden Finanstidningen* has pointed out that in 1969 in Sweden an old-age pensioner may be deemed to have insufficient wealth to justify stopping a special income tax concession, but at the same time have sufficient wealth to incur liability to wealth tax!

come in arriving at assessable income for income tax. But whatever method is chosen, it is difficult to see how some kind of ceiling provisions, relating income tax and wealth tax, can be avoided.

Let us turn to *valuation* procedures and problems. The Swedes have developed a valuation structure which utilizes the same procedure for various taxes. This is an essential principle for any wealth tax which is not to be inordinately costly to administer or inordinately inequitable. Thus, valuations for real property are used not only for all the wealth taxes in Sweden—the annual wealth tax, gift and legacy duty (and as a fall back for capital gains tax)—but also for assessing an assumed income for income tax purposes for real property yielding no money income; the value of unquoted shares for wealth tax purposes is used for gift tax and taken as a guide for succession duty whilst the information from which the valuations of unquoted shares are derived is collected for income tax purposes.

Any application of a wealth tax for Britain should seek to use the same kind of procedure: a structure of wealth tax valuation used for all capital taxes and associated if possible with other taxes.

The basis of a structure already exists. Valuation of real property is periodically undertaken for local rates though the valuation used is an assessed annual rather than an assessed capital value. But there would be no great problems either in levying rates on the basis of an assessed capital value or capitalizing the annual value for wealth tax purposes. Again, whilst in one sense the capital gains tax has made the wealth tax less necessary it has also made it more practicable; the experience gained from the capital gains tax and the actual valuations needed for this tax, could be used for wealth tax purposes. The United Kingdom has already gone some way towards a gift tax with the seven year gifts inter vivos provision in the estate duty and the treatment of gifts as 'realization' under the capital gains tax; moreover a comprehensive gift tax is essential for any system of death taxation which is not to be widely avoided: wealth tax valuations could and should be linked with a gift tax valuation; similarly, wealth tax and death duty valuations of real property and unquoted shares and perhaps also other possessions such as jewellery and art, could be linked together.

But the establishment of a valuation procedure of this kind, whilst essential, does not resolve the problems inherent in the valuation process. The Swedish system revealed marked undervaluation of personal assets—cars, jewellery, etc.—and of real property and uneven valuation of unquoted shares. Can any better procedures be devised for valuing these items?

If personal chattels are to be included within the wealth tax, the valuations used must be made to approximate to market value. Simply to take them on trust is not good enough. There are various possibilities; one suggestion has been that insurance values should be used; it is argued that in his own interests a property owner would not wish to insure at a value which would leave him a substantial loss if the article were stolen, damaged or destroyed and this consideration would act as a check to under-valuation. Again, it has been suggested that, as with the Swedish tax, the responsibility for valuation should rest with the taxpayer, but that the Revenue should conduct detailed sample investigations of returns and taxpayers who had been found to under-value significantly should suffer severe penalties. Further, it has been suggested that to check under-valuation the Revenue should possess the right to buy from a taxpayer any asset at 10 per cent above his valuation of it. None of these devices is perfect; the first would require compulsory insurance of all valuable assets and the taxpayer might still be willing to take the risk by insuring low to keep down wealth tax liability; the third procedure smacks of arbitrariness; and both the second and the third would impose on the taxpayer the need to obtain professional valuations of his property to safeguard himself. Where this happens, valuation costs have been transferred from the Revenue to the taxpayer but the social cost remains.

The existence of a capital gains tax does something to ease the under-valuation problem in that, provided the two taxes were closely integrated, anyone under-valuing property for the purposes of wealth tax would pay higher capital gains tax when the asset was 'realized'.

The second area of undervaluation, real property, raises intractible problems. Any assessed value basis, such as the Swedish or our own method of valuation for local rates, is bound to be cautious in case values should drop, but in general will be increasingly an under-valuation the further the time from the assessment date. With local rates this does not matter as much as for valuation for a wealth tax, because, when *only* real property is being taxed the inequity is limited to the instances in which real property of different kinds or in different areas moves out of line with the values of real property in general. With a wealth tax covering a generality of assets, inequity results as between the owners of (under-valued) real property and of other property such as ordinary shares, where a genuine market value applies. Is it possible for real property to be valued more frequently and hence to reduce the divergence between assessed and market value? This must be regarded as very doubtful at present, when the Inland Revenue has failed to carry through comprehensive quinquennial reviews for rating purposes.

To return to the last of the areas of valuation difficulty; experience of the valuation of private businesses for death duty purposes in the United Kingdom reinforces Swedish wealth tax experience, that it is almost impossible to avoid the unevenness of valuation of unquoted shares. The problem is so inherently intractible that little can be said of methods to improve valuation procedures.

Finally, if Britain should adopt a wealth tax, *at what level of wealth should it become applicable*? This must depend partly on the objective. Thus, if only a very small wealth tax was sought to offset a reduction in surtax, the limit could be kept as high as £100,000; if a much higher yield was required, say, equivalent to the elimination of surtax and the abolition of the differential income tax rates, then the limit would need to be set lower. But there are three general arguments for setting the exemption limit at a figure of not less than £20,000. First, there must be every expectation of a continuation of the secular upward trend in prices which we have known since the second World War; to set a limit as low as the present Swedish limit set in 1965 would be to make no allowance for the effect of continuing price rises in pushing down the exemption limit in *real* terms. Second, the administrative problems; at a £20,000 level, on the basis of 1967 figures, the number of taxpayers would be 600,000. As an exemption limit moves downward from £20,000 the proportionate increase in the number of taxpayers is much larger than the proportionate increase in revenue. Third, a high exemption limit eliminates, or at any rate reduces, some of the special problems to which a wealth tax may give rise, in particular the low income yield of modest wealth holders, referred to above.[1]

GENERAL CONCLUSIONS

Should Britain adopt an annual wealth tax? Our examination of the Swedish wealth tax in chapter 5 and our subsequent discussion of the possibilities for Britain make it clear that an annual wealth tax can never be entirely freed from inequities, nor can it be a simple tax to administer. Some of the benefits claimed for it are problematical in effect and the tax might have a detrimental effect on saving. There may be a need for special provisions in the tax to meet special problems, such as those of the owner-occupier in agriculture, and experience suggests that special provisions create new inequities, open up loopholes for avoidance and often have consequences neither expected nor intended. But so much depends on the form of wealth tax.

1 Pp. 217–18.

If Britain were to adopt an annual wealth tax, what form should it take? This is an area of political economy where individual value judgments and philosophies intrude, if not dominate; the author's views are that an annual wealth tax, TUC style, would be too extreme in its effects; that a wealth tax to raise £50m. or so to reduce surtax levels is hardly worth the trouble; that the most attractive kind of wealth tax would be that which enabled the distinction between 'unearned' and 'earned' income to be abolished and which reduced combined surtax and income tax to a maximum marginal rate of some 50 or 60 per cent. Even this form of annual wealth tax would raise considerable difficulties. Before adopting it we should need first to develop an adequate valuation structure. Improvement of the other wealth taxes would help here; the development of a system of death duties, capital gains and gift taxation makes easier the introduction of an annual wealth tax. This serves to emphasize that an annual wealth tax should not be adopted in a hurry and that we ought *first* to concentrate on reforming and improving the wealth taxes we already have—the death duty, capital gains tax and as part of this process, the development of a comprehensive gift tax. Thereafter serious consideration should be given to the introduction of an annual wealth tax in the context of a reform of income tax and surtax.

Part IV

A COMPREHENSIVE SYSTEM OF WEALTH TAXATION

Chapter 7

Capital Gains Taxation

ARE CAPITAL GAINS INCOME?

A capital gain may be taken as 'that form of gain that arises to the owner when some of his property appreciates in value'.[1] One of the unresolved tax controversies is whether capital gains constitute income, or at any rate should be treated as income for tax purposes. Those who argue for the inclusion of capital gains within income maintain that only if they are so treated does income taxation accurately reflect differences in the ability to pay of different taxpayers 'Receipts for services rendered, transfer income and the gain or loss from revaluations of property are all appropriately included in a concept of taxable income.'[2]

The crux of the issue is that capital gains arise from different circumstances; they do not all have the same characteristics. Some are easily equatable with income; others it seems reasonable to treat as income; still other capital gains arise in circumstances where the equation with income, or treatment as income, is very debatable Let us consider various circumstances in which capital gains arise and let us test the reasonableness of treating them as income by whether a man could spend the whole of the gain on consumption and still be as well off as before the gain accrued.

1. *An increase in share values because the retention and reinvestment of profits has increased the real assets of the company.* In such a case the rise in share value is a direct result of income not being distributed; it is the alternative to a distribution of profits as income to the shareholder. This would seem to suggest the characteristics of income and the reasonableness of treating the gain as income. Moreover, if the shareholder realized the whole gain by selling some of his shares and consumed the proceeds, he would still be as well off as before the gain accrued.

[1] *Royal Commision on The Taxation on Profits and Income, Final Report*, Cmd. 9474, 1955, p. 26.

[2] Martin David, *Alternative Approaches to Capital Gains Taxation*, Washington: The Brookings Institution, 1968, London: George Allen & Unwin.

2. *A rise in share prices reflecting the constant capitalization of larger expected income.* Some increases in share prices are attributable to a change in expectations about future income. (Such gains are often inextricably interconnected with the first kind, but it is helpful to distinguish the different causes.) Suppose, for example, that because of a change in expectation of future income, share prices double. Then it could be argued that a shareholder could spend half his capital and still be as well off as before the change took place. On the other hand, the contrary argument could be put that it was the valuation at the beginning which was wrong, and that, if the shareholder had spent all his gain he would in fact have become worse off; that had the expectations been right at the beginning, then he could *not* have sold half his capital and still left his capital and income intact. But this only pushes the point of revaluation of expectations further back in time; it is still possible to argue that the capital gains are the income of *some* period.[1]
3. *A rise in value of land because of community development.* Suppose a man owns a piece of unused site land worth £10,000; as a result of transport improvements in the area the land appreciates to £15,000. The owner could sell one third of the land and still be as well off as before the appreciation. This is a very similar case to the previous one—a change of expectation of future income. But the revaluation of expectations has resulted from a specific external phenomenon at a specific time.
4. *An increase in asset prices from a fall in interest rates.* Consider the holder of an irredeemable bond. If interest rates fall the capital value of his bonds rises; the income he receives from them is unchanged. If he realized the whole of the gain by selling bonds, he could retain the value of his capital intact, but at the cost of a fall in his income.

   If the bond holder owns redeemable bonds, then the value of his capital rises; but he will only regard himself as better off if his time horizon is limited; when the security matures he will have to reinvest at a lower rate of interest. For example, if the rate of interest fell from 5 to 4 per cent, a bond with 20 years to run would rise to about 112. During the 20 years, income from the bonds would remain unchanged and the price would gradually fall to 100 at maturity. If the rate of interest is still 4 per cent, a reinvestment by the bondholder would lead to a reduced income. If he had sold some of his bonds to realize his capital gain,

[1] For a development of this argument, see A. R. Prest, *Public Finance in Theory and Practice*, Weidenfeld and Nicolson, 3rd edition, 1967, pp. 287–8.

on reinvestment his income would have been still further reduced.

In the first case, *prima facie*, the bondholder with irredeemable bonds was better off as a result of the capital gain, but not to the extent of treating the whole increase as income. In the second case the bondholder was only better off in the short run.

5. *A rise in asset prices reflecting a rise in the general price level.* If the value of capital assets (and presumably also the income flow) rose simply in proportion to the rise in the price level, then there is no *real* gain. If the asset owner spent the money gain on consumption he would finish up with less capital and less income than before in *real* terms.

Prima facie, the first two instances are gains which are closely related to normal income concepts; the third (a rise in site values through development) gives rise to a gain all of which the recipient can consume and still be as well off as before. (i.e. he maintains his pre-gain income and capital intact.) In all these three cases it would seem appropriate to treat the gain as income for tax purposes. In the fourth case, gains resulting from reductions in interest rates, the bond holder cannot spend the whole of the gain and be as well off as before; and such gain as there is on redeemable bonds is short-lived. Finally, gains which are simply proportional to changes in the price level are illusory. However, the position is more complicated than this. For example, take the first case, of gains resulting from reinvestment in profits. The retained profits may have paid some tax—e.g. standard rate income tax and a low profits tax as in the UK before 1965; or corporation tax post 1965. Is it right, therefore, to subject the gains to the full severity of income taxation? The appropriate answer probably depends on what further taxation is necessary to keep the tax on gains in line with that on distributed profits. Under the UK pre-1965 system it would not have been right to tax the gain fully to income tax, as some had already been paid on the retained profits; post-1965, with corporation tax applying to both distributed and undistributed profits, but only dividends being liable to income tax and surtax, it would be much more reasonable.

Again, the supporters of treating gains as income maintain that the arguments we have used about gains from interest rate changes and price rises (cases 4 and 5) do not justify their exclusion from the income base because it is the relative position that matters. Compared with someone with new savings to invest, the irredeemable bond holder, for example, is indeed better off by the full amount of the capital gain. On the issue of capital gains which only keep pace with price rises, they argue that inflation affects other incomes by reducing their real value; why should capital gains be treated in a different way? There *may* be a case for making allowances for inflation in the taxation of *all* incomes; there is no case for making allowances for this one form alone. To this particular issue we shall return in the final section of this chapter. But it is clear that there is no simple answer to how capital gains should be treated in principle.

Another approach is to ask the question, how do people themselves treat capital gains? Do they treat them as income as or capital? Professor Wallich argues that 'If people consume their capital gains in the same proportion in which they consume their ordinary income, the case would be strong for treating gains as income'.[1] In fact he maintains that there is strong evidence that people make a sharp distinction between ordinary income and capital gains and that they respond to capital gains very much as they respond to wealth they already own. Both lead them to spend a higher fraction of current income. In brief, capital gains are treated as capital, not income.

How do the countries with capital gains taxes treat the gains? Although the taxation of capital gains is normally related to income, invariably any capital gain other than a short-term one is protected against the full rigours of the income tax. Thus the USA, one of the first countries to introduce taxation of capital gains as part of the income tax structure, distinguishes between short-term and long-term gains; short-term are taxed as income; *half* the long-term gains is taxed as income, with a maximum rate of 25 per cent in 1969.[2] The Swedes have a capital gains tax which applies to certain assets only; their method is to count as income a *proportion* of gain, the fraction diminishing with the length of time the asset has been held. As we shall examine in more detail below, under the United Kingdom capital gains taxes, short-term gains are treated as income, long-term gains are taxed at 30 per cent or at a lower rate depending on the size of the gain and the recipient's income.

It is interesting that the Minority Report of the Royal Commission on the Taxation of Profits and Income, 1955, whilst arguing strongly that capital gains should be treated as income, nevertheless concluded somewhat illogically that gains should be subjected to income taxation but not to surtax because 'the taxation of capital gains beyond a

1 Henry C. Wallich, 'Taxation of Capital Gains in the Light of Recent Economic Developments', *National Tax Journal*, June 1965.

2 The Tax Reform Act of 1969, which came into effect in 1970, provided that the 25 per cent alternative tax rate should apply only to the first $50,000 of gain received each year. The remainder is subject to a new maximum rate of 29·5 per cent for 1970, 32·5 per cent for 1971 and 35 per cent for 1972 and later.

certain rate would have highly undesirable effects on risk-bearing, saving and capital formation'.[1]

Besides disagreement on whether capital gains should in principle be treated as income; and the expediency argument of the Minority of the Royal Commission; there is another practical consideration which makes it difficult to tax capital gains precisely on a par with income. For administrative reasons, gains are taxed not as they accrue but when 'realized', i.e. when the asset is disposed of. This means that in any one year a man may dispose of assets on which gains have accumulated over a number of years; also the actual disposal of assets with gains may be irregular and hence may sometimes be 'bunched' in a particular year. If income tax was progressive and gains were taxed as income in the year in which they were realized, bunched gains would give rise to a tax liability much bigger than if the gains had been taxed evenly over the period in which they accrued. In equity, therefore, either long-term capital gains must be taxed at a low or flat rate, or complicated averaging provisions need to be introduced.

Enough has been said to indicate that, in principle, capital gains have much affinity with income, but it is debatable whether they should be taxed as income. In practice, whilst capital gains taxes are usually linked to income tax provisions, they are not taxed at full income tax rates. Capital gains taxes in practice are the outcome of a compromise reflecting the uncertainty of principle and economic and administrative considerations.

It is clear that full consideration of capital gains taxation is more appropriate to a treatise on income tax than one on wealth taxation.[2] Our prime object here is to examine how capital gains taxes in the United Kingdom fit in, or should fit in, with other capital taxes—in particular with the reformed death duties that we have proposed. Our procedure in the remainder of the chapter will be, first to indicate the case for capital gains taxation in the context of taxes on personal wealth; second to outline the gains taxes of the United Kingdom, with some incidental suggestions for reform; third, to concentrate on two inter-related aspects of capital gains taxation which particularly need reconsideration if death duties are reformed

[1] Cmd. 9474, p. 374.

[2] Some excellent general treatments of capital gains taxation are: A. R. Ilersic, *The Taxation of Capital Gains*, Staples Press, 1962; Martin David, *Alternative Approaches to Capital Gains Taxation*, The Brookings Institution, 1968 (Allen & Unwin); and, particularly on the same issue of whether capital gains constitute income, Henry C. Wallich, 'Taxation of Capital Gains in the Light of Recent Economic Developments', *National Tax Journal*, June 1965, and the comments by Walter J. Blum in the December 1965 issue of the same journal.

—the problem of whether death and gifts should continue to count as realization; and the problem of inflation.

THE CASE FOR CAPITAL GAINS TAXES

As we have already seen, the main arguments for capital taxes—death duties and annual wealth taxes—can conveniently be grouped under the headings of equity (horizontal equity), efficiency (in resource use) and equality (i.e. diminishing inequalities). What do capital gains taxes contribute under these heads? How far is the case for a capital gains tax undermined by the existence of an effective system of death taxation, or by an annual wealth tax? To what extent do they complement each other? These are the questions we seek to answer in this section.

The equity argument for a capital gains tax is that, whether or not capital gains should be treated precisely on a par with income, they constitute economic power or spending power; they add to taxable capacity. The argument is strengthened because unless gains are taxed, income tax can be avoided by converting (taxable) income into (untaxed) capital gains.[1] Whilst an effective death duty and an annual wealth tax do something to reduce the need for a capital gains tax, they do not eliminate it. A death duty can 'catch up with' accumulated capital gains which are not spent. An annual wealth tax comprehends the value of all net assets, including their appreciation, within the tax base, but cannot tax capital gains spent between assessment dates. Neither death duty nor wealth tax are a levy on gains as such; hence they do not distinguish between an addition to net assets from, on the one hand, personal saving which has borne tax as income, and on the other, capital gains, which in the absence of a capital gains tax have borne neither income tax nor an equivalent.

In terms of efficiency it can be argued that a capital gains tax corrects a distortion in the pattern of investment, which otherwise would move disproportionately into assets generating capital gains rather than income; the most extreme example is investment yielding no money income but substantial capital gain—e.g. stamp collections, pictures and the like.

The argument on grounds of equality is that capital gains can occur only to those who have capital; and further that, generally speaking, the more wealth a man possesses, the bigger the proportion of it likely to be held in a form which attracts capital gains.[2] To tax

[1] For examples see *Minority Report* of the *Royal Commission on the Taxation of Profits and Income*, Cmd. 9474, June 1955, pp. 368–70.

[2] See Appendix A, p. 258.

capital gains checks or offsets this powerful tendency to inequality. In this book we are primarily concerned with inequality in the ownership of wealth. But if it is appropriate to regard capital gains as income, then a policy of progressive income taxation to diminish income inequalities founders without the taxation of capital gains.

Whilst a case for taxing capital gains can be made under each of these headings, there are also reservations or offsets under each heading. As always, the big problem of taxes based on capital values is administration and valuation, and the methods adopted to make the tax practicable tend to reduce its equity and its contribution to equality. A capital gains tax suffers from a *particular* disadvantage as compared with death duties or annual wealth taxes; because gains tax is levied on the appreciation in asset values, *two* valuations are required, not just one. But this is a difficulty of *establishing* a capital gains tax; once the *initial* valuations are completed, only one subsequent valuation is necessary to arrive at the size of the capital gain. In principle tax could be levied regularly on accrued capital gains whether or not they were realized—but this would require an annual valuation for every asset. Hence the adoption of the realization basis, i.e. that on the *disposal* of an asset, tax is levied on the difference between acquisition value (or the value on the date from which the tax law was introduced) and realization value. Because of the problem of 'bunched' realizations which we have already described, a long-term capital gains tax has to be levied at a flat rate—or at least, any progression has to be given a fairly low ceiling. This both restricts the equity of the tax and also limits its value as an instrument for diminishing inequality.

The kind of valuation problems which we have already discussed fully with death duties and annual wealth taxes apply to a capital gains tax in relation to the starting date of the tax and any disposals which do not constitute an 'arm's length' sale, e.g. the deemed disposal at death or by gift.

Difficult problems arise in the treatment of losses; the tendency is for tax treatment to be one-sided; a capital gain is taxed, but a capital loss is only allowed for when there is a capital gain against which to offset it; capital losses cannot generally be offset against ordinary income.

The usual distinction in capital gains taxation between short-term and long-term is also a source of inequity. Short-term gains are normally taxed progressively as income; long-term gains at a much lower rate; but the demarcation line is arbitrary and creates hard cases which fall just the wrong side of the line, e.g. if a short-term gain covers disposals within a year, there is the discrepancy in treatment between the man who realizes a gain after 364 and another who realizes after 366 days.

In short, enough has been said to show that 'a tax on capital gains . . . cannot be expected to prove a tax of simple structure or one that would be free from a number of rather arbitrary solutions of its various problems'.[1]

The efficiency argument for a capital gains tax is the least strong and suffers most when other economic effects of the tax are taken into account. If, as Wallich argues, taxpayers treat capital gains as capital rather than income, the tax is largely paid from saving; and hence it cannot, like a low annual wealth tax, be used as a partial substitute for income tax or surtax. Because the reward of risk-taking is often in the form of capital gains, a gains tax may be detrimental to enterprise.[2] Because a capital gains tax provides an incentive to defer realization of gains, it makes for immobility of capital; this 'lock in' effect we examine more fully below.

CAPITAL GAINS TAXES IN THE UNITED KINGDOM

The first general capital gains tax in the United Kingdom dates from 1962. Earlier attempts have been made to tax capital gains of a sort, gains in land values resulting from community development; those go back at least to the land taxes of Lloyd George's famous budget of 1909 and have continued in the more recent attempts (Acts of 1947 and 1967) to impose charges on betterment These special levies have not been notably successful.[3] In any case, the 1962 tax is the more significant for our purposes, as the first general tax on capital gains, paving the way for the more comprehensive one of 1965.

The 1962 tax, introduced by the Conservatives, applied to short-term gains only; short-term was defined as six months, except for land and buildings where the period was three years. Chargeable assets disposed of within these periods were assessed for income tax as unearned income. The tax applied to acquisitions and disposals after April 10, 1962, and covered all forms of assets except those specifically excluded.

The 1965 act introduced a long-term gains tax and modified the short-term tax. The period within which a gain counted as short-

1 *Royal Commission on the Taxation of Profits and Income, Final Report*, Cmd. 9474, 1955, p. 31.

2 See the views of the minority of the Royal Commission, above p. 228.

3 The Conservative government of 1970 decided to repeal the Land Commission Act and end the Land Commission and the betterment levy, thus leaving all appreciation in land values to be taxed on the same basis as other capital gains.

term became one year for all chargeable assets. Assets held for longer than a year were chargeable to long-term gains tax. Both taxes covered all assets except those exempted—amongst which were one residence, savings certificates, premium bonds, life insurance policies, chattels under £1,000 and 'capital' receipts not derived from assets, e.g. football pool winnings. The 1969 Finance Act added government securities to the list of exempt assets (which, of course, meant that whilst capital gains were relieved of tax, losses on government securities could no longer be set off against other gains). The 1968 Finance Act provided for the exemption of net gains of less than £50 per annum.

As under the 1962 Act, short-term gains are treated as income. Long-term gains are taxed at a flat rate of 30 per cent; alternatively, as a concession to those with small incomes, income tax and surtax at the marginal rates applicable to the taxpayer can be charged on a fraction of the net gain: for net gains under £5,000 the fraction is one-half; for net gains over £5,000, tax is charged on the sum of £2,500 plus the excess of the net gain over £5,000. For gains under £5,000 this concession is the equivalent of taxing the whole gain to half the marginal rate of income and surtax; with standard rate at 8s 3d (1970) the effect is to charge the standard rate income tax payer at 20·6 per cent. Charities and approved superannuation funds are exempt from capital gains tax. Capital gains by companies are treated on a par with income and assessed to corporation tax. If a firm makes a gain on a physical capital asset there is a 'roll over' provision by which it is not subject to tax, provided that the proceeds are reinvested in another physical asset within a year.

The capital gains taxes inevitably adopted the realization basis, requiring valuation on acquisition (or budget day 1965) and on disposal; an asset is deemed to be realized not only when sold but also when given away and at death. The donor is liable to capital gains tax on any gain or gifts (subject to an annual exemption of £100 of gifts per donor); the gains tax at death is deducted from the estate, subject to an exemption of £5,000 of gains. There is also a special family business relief.[1]

Realized losses can be offset against realized gains, but only long-term losses can be offset against long-term gains and short-term losses against short-term gains. Where losses exceed the corresponding gains in any year, they can be carried forward.

There is no doubt that the introduction of the tax caused administrative costs and headaches to both tax officers and to taxpayers and their advisers. Inland Revenue men had to be awarded an un-

[1] See p. 120.

precedented bonus of £50 for mastering the details of the tax and heavy compliance costs have been laid on taxpayers by way of professional advice in completing their tax returns and professional valuations of assets. It is a sobering thought that in sixty years time there will still be occasions to try to discover the value of an asset on April 6, 1965. Some of this high cost of administration and compliance was doubtless transitional, but, although quantitative evidence is difficult to come by, it seems likely that much remains. The exemption of net gains under £50 was an attempt to cut down some of the costs which, on small gains, were disproportionate to revenue; but it is still often necessary for an accountant to undertake extensive calculations before he can determine that the net gains of a client are below the exemption limit.

In the first two years of its existence the yield from the capital gains tax was minuscule: £7m. in 1966–7 and £15m. in 1967–8. The yield increased to £47m. in 1968–9, and to £127m. in 1969–70; the budget estimate for 1970–1 was £150m. In considering its *net* contribution to revenue it should be remembered that in so far as it has discouraged avoidance by the deliberate switching of income to capital gains, income tax and surtax yields have increased. On the other hand, an effect of counting death as realization is to *reduce* the yield of estate duty, capital gains tax being deductible from the estate before calculation of death duty.

Before we turn to those aspects of capital gains taxes which are most relevant to considerations of death duties and annual wealth taxes, some incidental suggestions might be made for reform.

(1) To reduce costs of administration and taxpayer compliance, it might be helpful not only to exempt net gains below a certain figure (£50 by the 1968 Finance Act) but also to exempt from gains tax all disposals in a year which totalled less than a specific sum, say £1,000. Qualification for exemption under this provision could often be calculated much more easily than that of the minimum net gain and some small loss in equity might be worth trading off against the saving in administrative and compliance costs.

(2) The exemption of one residence is one of several examples of the favoured treatment of owner occupiers in our tax system; but if by deliberate policy we wish to continue that exemption, or are afraid that to remove it would restrict labour mobility, why not a roll-over provision?[1] It seems ludicrous that capital gains should be

[1] A roll-over provision for the sale of homes is included in the Canadian government's proposals for a new capital gains tax. See *Proposals for Tax Reform*, Ottawa, 1969, pp. 38–9.

exempt on one house even if the seller does not buy another, and still more so when realized at death.

(3) As we have already pointed out, the provisions of capital gains taxes are biased against losses. If we rule out any offset of losses against general income because of the fear that the state would be subsidizing unwise and unsuccessful speculators, at least the loss offsets might be made less rigid so that losses, whether short- or long-term, could be offset against gains which were short- or long-term.

(4) The technical argument against including gambling winnings within the ambit of the tax is irrefutable—since there is no capital asset there can be no capital gain! Nevertheless to exclude large gambling winnings from income tax and capital gains tax is contrary to the whole essence of the equity argument for a gains tax. It has been said that if gambling winnings are taxed, gambling losses would have to be allowed.[1] To this there are two replies: for individuals with large winnings (though not the community as a whole) winnings are disproportionate to losses; there should be a minimum exemption limit for gambling winnings which would only bring the big winnings within the tax. Second, the 'losses' (what is paid for the gamble) can be regarded as providing a utility to the taxpayer, win or lose, i.e. the excitement of engaging in the gamble; hence it does not need to be computed as a loss to offset against gains. An alternative way of taxing big gambling winnings is to include them within a capital receipts tax, as outlined in the next chapter.

Finally, when progression in tax rates is generally regarded as reflecting ability to pay and is in line with prevailing political philosophy, it is a defect in the capital gains tax that administrative considerations make it necessary to levy it at a flat rate. Its lack of progression restricts its effectiveness in diminishing inequalities. A possible solution is discussed in the next chapter.

INTEGRATING CAPITAL GAINS TAX WITH A REFORMED DEATH DUTY

Two inter-related problems of capital gains taxation particularly need to be considered if death duties are reformed—whether an estate duty is retained or an accessions tax adopted. Assuming an effective death duty integrated with a general gift tax, should

[1] *Royal Commission on the Taxation of Profits and Income*, Cmd. 9474, 1955, p. 86.

death and gifts continue to count as realization under the capital gains tax? Further, should some provision be introduced into the capital gains tax to allow for inflation?

Capital Gains Tax Treatment of Death and Gifts

There are three principal ways in which gifts and death might be treated:

(1) *Gifts and death might count as realization* (called the 'presumptive realization' solution). With the estate duty form of death duty the capital gains treatment at death would be as at present in the United Kingdom. Gifts would also be liable to capital gains tax (paid by the donor) as at present in the United Kingdom, but then gift tax would also be paid on the value of the gift less the amount of capital gains tax paid on it.

With an accessions tax the position would be similar except that liabilities would fall on different people at death. Capital gains tax would be paid from the estate before the distribution of bequests—on which accessions tax would then be paid by the recipients. Capital gains tax on gifts would be paid by the donor, general gift tax by the donee.

The disadvantage is the administrative complications of the double set of calculations. Moreover, as we have demonstrated earlier, inflation converts estate duty into a powerful long-term gains tax.[1] With a reformed and effective death duty, which includes an integrated gift tax, is it any longer necessary or desirable to treat death and gifts as disposals?

(2) *Death and gifts do not count as a disposal; death duty or gift tax valuation becomes the acquisition value for future capital gains tax.* (The 'no disposal' solution). This method avoids the disadvantage of the first: it simplifies the capital gains tax and facilitates the winding-up of estates. It recognizes the effect of inflation in increasing the real burden of estate duty and gift tax. It would ease the tax problems associated with the owner-occupied farm and the private business. But it has its own disadvantage; it would accentuate the 'lock in' effect. Let us examine this effect more closely. A capital gains tax provides a deterrent to realizing gains and an incentive to realize losses provided some gains are realized at the same time so that losses can be offset against them. In practice, with real growth and inflation, we can expect gains to exceed losses and thus the

[1] See pp. 55–9.

lock-in effect to exceed the reverse lock-in effect. Thus a capital gains tax will reduce the mobility of capital.

From the point of view of the economy, does this matter? As Wallich puts it: 'Unlocking of high gains situations will not increase the total demand for equities. More likely it will reduce it. If Jones, who previously felt locked in, sells to Smith, Smith's funds are now tied up. Jones buys some other stock that Smith might otherwise have bought. But Jones may also take his money out of the market, reducing the total demand for equities.'[1] Nevertheless there are some grounds for believing that the lock-in reduces the demand for a certain kind of equities—of new, risky, ventures; investors successful in one situation are those more likely to transfer to new promising investments if their funds are not 'locked-in'. Thus the lock-in effect may reduce the supply of risk capital. How significant this is, we do not know.

There is always some lock-in effect with a capital gains tax, because the longer the realization of a gain is deferred the less is the present value of the tax payment; but this lock-in effect would be much more pronounced if capital gains tax liability fell to zero on assets retained 'till death. In making gifts there would also be a distorting tendency to include assets on which the gains had been biggest.

(3) *Death and gifts do not count as a disposal, but the previous acquisition value is carried over.* (The 'carry-over' solution.) Under this proposal death and gifts would not count as realizations, but the deceased's acquisition value and the donor's acquisition value would be carried forward to the inheritor and the donee, so that when the asset was eventually sold, capital gains would be paid on the gain over the holding period of two (or more) owners. If part of the estate was sold to meet death duties, capital gains tax would be paid on these assets. This solution presents few administrative difficulties for gifts, but its application at death raises complications. Where the distribution of assets amongst the beneficiaries of a will was specified in value terms, the division of the estate would be immensely complicated by the capital gains tax liabilities (and indeed loss offsets) attaching to the various assets and hence carried over to their recipients. It would be necessary to have a 'testamentary formula' not only for the distribution of the estate but also for the distribution of the capital gains tax liabilities and offsets. A

[1] Henry C. Wallich, 'Taxation of Capital Gains in the Light of Recent Economic Developments', *National Tax Journal*, June 1965, p. 146.

further disadvantage is that there would still remain a considerable lock-in effect—even though it would be less than with presumptive realization at death.[1]

In deciding which is the most suitable (or the least disadvantageous) procedure to adopt we are hampered by ignorance—in particular there are few hard facts on the extent and significance of the lock-in effect.

Experience elsewhere is very little guide. The USA capital gains tax does not count death as presumptive realization nor is there a carry forward of valuation. But many Americans are unhappy about this solution and are concerned about lock-in; there is a strong lobby for changing to presumptive realization and it is not at all improbable that the Americans may adopt it. Under the US tax the carry-over basis is applied to gifts. In the more limited capital gains tax provisions of Sweden, the no disposal solution applies to gifts and at death. The Canadian government, on the other hand, is proposing to introduce a capital gains tax by which gifts would count as presumptive realization, but the carry-over basis would apply at death.[2]

On this complex issue the author does not feel competent to make more than a suggestion which might prove a basis for more detailed discussion—i.e. that presumptive realization should apply to gifts and at death, with the exception that for a very restricted range of assets, characterized by limited marketability, most notably agricultural farm units and unincorporated businesses or close companies, an option to 'carry forward' might be permitted. The solution to this problem, however, partly depends on what action, if any, is taken on the inter-related issue of inflation.

An Allowance against Inflation in the Capital Gains Tax

There are two issues to be considered. In principle, should there be some provision against inflation in a capital gains tax? If so, what form should it take?

We have already pointed out that in so far as gains are a product of price increases they are monetary only, not real. On the other hand, it is argued that what matters in taxation is the relative rather than the absolute position of taxpayers. A capital gains tax is primarily thought of as a substitute for income tax if not an equivalent

[1] For a fuller discussion of the implications of adopting the carry-over basis, see Martin David, *ibid.*, chapter VII.

[2] *Proposals for Tax Reform*, Ottawa 1969, p. 42.

to it. No correction against inflation is allowed on income tax. Why then allow a relief on taxation of capital gains?

One answer to this question is that whilst the lack of a corrective against inflation increases income tax on ordinary income, it does not entrench on the assets which give rise to that income. For earned income these are the abilities of the individual.[1] Personal abilities have a capital value equal to the present value of the future earnings to which they give rise. Sometimes these future earnings can be capitalized, for example, when an entertainer contracts to work for a company in exchange for a low salary and a capital sum. Also borrowing on the strength of future earnings is a form of capitalization. As Professor A. J. Merrett has written:

> 'It is perfectly true that *ordinary taxable income*, whether earned or unearned, is subject to tax without correction for inflation. But individuals are not subject to tax at all *on the changes in the capital values* of the asset—namely personal abilities—which produces earned income.
>
> Hence taxation of earned income involves no comparable case on which to base the taxation of changing capital values of unearned income and financial wealth.'[2]

In other words, in so far as a capital gains tax is levied on monetary gains, i.e. gains which simply reflect price increases, it becomes a tax not on capital gains but on wealth. It is possible to make out a case for the taxation of wealth in this way. First, the long-term capital gains tax of the United Kingdom is at a comparatively low rate compared to the full rigours of income tax and surtax. Second, nominally, except for the concession to small incomes, it is not progressive; but by and large, the wealthier a man is, the larger the proportion of his wealth which he holds in assets benefiting from capital gains;[3] hence a flat rate gains tax in times of inflation may effectively be progressive.

When one thinks of the fixed income receiver the value of whose capital has *fallen* as a result of inflation, it is not easy to feel compassion for the holder of equities, the capital value of which may have risen enormously. Yet the argument for taxing monetary gains as a form of wealth tax is fundamentally unsound. If we want to tax wealth, let us have a wealth tax. And if we wish to make a capital gains tax progressive, cannot we find a more systematic method of

1 See the discussion of human capital above, p. 184–5.

2 'The Capital Gains Tax', *Lloyds Bank Review*, October 1965.

3 See Appendix A.

doing it than relying on this haphazard way of taxing monetary gains? Our answer must surely be that these deficiencies should be remedied by other means and that in principle we should introduce a provision against inflation into the capital gains tax.

How should this be done? One suggestion has been to taper the rate of long-term gains tax—so that the longer the asset was held the lower would be the rate of tax.[1] This solution has two main disadvantages; the reduction in rate of tax would have to be according to a fixed scale and would not bear any relationship to the *actual* rate of inflation. Second, it would seem to accentuate the lock-in effect, for postponing realization would reduce the rate of tax.

A more attractive proposal is to allow a percentage addition to the acquisition price of assets equal to the percentage increase in a specified index of prices. There is room for argument about the nature and composition of the index, but because of the links between capital gains tax and income, the index of retail prices would probably serve well enough. It could be a corollary that if prices *fell* there would be a corresponding *deduction* to the acquisition price. There is a partial precedent for this procedure in the Swedish capital gains tax applicable to gains on real property sold on or after January 1, 1968. These are taxed as income to 100 per cent if the property was held for less than two years and to 75 per cent in other cases. 'In calculating the capital gains, however, the historic cost of the real property is recalculated by an index so as to take into account the rise of the general price level up to the time of sale.'[2] These provisions, it is of interest to note, replaced previous ones which had provided for a tapering rate falling to zero after ten years.

If a provision to correct for inflation was introduced into the capital gains tax, it would strengthen the case for treating gifts and death as a presumptive realization.

SUMMING UP

The strongest argument for a capital gains tax is equity; without it taxable capacity goes untaxed; income tax can be avoided by the conversion of income to capital gains. Yet the tax has many unsatisfactory features. It is difficult wholly to sustain the argument that capital gains should be treated as 'ordinary income' despite affinities

[1] A. R. Prest, *Public Finance in Theory and Practice*, 3rd edition, 1967, pp. 298–9.

[2] *The Swedish Budget 1968/69*, A Summary published by the Ministry of Finance, Stockholm, 1968, pp. 114–15.

with it. To the best of the author's knowledge, no country consistently so treats it; and even the Minority of the Royal Commission on Profits and Income, who argued strongly that capital gains should rank as income, failed fully to apply this logic in their recommendations. A gains tax gives rise to a series of complex questions; and a measure of their complexity is the diversity of practice in seeking to solve them. In short the features of a gains tax mirror the uncertainty about its nature. Its characteristics reflect compromise solutions. The justification for a capital gains tax is simply that the inequities of having one are less than the inequities of not having one.

Chapter 8

Programme for Reform

OBJECTIVES, IGNORANCE AND JUDGMENT

Chapter 4 set down alternative possibilities for a major reform of the death duties in the United Kingdom with a number of suggestions for detailed amendment and modification; in chapter 6 we considered various possible forms of annual wealth tax; and in chapter 7 some improvements in the capital gains tax were proposed and in particular we examined issues raised by the need to integrate a capital gains tax with a reformed death duty. In these earlier chapters, whilst a preference was usually indicated, the various possible treatments of each tax in turn were considered at some length and often in detail. In this chapter we are concerned to present a programme for a comprehensive system of capital taxation. The modifications of detail already recommended will generally be taken for granted, and we shall be concerned to restate the main conclusions; to relate the capital taxes recommended to each other; to relate the system of capital taxation to income taxation; and to develop the proposals further, even beyond the conventional confines of wealth or capital taxation. We shall also examine some of the problems of implementing the suggested reforms.

Let us begin by reverting to the objectives behind capital taxes. In chapter 1 we indicated that arguments of equity, equality and efficiency could be presented to support the taxation of wealth, but suggested that the relative strength of those arguments depended very much on the nature and form of the wealth tax. As we have proceeded to analyse each form of capital tax, this point has emerged more clearly. Thus a modest annual wealth tax meets the equity criterion more effectively than death duties, because it would *regularly* take into account that capital confers benefit on its owner (and thus adds to his taxable capacity) over and above the income derived from it. A death duty, on the other hand, has particular advantages for reducing inequality in the ownership of wealth because no alternative capital tax could achieve the same result with less resentment and with so few adverse economic consequences. The objectives, too, may conflict with each other; most obvious is the oft met clash between efficiency and equality. A modest annual wealth tax which could be paid from income might promote efficiency in resource use by encouraging investors to seek high returns, and the efficiency benefits would be the more pronounced if the wealth tax replaced surtax; yet such a wealth tax would do little to promote equality. If, with equality as our objective, we step up the rates of tax so that it has to be paid from capital, then it is likely to have adverse effects on resource use—to discourage saving and to stimulate the flight of capital and capitalists. Again, if in seeking to promote equality we continue to raise death duty rates, then, for a variety of reasons,[1] we may accentuate the inequities which can never wholly be excised from the tax; and, indeed, we may not even be very successful in promoting equality, for the more inequitable the tax appears, the less the moral compunction about avoidance and evasion.

Thus, what emerges from the analysis is the need to select the objective or objectives which each genus of wealth tax is best able to achieve and then to choose the form of wealth tax within that genus most suitable for that purpose.

It also emerges that the various forms of capital tax overlap very little in achieving their purposes. The establishment of an effective combination of death duty and gift tax does little to undermine the case for an annual wealth tax, nor does a system of death duties and annual wealth tax render a capital gains tax unnecessary. Indeed there is as much complementarity as substitutability in such a series of capital taxes; the more taxes to which the same valuations of assets can be applied, the less the administrative costs as a proportion of revenue.

In seeking to arrive at recommendations about wealth taxes we must admit ignorance on some crucial issues and recognize the dependence of other issues on personal value judgments. We do not know whether heavy death duties exercise a significant net disincentive to save (or would do if the loopholes to avoidance were blocked); we do not know how many gifts or legacies are received by the same people, nor whether an accessions tax would have any significant effect in inducing the wealthy to change the disposition of their property. We are ignorant about how far an annual wealth tax would encourage big wealth holders, most of whom are over fifty-five, to reduce their liquidity and seek higher yields in their investment. We cannot accurately assess either the extent or the significance of the 'lock-in' effect of a capital gains tax with or without presumptive realization at death. These are but some of the matters on which we are ignorant. Policy forming governments

[1] See pp. 139–41.

and truth seeking universities should continually seek to reduce these areas of ignorance; but some are almost impossible to eliminate, and governments inevitably must exercise a practical judgment and act with imperfect knowledge.

As for value judgments, some people value equality more than others; and they may be prepared to 'trade off' more efficiency for a given gain in equality.

In the last resort a system of wealth taxation is some form of compromise amongst objectives. But some compromises have a firmer foundation in economic principles and empirical investigation than others; and some are more widely acceptable than others. The author hopes that both observations apply to the following summarized conclusions on the objectives appropriate to the different wealth taxes and the form of tax most likely to achieve them.

1. The singular merit of death duties is the facility to promote equality—an objective the more significant in the United Kingdom because of its very unequal distribution of wealth. The form of death duty most suitable for this purpose is an accessions tax.
2. An annual wealth tax is unsuitable as a means of promoting equality. But a modest wealth tax brings advantages of equity, and substituted for surtax and the unearned income differential, brings prospects of increased efficiency.
3. The particular merit of a capital gains tax is equity—to ensure that there is not too much disparity in treatment between those who receive 'normal' income and those whose economic power is increased by capital gains. A capital gains tax can also do a little to promote the equality objective.

Let us look somewhat further at the first two of these conclusions and in particular at their implementation.

AN ACCESSIONS TAX FOR EQUALITY

Reform of the United Kingdom death duties is long overdue; the weight of death duties should be reduced and a gift tax integrated with the death duty. To pursue the objective of equality, the form of duty should be changed from estate duty to inheritance tax and an accessions duty adopted—paid by the beneficiary on the cumulative total of legacies and gifts received throughout a life-time.

This form of tax opens up some further possibilities. The basis of the accessions tax could be broadened into a capital receipts tax[1]

[1] I have to thank Professor R. C. Tress for suggesting this name to me.

to include not only gifts and legacies but other non-income receipts. Clear candidates for inclusion would be football pool and other gambling winnings, which are taxed neither as income nor capital gains, and golden handshakes, of which only the excess over £5,000 is liable to income tax.

What of capital gains? Short term capital gains are assessed for income tax; why not tax long-term capital gains on the same basis as gifts, legacies and other non-income receipts?

It must be admitted that there is no irrefutable logic in the suggestion to treat long-term capital gains in this way. But then there is really no precise logic about the capital gains tax. It is difficult to sustain the view, either in theory or in practice, that all capital gains are equivalent to income. Every capital gains tax in fact is a compromise. A compromise that treated long-term capital gains as non-income receipts to be taxed along with other capital receipts would have some decided merits. First, it would remove the disadvantage of the long-term capital gains tax which we have previously noted, namely that it was proportional rather than progressive and hence of only limited use in promoting equality. If gains paid capital receipts tax, the man who had received much by gifts and legacies would pay more tax on his capital gains than the man with the same capital gain but who had received less in other capital receipts. Yet, whilst the tax would be progressive, long-term capital gains would in general not be taxed as severely as if they were treated as income. Again, whilst some who had received much in capital receipts might feel 'locked in', for the economy as a whole the lock-in effect might be small, for there would always be many owners of property subject to the lower rates of capital receipts tax who would not be deterred from realizing gains. It is assumed, too, that the kind of measures proposed in chapter 7 to correct for inflation would be adopted, so that tax would be on 'real' gains only.

A comprehensive capital receipts tax has attractions of conceptual simplicity. All receipts would be taxed either as income on an annual basis (and these would include short-term capital gains) or as capital receipts at rates determined by the cumulation of non-income receipts on a life-time basis (and these would include long-term capital gains). The general method of operation and the tax rates would be as recommended for the accessions tax in chapter 4.

This combination of income tax and capital receipts tax would bring us nearer to the 'comprehensive income tax base' or the 'economic accretions' principle, without going all the way. The comprehensive income tax base consists of treating as income all additions to 'economic power' over a period of time: or, expressed alternatively, income for tax purposes is taken as the sum of an individual's expenditure on consumption goods and services plus any change in net worth (wealth or capital) over a period of time. Under this concept, all accretions of wealth are included with income regardless of source or manner of use: wages, interest, legacies, gifts, capital gains, for example, would all be treated as 'income' and taxed on the same basis. This attractively simple proposition runs into various practical difficulties: in its purest form, accretions of wealth, whether realized or not, are included and this raises valuation problems; also a complicated averaging system is necessary to prevent bunched receipts from being too heavily taxed; and the comprehensive tax base is such a huge break with contemporary practice that the problems of transition would be mammoth. The proposals of the latest exponents of this principle—the Carter Commission—have not in fact been accepted by the Canadian government. Our proposals for a dual sustem of taxation—for 'income' taxed on an annual basis and 'capital' receipts, according to life-time accumulation—whilst they lack the extreme conceptual simplicity of the comprehensive income base proposals, avoid the need for averaging and are not such a complete break with present practice as to be ruled out of court.

Nevertheless, it must be admitted that the strongest argument in favour of continuing with estate duty instead of introducing an accessions tax, let alone a capital receipts tax, has nothing to do with the relative merits of the taxes as such; it is that we already have the estate duty. This is the sense in which 'an old tax is a good tax'. Any major restructuring of a tax involves a considerable cost and a long and complicated transitional period. This cost is the administrative effort needed, by both the Revenue authorities and the tax payer and advisers, to master the details of the new tax; the years of experience and expertise built up through knowledge of the intricate details of the old tax are rendered obsolescent like out-dated capital. In short, a new tax does not only have to be better than the old, but so much better as to justify the change. The costs of transition from estate duty to accessions tax would also include the necessity to re-draw wills. Not only would some people wish to re-draft wills to take advantage of the new tax situation, if others did *not* do so their clear intentions might be frustrated. For example, under estate duty most specific legacies and pecuniary legacies will have been free of duty (the total duty being paid from the residuary estate). If the testator did not make a new will, then his intention would not be carried out unless there was some deliberate grossing up of these legacies during the transition period.

Some interim provisions would also be necessary in relation to gifts inter vivos which might otherwise have been caught for estate duty; also provisions might be needed for gifts made whilst the new tax proposals were being discussed.

What is clear, however, is that the estate duty, as it stands, simply will not do. It would have to be changed anyway; rates would have to be reduced and a new and comprehensive gift tax integrated with it. Many other changes of detail are also necessary—the abolition of the special reliefs on agricultural and industrial property; and the development of payment in kind. With these changes due anyway, now is the time to change to an accessions tax. Were the estate duty to be improved and a gift tax integrated with it, the case for subsequently adopting an accessions tax would, on these practical grounds, be much weakened.

First and foremost then, in our programme of reform to develop a comprehensive system of wealth taxation, is the introduction of an accessions tax with the minimum of delay. At the same time, or subsequently if there were administrative advantages in proceeding in stages, the accessions tax could be broadened into a capital receipts tax.

A WEALTH TAX FOR EFFICIENCY

A second and less urgent recommendation is that very serious consideration should be given to the introduction of a wealth tax of a kind to meet the objectives of equity and efficiency. This would be a modest tax to raise sufficient revenue largely to replace surtax and to enable the income tax differential on unearned income to be abolished. As the calculations in chapter 6 indicate, a wealth tax imposed on wealth in excess of £20,000 with marginal rates rising from ½ per cent to 2 per cent in steps of ½ per cent, would make possible the reduction of marginal rates of tax on income to a maximum of 50 or 60 per cent. A detailed discussion of the restructuring of income tax is outside the scope of this book; but (as figure 8.1 shows) the rates of income tax have become less and less progressive with the abolition of the 'reduced rates' in the budgets of 1969 and 1970; and the substantial modification of a genuinely progressive surtax and the abolition of differential income taxation, would provide the needed opportunity to devise a new consistently progressive structure of income tax rates.

With a modest wealth tax of this order, which simply compensated for a reduction in income tax and surtax, and with the lower tax on income, special ceiling provisions should not be necessary; but

FIGURE 8.1. UK Marginal Rates of Income Tax and Surtax, 1970–71 (Married man with two children under 11)

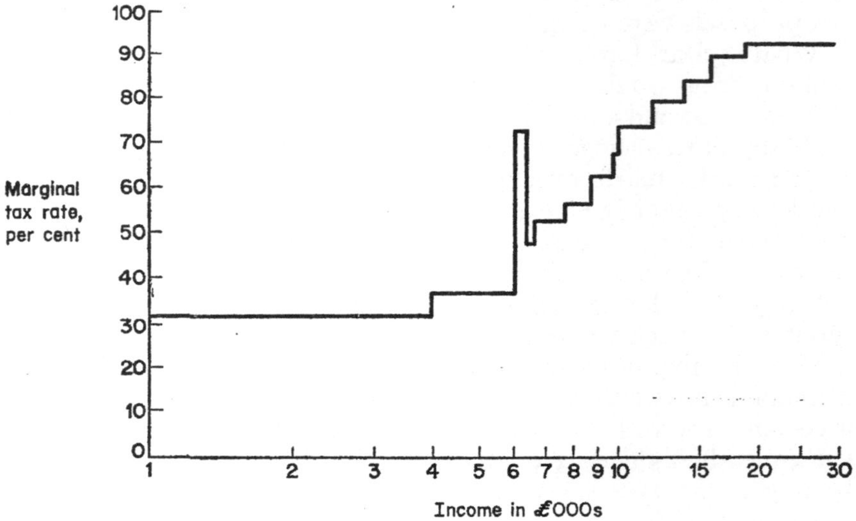

Note: The peculiar marginal increase round the £6,000 range resulted from the 1970 budget. The Chancellor raised the exemption limit for surtax but recouped the revenue from those who paid surtax, with a maximum rate of 40 per cent on those whose incomes just exceeded the exemption limit.

the possibility of something like the Swedish 'eighty per cent' rule[1] should be borne in mind. The more special provisions are introduced, however, the more the purposes of the tax are likely to be distorted. There remains, of course, the biggest problem of an annual wealth tax—that of administration centring round valuation. We should learn from Swedish experience and try to improve on it. A pre-condition of the introduction of a wealth tax is the development of an adequate valuation structure, the fundamental principle of which should be the utilization of the same valuations for a series of taxes. Valuations for annual wealth tax purposes should be used also for death duties and gift tax and vice versa; and they should be integrated with valuations for capital gains tax. These taxes complement each other in this sense that an asset under-valued for wealth tax may pay more gains tax and *vice versa*. The annual wealth tax valuations should be recorded on the same form as the income tax so that there would be an automatic link and cross-check with income. If local taxation were based on the capital value of property

[1] See p. 192.

rather than an assessed annual value, whether or not cadastral values were used, the same valuations could apply for local property tax and the wealth taxes.

The acceptance of an accessions tax or a capital receipts tax, which requires life-time records of receipts by gifts and legacies, probably makes it easier to keep track of the more valuable asssets and to ensure, for example, that the valuation of a piece of jewellery for death duties is also available for annual wealth tax.

One of the least satisfactory aspects of the Swedish annual wealth tax is the valuation of personal assets, like jewellery.[1] The suggestion of insurance valuations is probably worth trying. As indicated in chapters 5 and 6, exemptions to an annual wealth tax should be kept to a minimum and, when allowed, take the form of a limit by value rather than the wholesale exemption of a particular class of asset; this way investment patterns are distorted less.

In implementing a wealth tax Professor G. S. A. Wheatcroft has suggested that it would be wise to start at a low rate with a very high exemption limit (say 1 per cent on holders of over £200,000 wealth) and then subsequently extend downwards, and introduce progression as experience was gained in working the tax.[2] A stage by stage introduction of a wealth tax could be accompanied by a phased reduction of surtax, the final stage taking the form of the abolition of the unearned income differential and the re-structuring of income tax.

A NEGATIVE WEALTH TAX

An annual wealth tax, of the kind outlined, could prove a very useful and desirable measure to promote efficiency. But, to the author, the prime attraction of wealth or capital taxation is what it might do towards evening out the distribution of wealth. The author was once indicted by a student for his 'bourgeois liberal philosophy'. He admits his guilt. For that reason he prefers to seek equality through the gradualism of an efficient system of death duties rather than through the disturbance of capital levies or annual wealth taxes which could only be paid from capital.

Even if the accessions tax or capital receipts tax is introduced, its effect in reducing inequalities of wealth will be slow. Even with this form of death duty, reductions in inequality are likely to be brought about more by the diminution of large inheritances by high taxation than by widespread small bequests from the tax

1 See pp. 193–4.

2 'The Administrative Problems of a Wealth Tax', *British Tax Review*, November–December 1963.

incentive to dispersion. And if an accessions or capital receipts tax does lead to increased diffusion in wealth, will this result in a meaningful reduction in inequality? Might it not simply mean that, say, the upper quartile of property owners retained as much property as before, but distribution within that upper quartile was more even; for example, that property owners gave or bequeathed their wealth more widely and more evenly within their families or at any rate their own social circle?

Herein lies the fundamental limitation of *orthodox* taxation, be it income tax or wealth tax, to promote equality. It can cut down but it can do little to build up.

It is with the idea of building up *incomes* at the lower end that a negative or reverse income tax has been much discussed in recent years and indeed has become one of the bases of President Nixon's welfare proposals. If a negative income tax, why not a negative wealth tax? A negative income tax is designed to bring low incomes up to a specified minimum. A negative wealth tax would be designed to ensure that, by lump sum payments at one or more stages of their life, capital receipts for everyone attained at least a certain minimum.

It has been said that, to improve state welfare services, first see what the 'middle class' do for themselves and their families and then do the same for all. There are perhaps three or four occasions in life when the wealthy provide lump-sum gifts for their children, or near relatives, or for themselves. At the birth of a child a sum may be put aside for the new arrival; at coming of age; at marriage; and at retirement—when, for example, some middle-class pensions arrangements provide for a lump sum.

Although there is an attractive symmetry about 'birth bounties' as a sort of balance to death duties, the more realistic times for payments under a negative wealth tax would be at coming of age and retirement.

Let us concentrate on the first. The idea would be that, on attaining the age of eighteen, every person residing and born in this country should receive from the state a capital sum of, say £500. (There might be a case for making the age twenty-one, the former age of majority, allowing the sum to be available, in whole or in part at age eighteen but only for approved purposes, like education.) The big merit of the scheme would be that it provided everyone with the minimum security of a small 'nest egg'; it would do something at the lower end to promote a wider distribution of wealth. But the scheme would have other advantages. In general the various state welfare and social service benefits are 'income' benefits; yet some needs can better be met by the provision of 'capital' benefits. Such a need is that of a young couple setting up house. Many couples can meet annual mortgage payments on a house but lack a deposit. Under this scheme their combined 'bonuses' give them £1,000. Apart from the possible purchase of a house, a lump-sum at this particular time in life can be very useful for furnishing. (In Sweden the need for a welfare provision to help young couples setting up a home is recognized by the facility of state loans.)

The proposal has the further merit that it would benefit the less intellectually able members of the community. At the moment the intellectual élite gain the benefits of state subsidization in the later stages of secondary and in higher education as a result of which (on average) they derive the personal benefits of higher life-time earnings. Education provision helps those who are in any case the fortunate ones. A negative wealth tax would benefit all. The intellectual high-fliers could use the bonus towards the costs of higher education, but, as we suggest below, might be required to supplement with loans.[1] The less intellectual could use the bonus to develop their talents in other ways, for example to help them to establish a small business. Also, because the bonus is given equally to men and women, it is fairer between the sexes than the present situation in which state expenditure on higher education predominantly benefits men.

There is a further merit of a negative capital tax which deserves to be noted. Just as a wealth or capital tax has little or no deterrent effect on effort because the tax base is related to past and not present action, so a 'once and for all' payment under a negative wealth tax would not have the disincentive effects of some income benefits which affect the terms on which income can be earned.[2]

Two arguments are particularly likely to be presented against the scheme. First, the cost: at £500 per person at age eighteen the cost would be of the order of £400m. per annum.

A substantial part of the cost could be met by ending certain income benefits for those who receive the bonus—in particular the lower interest rates or tax relief on house mortgage payments; and

1 An alternative way of seeking to do 'justice' to the less intellectually able would be to give the bonus only to those who did *not* receive full-time higher education. I am indebted to John Hughes of Ruskin College for the idea that income tax paid by young people who left school without proceeding to higher education might be credited to them and paid out in a lump sum when they became of age. This arrangement might, however, particularly discourage some intellectually able 'working class' children from extending their secondary education and continuing to higher education.

2 For a number of examples, see A. R. Prest, *Social Benefits and Tax Rates*, IEA Research Monograph 22, 1970.

the partial replacement of student grants by loans in the finance of higher education. The mortgage relief schemes could be gradually phased out; people too old for the bonus would continue to get mortgage relief but, if the bonus were introduced in, say, 1970, no one born after 1952 could obtain the mortgage interest concession. The coming of age bonus would provide assistance for the house purchaser without at the same time discriminating in his favour as compared with the private tenant. The continuation of mortgage and student grant benefits for those born too early to receive the bonus, would make its introduction more acceptable; those just too old for it would feel less sense of grievance. The bonus would likewise facilitate the change to loans in financing higher education.

Not all the cost of the scheme would need to be met from reduced government spending elsewhere or from higher taxation; in so far as bonuses were saved they would not constitute a claim on current output other than the interest or profits derived from them. In this way there is a match up with revenue from death duties. Thus suppose, for purposes of illustration, that the bonus was in the form of government securities which had been paid to the government in death duties. Suppose £500 of securities were received by the government as accessions tax from A and then passed over as bonus to B; if B did not attempt to cash the asset and spend the proceeds on consumption, the cost to the government would simply be the annual interest (less income tax) on the securities.

Moreover, if an accessions tax or capital receipts tax were adopted, the net cost could be reduced in either of two ways. The bonus could be paid *only* to those whose previous capital receipts amounted to less than a specified sum. Alternatively, if all received the bonus, it would in any case count as a capital receipt for purposes of the tax. Thus those who had already received sufficient receipts to bring them above the exemption limit would pay tax on it—the rate depending on cumulative receipts to that date. Those who had not would have the bonus recorded against them so that subsequent receipts would bring them more quickly into the taxpaying brackets. Thus the net cost of the scheme would ultimately prove to be considerably less than the gross figure.

The second argument likely to be used against the proposal is that the bonus would be used irresponsibly—that some beneficiaries would embark on a rash spending spree. This may not always be bad; if a young man spends his bonus on a trip round the world, he benefits from a valuable experience and there is something to be said for having a little wealth when you are young enough to enjoy it. However, some forms of expenditure would undoubtedly be matter for regret and would just have to be accepted. People become responsible only when given responsibility: it is one of the attractions of the negative wealth tax proposals, as compared with income-type benefits, that more responsibility and initiative is left in the hands of the individual. To encourage the saving of the bonus, it need not be paid in cash, but, say, half in saving certificates and half in unit trust certificates or some other security which provided some 'hedge' against inflation and enabled the recipient to share in the prosperity of the community.[1] One or both components of the bonus might also carry attractive premiums if left untouched for a specified term of years.

The other possible time for a bonus would be at a specified retirement age; the procedure might be similar to that of the 'coming of age' bonus. A 'nest egg' has particular value at retirement and the 'hedge' against inflation would be especially useful. There is more likelihood that much of the retirement bonuses would be saved and for other reasons also the net cost would be much less than the gross. Bonuses might be paid only to those who had received less than a specified sum in capital receipts. Or they might go to everyone at retirement. But in any case they would count as capital receipts for purposes of tax, so that the rate of tax paid on many of them would be high. They would also tend to increase the subsequent yield of a capital receipts tax, both because they would raise the tax revenue from capital receipts later received by the beneficiaries of the retirement bonus and because they would increase the wealth entering into the accessions or capital receipts tax when the beneficiaries parted with their property by gift or bequest.

Some may hold up their hands in horror at these radical suggestions. Yet there is nothing inherently impracticable or inherently expensive about them. Compensation for redundancy now takes the form of lump-sum payments. 'Gratuities' have regularly been made to servicemen on demobilization. In pre-war days post office women workers who were expected to leave employment when they married received a dowry depending on length of service. And the superannuation schemes of many who (like university teachers) are effectively state employees, may partly take the form of lump-sum payments. Why should they not be extended to the population at large at those particular times in life when a lump sum meets a particular need?

[1] For example, the kind of 'ordinary share' proposed by *The Economist* ('A Government Ordinary Share', May 2, 1970) by which the government undertook to pay as annual dividend a specified proportion of GNP in money terms, e.g. 0·02 per cent of GNP paid on a nominal issue of £100m.

In a leading article, 'Spreading the Wealth',[1] *The Times* commented: 'The right way to approach the problem of the ownership of wealth is to encourage the creation of capital among people who have not in the past had the habit of capital formation or indeed the opportunity.' *The Times* proceeded to consider various ways in which this might be done—the encouragement of home ownership (including the purchase of council houses), the widening of share ownership and the novel suggestion that one or more of the nationalized industries should be denationalized by a general distribution of shares. A negative or reverse wealth tax could be part of such a policy —complementary both to capital taxes and to measures to increase the wealth of those with little or none. Let us conclude with a further quotation from *The Times* leader:

> 'Quite moderate private wealth can give real independence to the private citizen—independence such as the possibility of private retirement rather than the public home, the ability to leave one's job without the family going short, or the ability to travel. Private property is the best safeguard the individual has against public power. There is no state in the world in which private property has been destroyed without private freedom being destroyed with it. What we need to do is to see that the personal independence of property ceases to be the prerogative of the rich and becomes a natural and realizable ambition of all citizens.'

[1] September 28, 1968.

Appendix A

The Calculation of a Property Price Index, 1949–1967

This appendix sets out an attempt to calculate changes in the money value of property for the years 1949–67 which can provide a useful if imperfect indication of the effect of inflation on the incidence of estate duty. The year 1949 is a convenient starting point because in that year Sir Stafford Cripps abolished the legacy and succession duties and increased the rates of estate duty to a level at which they have remained (with minor adjustments) since.

A high degree of accuracy is not claimed for the property price index. Data for the compilation of a refined index is lacking and some rather arbitrary assumptions have been made. Also no attempt has been made to separate out, quantitatively, how far the rise in price of a particular class of assets is a monetary phenomenon and how far a change in the real content of the assets themselves. Despite those limitations, there is no doubt that the property price index reveals indications of the direct and indirect effects of inflation on the incidence of estate duty which would be obscured if it were simply to be assumed that all assets had risen equally in price in line with an index such as the retail price index.

METHOD OF CALCULATION

The annual reports of the Inland Revenue contain data on the types of assets comprising estates. To simplify the compilation of a property price index the assets have been combined into four groups (A–D) each believed to be reasonably homogeneous in terms of the likely price variation of its components. The weight assigned to each group of assets in the index is determined by their values as a proportion of the total value of estates in 1957–8—a year mid-way between 1949 and 1967 and hence convenient as a base.

Group A consists of assets in the form of cash, balances at clearing banks, trustee and Post Office accounts, mortgage loans, ordinary life policies, farming stock, trade assets of individuals, household goods, government securities, preference and debenture shares and some miscellaneous assets. The somewhat heroic assumption is made that, on balance, these will not have changed much in monetary value, and the price index for them can be assumed constant. For 57 per cent of this group (in 1957–8), i.e. cash, bank balances, and other very liquid assets, this is a very reasonable assumption. Undoubtedly Group A includes a few possessions like paintings, precious metals

TABLE A1. *Price Index of the Main Components of Personal Estates, 1949–67*

	(1958=base year 100)					
Year	Group A cash, etc.	Group B ordinary shares	Group C land, etc.	Group D buildings, etc.	Property index all estates	Retail price index
1949	100	60	88 (est.)	84	87	66
1950	100	61	89 (est.)	87	88	68
1951	100	71	96	92	91	75
1952	100	59	89	92	88	81
1953	100	63	86	87	88	84
1954	100	84	88	86	93	85
1955	100	98	94	88	97	89
1956	100	91	92	95	97	94
1957	100	98	86	97	99	97
1958	100	100	100	100	100	100
1959	100	143	119	102	112	101
1960	100	181	145	111	123	102
1961	100	187	146	123	127	105
1962	100	176	158	130	126	110
1963	100	199	198	143	135	112
1964	100	212	252	161	143	115
1965	100	199	276	177	143	121
1966	100	201	285	185	147	126
1967	100	215	304	197	151	129

or jewels, antiques and rare collections, which will have appreciated markedly, but these form a very small proportion of the whole. (Household goods constituted 3–5 per cent of the Group.) Government securities (14 per cent of Group A) are difficult to assess. Holdings of undated securities have depreciated considerably; on the other hand many dated securities will have risen towards par value as they approached maturity. Clearly the assumption of constant monetary value for Group A is open to objection; but the difficulties of obtaining information to allow a more detailed breakdown of this category seemed too great in relation to the likely benefit to justify the attempt.

Group B consists of quoted and unquoted ordinary shares. The index used from 1949–61 is the ordinary share price index as given by the London and Cambridge Economic Service in *Key Statistics 1900–66;* this consists of Moody's index of the geometric mean of sixty 'blue-chip' companies. From 1962 the '500 share index' compiled by the Institute of Actuaries for the *Financial Times* is used. It is assumed that unquoted shares followed the same price pattern as the quoted. Unquoted shares were approximately 20 per cent of all ordinary shares but the proportion varied between estate sizes; in estates under £20,000 unquoted shares were a third of ordinary shares; in the estate range £20,000 to £500,000, on average 16 per cent; and in estates over £500,000, 36 per cent of ordinary shares held were in private companies.

Group C covers land and miscellaneous realty and the index used is an index of agricultural land values collated by G. H. Peters.[1] It represents the average weighted price per acre of land in varying sizes of farm (from 5 to over 300 acres) with vacant possession. Separate figures were not published for 1949 and 1950, only an average covering several years; the figures in table A1 for these years are therefore estimates. The index seems a not unreasonable guide for land in general, as land for development has influenced the price of agricultural land; but, we might expect it to under-estimate the rise in land prices as a whole.

Finally, Group D comprises residential and industrial buildings and miscellaneous rights over property. To measure price changes in this group an index for existing residential property has been used, compiled by the London and Cambridge Economic Service, which appears in *Key Statistics 1900–66*, supplemented for 1967 by the index published by the Co-operative Building Society. This index may be expected to be a reasonable guide to the value of property in Group D as similar considerations will affect the value of both residential and industrial buildings; in any case the total of non-residential building is very small and only amounts to about 4 per cent of residential building in personal estates, probably because most non-residential property is held in company form.

Table A2 shows the significance of the four types of asset in the

[1] Published in G. H. Peters, 'Recent Trends in Farm Real Estate Values in England and Wales', *The Farm Economist*, vol. XI, No. 2, 1966; and *British Farmer*, April 6, 1968.

composition of estates in each of a series of estate ranges and for all estates. Estates under £5,000 were exempt from duty after 1963; estates over £2 million occur irregularly and may distort the pattern. Thus the penultimate column (£5,000 to £2 million) may provide a better reflection of the overall position than the final column.

The table reveals marked differences in asset composition among different sizes of estates: notably the high proportion of 'constant

THE ASSET COMPOSITION OF ESTATES

TABLE A2. *Asset Composition of Estates of Different Sizes, 1957–8*

Category of weight	*Weighting for range of estate by gross capital value, thousands* £5–£20	£20–£50	£50–£100	£100–£500	£500–£2000	£5–£2000	All Estates
Group A Cash, deposits, fixed interest securities, etc.	66·4	50·5	43·0	39·4	32·0	53·7	55·7
Group B Ordinary shares (public and private companies)	8·1	35·3	45·0	48·9	39·8	27·8	24·5
Group C Land and other realty	1·9	2·9	4·0	6·4	21·3	3·7	3·4
Group D Residential and other property	23·6	11·3	8·0	5·4	6·9	14·8	16·4
Total weighting	100	100	100	100	100	100	100

Source: *Commissioners of HM Inland Revenue, Report No.* 101. Cmd. 628, table 113.

price' assets in the smallest estates; and the high proportion of 'growth' assets in the largest estates. The proportion of constant price assets (Group A) declines steadily with estate size. The assets which have risen most in price (Group B and Group C) taken *together* rise steadily with estate size from 10 per cent of the smallest to 61 per cent of the largest estates.

PRICE INCREASES FOR ESTATES OF DIFFERENT SIZES

As this would lead us to expect, when the property price index, weighted by asset distribution in 1957–8, is calculated separately for each estate range, substantial differences emerge between estates. Table A3 gives the indices for the five estate ranges in 1949 and 1967 and records the percentage increase. In the two lowest estate sizes the increase recorded by the property price index is less than the increase in the index of retail prices for the same period; but for the three largest estate values, the percentage increase recorded by the property price index is considerably more. On the basis of the property index, the asset prices rise consistently with size of estate. Small estates in the £5,000 to £20,000 bracket have risen by 46 per cent; all estates over £50,000 have more than doubled in value, whilst the largest estates, over £500,000, are almost two-and-a-half times their value in 1949.

TABLE A3. *Property Price Index applied to Estates of Various Sizes*

Estate range, '000	Property price index 1949	1967	% increase	Retail price index % increase 1949–67
£5 to £20	93	136	46	
£20 to £50	84	157	87	
£50 to £100	80	168	110	
£100 to £500	79	174	120	95
£500 to £2,000	81	196	145	
Average £5 to £2,000	86	154	79	
Average all estates	87	151	74	

For all indices 1958 = 100.

ESTATE DUTY PAYMENTS AND THE PRICE INCREASES

Where assets have risen in price, whether the rise is a real capital gain or a gain in monetary terms only, there are two effects on estate duty payments; at any given rate of duty the amount of tax paid in monetary terms, is increased; but also, because taxation is progressive, the estate is likely to move into higher tax brackets.

The effect of the price increase on the *rate* of estate duty payable, as measured by the property price index, is shown in figure A1. The broken line in the figure indicates estate duty rates for various sizes of estate at 1967 values. The circles indicate the rate of duty that would have been payable on that size of estate at 1949 values. The vertical dotted lines indicate the increase in rates of estate duty resulting from the rise in the prices of assets. Thus a typical estate valued at

£6,850 in 1949 and taxed at 2 per cent would have a value of approximately £10,000 in 1967 and be taxed at 4 per cent; the duty paid in 1967 would be £400 as against £137 in 1949. An estate valued at £21,250 in 1949 might be expected to have a value of about £40,000 in 1967; the rate of duty would have risen from 15 per cent in 1949 to 24 per cent in 1967 (an effective increase of 60 per cent in the rate of liability); actual payment of duty would have trebled, from £3,190 to £9,600. An estate valued at £47,200 in 1949 might have been expected to have a value of about £100,000 in 1967; this would mean a rise in the rate of duty payable from 31 per cent in 1949 to 45 per cent in 1967 (an effective increase of 45 per cent) with a tax liability of £45,000 as compared with £14,632 in 1949. At the upper end of the scale a typical estate of £510,200 in 1949 would probably have increased to a value of £1,250,000; rate of duty payable would have risen from 65·7 per cent to 80 per cent (an effective increase of 22 per cent); actual tax liability would be £1 million in 1967 compared with £335,200 in 1949.

In conclusion, several points about the limitations of this index should be stressed:

(1) It is illustrative only; the data is not sufficiently refined for the exact figures to be meaningful.
(2) No attempt is made to distinguish how far the price rises of the various assets are a product of inflation and how far of 'real' factors such as increases in productivity.
(3) Inflation has indirect as well as direct effects on asset prices. The direct effect is that the value of the physical asset rises; indirect effects are that certain forms of income rise at the expense of others; profit incomes usually benefit and the higher profits and expectations of increased profits raises the prices of ordinary shares. Also between 1949 and 1967, especially during the latter half of the period, the experience of continued inflation led investors to transfer from fixed interest investments to ordinary shares and land, in an attempt to 'hedge' against inflation. This accentuated the price rises in these assets.
(4) The period was one in which the upward movement in the prices of assets in Groups B, C and D was almost continuous. It cannot be assumed that the next twenty years will show the same pattern. In fact, 1969 saw a big drop in share prices and the stabilization of land prices.

FIGURE A1. Effective Rates of Estate Duty on selected Estates at 1949 values and at 1967 values (no nominal changes in duty rates on estates of £8,000+ during period)

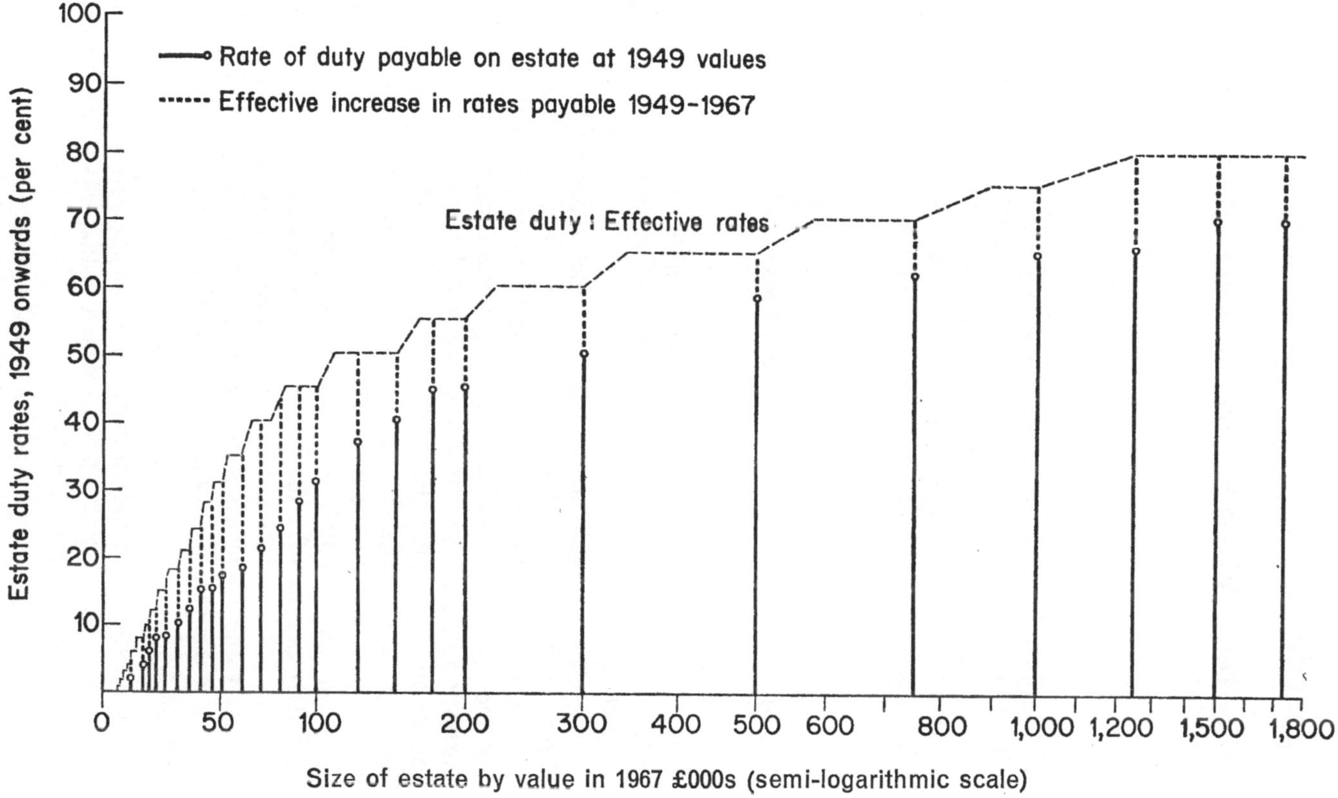

Appendix B

Gifts Inter Vivos Subject to Estate Duty

This appendix provides fuller details of the statistics from which was derived the graphical presentation of gifts inter vivos subject to estate duty as a percentage of the net capital value of all property subject to estate duty in the same years. (Figs. 3.1 and 3.2, chapter 3.) All the data are derived from the annual reports of the Commissioners of Inland Revenue.

THE PERIOD 1898–1931

The full statistical details are set out below in Table B1.

Explanatory Notes to Table B1

Statistics of Capital Values of Property Subject to Estate Duty. Two different bases are used for the figures of capital value of property subject to estate duty:

1899–1915 (inclusive), the capital values recorded by the Inland Revenue were those of which the department *had notice* during the year; (i.e. the full capital value brought to notice in that year and not merely capital which at the appropriate rate would yield duty corresponding in amount to the first instalments paid, subject to an exception that where the capital value of aggregable property was disclosed approximately merely for the purpose of determining the proper rate of duty and not definitely for the purpose of payment of duty on such capital, it was not included in the statistics until definitely declared for the purpose of payment.)

Post 1919 this system was abandoned in favour of that figure of capital value *on which duty was paid during the year*. The Inland Revenue Report for 1920 made the following comments on this change:[1]

1. Payment of the whole sum of estate duty was in the great majority of cases made in the year in which notice was given—hence the bases were largely coincident.

[1] Notes on the post-war statistics of capital values, *Report of the Commissioners of HM Inland Revenue*, year ended March 31, 1920 Cmd. 1083.

2. The second method had the advantage that the capital paying duty was fixed by the definite fact of payment.
3. The statistics compiled under the pre-1915 'notice' system did not accurately represent, for any one year, the total capital passing at death because of the exception, mentioned above, that approximate capital values notified were excluded.
4. The disadvantage of the break in comparability was minimized by the war-time gap in statistics, by the repeal of the settlement estate duty 1914, and by the fact that little disturbance in the total capital included in the statistics was likely to result, since the capital brought to notice in any one year, but omitted from the statistics of that year by reason of deferment of payment, was likely to be roughly balanced by the inclusion of capital brought to notice in the previous years, but paying duty in that year.

It is clear that the change in base makes no significant difference to the general comparisons for which we have used the figures.

Gross and Net Capital Value of Gifts Inter Vivos. Only the gross figures of the inter vivos gifts on which estate duty was paid were recorded in the pre-1914 tables, although the post war included both net and gross. The percentages of net capital value of gifts inter vivos to net total capital subject to estate duty have been calculated for the years in which they are both available (column 7), but since, as one would expect, they show a pattern not greatly different from the corresponding percentages of gross capital values (column 6), in view of the greater continuity of the latter these alone have been utilized for the graph in chapter 3, which plots the values recorded in column 8. Gross figures are the value of the estate (or gift) before the deduction of liabilities; the net figures are after this deduction.

Discontinuities in the Figures of Gifts Inter Vivos. Figures of gifts inter vivos were first compiled for the year 1898; they were discontinued 1916–19 (inclusive) as a result of the war and publication ceased in 1931. No explanation of the abandonment of the table was given in the Inland Revenue reports, but it probably resulted from the economy measures of the period.

Extension of the 'statutory period' of liability of gifts to estate duty, from one to three years, under the Finance (1909–10) Act 1910, must largely account for the substantial jump in 1911 in the figures of gifts inter vivos on which estate duty was paid.

TABLE B1. *Value of Gifts Inter Vivos subject to Estate duty in relation to the value of total Property subject to estate duty, GB, 1898–1931*

(1) Year ended March 31st.	(2) Gross cap. val. of gifts inter vivos subject to estate duty GB £000	(3) Net cap. val. of gifts inter vivos subject to estate duty GB £000	(4) Gross cap. val. of total prop. subject to estate duty GB £000
1898	858	—	260,220
1899	1,593	—	265,090
1900	1,061	—	311,067
1901	851	—	278,380
1902	980	—	305,558
1903	1,378	—	285,244
1904	1,222	—	278,500
1905	1,422	—	279,020
1906	1,735	—	290,548
1907	1,600	—	313,903
1908	2,143	—	298,401
1909	1,887	—	287,346
1910	1,761	—	298,126
1911	3,493	—	283,768
1912	2,652	—	292,146
1913	2,685	—	292,508
1914	3,171	—	310,407
1915	2,887	—	325,202
1916–1919	—	—	—
9 months to			
1920	2,344	2,339	315,026
1921	2,938	2,931	409,200
1922	5,995	5,985	441,026
1923	5,810	5,799	472,586
1924	6,337	6,332	479,362
1925	6,119	6,089	501,508
1926	5,670	5,657	495,521
1927	5,382	5,354	505,114
1928	7,059	7,033	550,803
1929	8,703	8,689	563,792
1930	7,971	7,654	579,618
1931	6,000	5,978	556,453

(5) Net cap. val. of total prop. subject to estate duty GB £000	(6) Col. (2). as per cent. of Col. (4).	(7) Col. (3). as per cent. of Col. (5).	(8) Col. (6). as Moving avge. with 3 Year span
—	0·33	—	—
—	0·60	—	0·42
—	0·34	—	0·42
—	0·31	—	0·32
—	0·32	—	0·37
—	0·48	—	0·41
—	0·44	—	0·48
—	0·51	—	0·52
—	0·60	—	0·54
—	0·51	—	0·61
—	0·72	—	0·63
—	0·66	—	0·66
—	0·59	—	0·83
—	1·23	—	0·91
—	0·91	—	1·02
—	0·92	—	0·95
—	1·02	—	0·94
—	0·89	—	—
—	—	—	—
288,773	0·74	0·81	—
372,890	0·72	0·79	0·94
402,085	1·36	1·49	1·10
431,197	1·23	1·34	1·30
441,896	1·32	1·43	1·26
461,135	1·22	1·32	1·23
456,390	1·14	1·24	1·14
466,467	1·07	1·15	1·16
511,070	1·28	1·38	1·30
525,133	1·54	1·65	1·40
538,376	1·38	1·42	1·33
516,800	1·08	1·16	—

THE PERIOD 1961–68

Information on gifts inter vivos subject to estate duty is again published in 1961, but on a basis different from that of the earlier years. Table B2 shows the form in which the information is now presented.

TABLE B2. *Estate Duty: Analysis of Gifts inter vivos, 1967–68. Estates over £5,000 net capital value, G B*

(Amounts £ thousands)

	Great Britain		England and Wales		Scotland	
	No. of cases	Amount	No. of cases	Amount	No. of cases	Amount
Charities	6	6	6	6		
Other:						
within 1st and 2nd years before death	4,649	23,719	4,235	21,334	414	2,385
within 3rd and 4th years before death	3,170	14,766	2,949	13,317	221	1,449
within 5th year before death	1,082	2,688	1,042	2,439	40	249
not known	144	353	94	196	50	157
Total gifts inter vivos	7,220	41,532	6,608	37,291	612	4,241

The amount of a graduated gift included in the table is the value as reduced for estate duty.
Source: *Commissioners of HM Inland Revenue, Report No. 111*, January 1969, table 133.

The data for Great Britain for the years 1961–68 are set out in table B3 in relation to the value of total property subject to estate duty.

Explanatory Notes to Tables B2 and B3

(1) *Net and Gross Gifts.* No distinction is made in the later figures between gross and net gifts which were distinguished in the earlier period; a glance at the earlier figures (table B1) demonstrates that the difference between the two categories was negligible.

(2) *Numbers of Estates with Gifts.* Table B3, column 2, gives the numbers of estates including gifts inter vivos subject to estate duty (the final figure of table B2, column 2). These totals were only

TABLE B3. *Gifts inter vivos subject to Estate Duty in relation to the Value of Total Property subject to Estate Duty, Great Britain, 1961–8*

(1) Year ended 31st March	(2) No. of estates including gifts inter vivos subject to estate duty	(3) No. of estates including gifts inter vivos in categories subject to estate duty*	(4) Capital value of gifts inter vivos subject to estate duty† £000	(5) Net capital value of total property subject to estate duty £000	(6) Col. 4 as per cent of Col. 5	(7) Col. 6 as moving average with 3-year span
1961	N.A.	7,206	25,198	1,036,000	2·43	—
1962	N.A.	7,323	31,108	1,126,900	2·76	2·66
1963	N.A.	8,990	31,354	1,127,000	2·78	2·75
1964	N.A.	8,818	31,435	1,162,400	2·7	2·80
1965	6,976	9,957	34,510	1,183,100	2·92	2·91
1966	6,592	8,265	35,568	1,228,000	2·9	2·97
1967	7,063	9,096	39,976	1,288,400	3·1	3·01
1968	7,220	9,051	41,532	1,376,200	3·02	—

Source: N.A.=not available. * See explanatory note 2, p. 266. † See explanatory note 3, p 267.

included in the Inland Revenue tables of 'Estate duty: Analysis of gifts inter vivos' from 1965. However the tables 1961–64 (inclusive) do include the various categories of gift as in table B2: charities, within 1st and 2nd years before death, etc. To try to give some idea of trend over the full period 1961–68, table B3 column 3 records the totals of the 'number of cases' in each category. The meaning of these figures must be made clear. The 'number of cases' in the Inland Revenue estate duty statistics is the number of estates containing the particular type of property. Thus, if an estate contained gifts made in *each* of the five years preceding the death, it would count (under table B2) (i) as *one* case with gifts within the first and second years before death; (ii) as *one* case within 3rd and 4th years before death; (iii) as *one* case with gifts within the fifth year before death; (iv) as *one* in the total gifts inter vivos. The figures in table 3, column 3, therefore are neither the total number of gifts inter vivos subject to estate duty (which would be larger) nor the total of estates including gifts subject to estate duty (a smaller figure, recorded in table B3 column 2 when available). They are a summation of the number of estates, which include gifts subject to estate duty, falling within the various categories of table B2; an estate appears more than once when gifts falling into more than one category were made from the same estate.[1]

(3) *Capital Value of Gifts inter vivos subject to Estate Duty.* The figures in this column are the totals of the amounts of gifts listed by the Inland Revenue as in table B2 column 3. However, 'The amount of a graduated gift included . . . is the value as reduced for estate duty.' The 1960 Finance Act (amended for deaths after March 19, 1968 by the Finance Act 1968) provided that the value of a gift should be reduced for estate duty purposes by 15 per cent if the death took place in the third year after the gift; 30 per cent if the death took place in the fourth and 60 per cent if the death took place in the fifth year after the gift. The amounts of the gifts shown are thus the values for estate duty purposes, appropriately reduced where the death took place in the third, fourth or fifth years before death; for our purposes it would have been preferable to have had the full value of gifts subject to estate duty not the estate duty value. The published data do not enable us to gross up satisfactorily the value of gifts for estate duty purposes to the full value because gifts in the third and fourth year before death are combined (although the reduction

[1] I am indebted to Mr W. Gonzalez of the Statistics and Intelligence Division of the Inland Revenue for clarifying for me the meaning of these figures and for explaining the 'graduated gift' reduction (explanatory note 3.)

in valuation differs for each year) and there are also a number of cases in a 'not known' category. The figures in table B3 column 4 (and those used in the graph in chapter 3) thus under-estimate the value of gifts, but probably do not seriously affect the *trend*.

(4) *Changes in the Exemption Limit of Estate Duty* (referring to table B3, columns 4 and 5). At the time the statistics of gifts inter vivos subject to estate duty were compiled for the earlier period, 1898–1931, all estates over £100 were liable for estate duty. In 1946 the exemption limit was raised to £2,000 and by 1961, when statistics of gifts again became available, it had been raised to £3,000. During the period of our later statistics the exemption limit was further increased to £5,000: from 1964–68 inclusive it remains at £5,000. All our figures of gifts inter vivos relate to estates above the exemption limit and these are compared with the corresponding total of net capital value of total property subject to estate duty. Thus the figures for 1961 and 1962 refer to gifts from estates over £3,000 compared with the net capital value of estates over £3,000; the 1963 figures compare gifts from estates over £4,000 with the net capital value of estates over £4,000; and for the remaining years gifts from estates over £5,000 are compared with the net capital value of estates over £5,000.

Appendix C

Statistics of Land Ownership

POPULATION—OWNERS OF LAND 1873 (c. 1097)

The return was compiled on a county basis for England and Wales except London. It included the name of owner, address, acreage and estimated gross rental of estates of one acre and above, together with the county totals. The number of owners and total acreage of all estates below one acre and the amount of common and waste land in each county were also estimated.

The information was derived almost entirely from parish rating valuation lists and covers, therefore, all land at that time subject to rates; there are very few exclusions, e.g. crown property not let and churchyards.

Absolute accuracy is not claimed for the return. Parish lists were sometimes defective and out of date on the names of owners and the name of an agent or trustee may often have been inserted. The estimated extent of lands is also liable to inaccuracies of detail, but support for the general accuracy of the return is provided by a comparison with the total acreage in England and Wales given in a contemporary census report.[1]

Land Ownership in the Eastern Counties 1941. (University of Cambridge, Department of Agriculture, Farm Economics Branch, Report No. 30, 1948).

This report was based on the National Farm Survey carried out in 1941 for the Ministry of Agriculture by members of the War Agricultural Executive Committees. The National Farm Survey covered all agricultural holdings of five acres or more recorded in the agricultural census for 1941 (June). Ownership received little attention in the National Farm Survey; the Cambridge Agricultural Department obtained further information on ownership, allocated the acreage of each holding to its owner, and presented this information in convenient tabular form showing the number of owners and the total acreage for various sizes of estate in each of the ten adminis-

[1] Further details are provided in the Explanatory Statement prefacing the Return.

trative counties of Cambridge, Bedford, Essex, Hertford, Holland (Lincs.), Huntingdon, Norfolk, Soke of Peterborough, East and West Suffolk. Except West Suffolk (where the acreage of woods and waste land is included) the figures from this report cover agricultural area only, derived from holdings of five acres and above.

Whilst the general accuracy of the return cannot be doubted, certain war-time difficulties in collection and deficiencies in some of the census returns, have made for minor inaccuracies of detail.[1]

The Farms and Estates of Buckinghamshire, (Thomas and Elms, Faculty of Horticulture and Agriculture, University of Reading, 1938).

The figures of estate ownership in this county survey are compiled on exactly the same basis as the Cambridge survey, but cover a sample of 93·6 per cent instead of the whole of the agricultural area of the county.

COMPARISON OF ESTATE SIZES FROM THE VARIOUS SOURCES

Tables C2–C7 show comparisons in land ownership in 1873 and 1941 for each of the six geographical[2] counties covered by *Land Ownership in the Eastern Counties*. The 1941 figures are taken directly from the tables in the Appendix of the Eastern Counties Report (except for Suffolk, where the figures for the administrative counties of East and West Suffolk have been aggregated to obtain those for the geographical county). The 1873 figures have been compiled in categories corresponding to those for 1941. Except for Huntingdon (where estates of all sizes are compared) the comparison has been limited to estates over 1,000 acres. In table C8 the results for four eastern counties are combined.[3] Table C9 compares the figures drawn from the Buckinghamshire survey of 1936 with the 1873 data compiled in similar categories.

[1] See *Land Ownership in the Eastern Counties 1941*, pp. 4–6.

[2] Since the 1873 return was compiled for geographical counties, only where the 1941 data (which was compiled for administrative counties) covers a geographical county, is comparison possible. Thus comparisons can be made for the six Eastern counties of Huntingdon, Bedfordshire, Essex, Hertfordshire, Norfolk and Suffolk.

[3] Bedfordshire, Huntingdon, Norfolk and Suffolk. These four have been chosen because in each case the margin of error—i.e. the difference in the extent of estates of one acre and above in 1873 and 1941 respectively—is less than twenty per cent. With the remaining two Eastern counties the margin is considerably larger.

The 1873 return covers practically all land of whatever description, including urban and forest; the 1936 and 1941 surveys cover not quite all *agricultural* land and thus exclude urban, forest, and some agricultural land. Thus the total extent of land covered by the 1873 return is larger than that of 1941 and 1936 for each county. This 'excess acreage' can be conveniently thought of as the margin of error. In an attempt to clarify and define limits to the extent of the changes in large estates (defined as (*a*) estates over 1,000 acres and (*b*) estates over 2,000 acres) we distribute the excess acreage in each county over the estate sizes for the later year of the comparison on the basis of three assumptions:

(i) that the whole of the excess in acreage (for estates of one acre and above) of 1873 over 1941 consisted in 1941[1] of private estates over 2,000 acres;
(ii) that the whole of the excess in acreage (for estates of one acre and above) of 1873 over 1941 consisted in 1941 of estates below 1,000 acres;
(iii) that the excess in acreage (for estates of one acre and above) of 1873 over 1941 consisted in 1941 of estates of all sizes and categories in exactly the same proportion as the estates already analysed for that year.

Both assumptions (i) and (ii) are completely unrealistic, but represent extremes between which the exact figure—if it were obtainable—would almost certainly lie.[2] Assumption (ii) probably would not be far out but for the presence of forest land, which is likely to be grouped in large estates. Assumption (iii) probably gives the nearest approach to the truth, but there is no reason to believe that the assumption exactly corresponds with the reality.

For Buckinghamshire, Hertfordshire and Essex, where for each the margin of error is over 28 per cent, it is not surprising that assumption (i) gives a negative decline in large estates. But in the other counties with the smaller error margin, the extent of large

1 For Buckinghamshire substitute 1936 for 1941 throughout the statement of assumptions and analysis.

2 Strictly speaking assumption (i) does not give the minimum *conceivable* figure. This can be obtained by assuming that all the excess acreage consisted, in 1941, of land belonging to existing estates just below 1,000 acres in size. The addition of the excess acreage to these estates would then bring not only the extent of the excess, but also a large acreage from estates previously classified as under 1,000 acres, into the category of large estates. Such a possibility can be ignored in practice, and there can be no doubt that the true figure of the decline in large estates lies between the limits prescribed on the basis of assumptions (i) and (ii).

estates can be shown to have declined even on this most unrealistic assumption.

The figures of commons and waste and the total acreage of land in holdings of less than one acre, given in the 1873 return, are noted with each table, but ignored in the comparison. Similar categories are not included in the later figures (except partly in the case of West Suffolk[1]) but in any case the combined extent is very small and for no county in 1873 is it above 2 per cent of total acreage. Thus, even if the extent of waste, etc., had declined 100 per cent by the later year, it would have no appreciable effect on the general comparison.

By adding the excess acreage of 1873 over 1941 to the figures of 1941, we can measure changes in the sizes of *all* landed estates. Although appreciable changes in the extent of all large landed estates can be safely taken as an indication of changes in large agricultural estates, because the latter form an overwhelming proportion of all large estates, nevertheless, this is not an ideal basis for assessing changes in the ownership of *agricultural* land. A comparison of agricultural land plus forest land, in each period, would probably be ideal, but such a comparison is not possible with present data. However we could have adopted the alternative procedure of *deducting* the excess acreage from the figures of 1873. This might, perhaps, be expected to give a better indication of the changes in the ownership of agricultural land alone (excluding forest land). Nevertheless such a comparison would be far from exact; the 1941 return omitted agricultural acreage farmed in holdings of under five acres. More important, there may have been considerable differences in the extent of agricultural acreage in the two periods. It does not follow, because the excess of 1873 over 1941 represented roughly the extent of urban and forest land in 1941, that forest and urban land was even approximately of the same extent in 1873. Thus this alternative method offers no significant advantage over that adopted for measuring changes in the ownership of agricultural land. In fact, whether the excess acreage is deducted from that of 1873 on the basis of certain assumptions, or added to that of 1941 on the basis of similar limiting assumptions, little difference is made to the result. Thus, suppose the excess acreage be *deducted* from the figures of 1873 utilizing the following assumptions:

(i) that the excess consisted, in 1873, of large private estates over 2,000 acres;

[1] See above, p. 271.

(ii) that the excess consisted, in 1873, of small estates under 1,000 acres;

(iii) that the excess consisted, in 1873, of all sizes and categories of estates in the same proportion as the existing distribution of estates in 1873.

Then assumptions (ii) and (iii) would give exactly the same percentage decline in large estates as that given by assumptions (ii) and (iii) used in the tables. Assumption (i) would give a slightly different minimum[1] figure of the decline in large estates.

The figures of the decline in large estates on the basis of the assumptions appropriate to *deducting* the excess, have been calculated (table C1) from the combined table of the four eastern counties. A comparison of the alternative methods gives the following results:

TABLE C.1. *Percentage Decline in the Extent of large Estates 1873 and 1941 (Bedfordshire, Huntingdon, Norfolk and Suffolk combined)*

Adding the excess acreage to 1941. Assumptions	Deducting the excess acreage from 1873. Assumptions	Over 1,000 acres	Over 2,000 acres	Private over 2,000 acres
(i) above		8·0	5·4	17·4
	(i) above	11·0	8·2	26·5
(ii) above		35·0	39·0	51·8
	(ii) above	35·0	39·0	51·8
(iii) above		23·6	28·1	43·3
	(iii) above	23·6	28·1	43·3

The data for the Eastern Counties enables us to distinguish between public and private estates[1] over 2,000 acres and thus to assess relative changes in large public and private estates. But several qualifications should be noted:

(i) Church land: in 1941 church estates include glebe land which is aggregated with other properties held by the Ecclesiastical

[1] In similar manner to that pointed out in footnote (2) p. 272, assumption (i) immediately above would not provide the minimum *conceivable* figure because of the possibility of the excess acreage all belonging to estates just over 2,000 (or 1,000) acres in 1873, in such a way that its subtraction reduced the total acreage of large estates by more than the extent of the excess itself.

[2] The term 'private' covers not only estates of individuals, but also partnerships and estates in the hands of executors or trustees of private individuals.

Commissioners; in 1873 glebe land is not combined with the holdings of the Ecclesiastical Commissioners and no useful purpose would be served by attempting to aggregate it as the report warns that the name of the person managing glebe land must often have been inserted as the owner. As a result of these different procedures, our figures will under-estimate somewhat the decline in total large estates and exaggerate the increase in land held by public bodies in 1941. Figures of the decline in large private estates are unaffected.

(ii) Land held for charitable purposes: in 1941 parishes have been treated as the owners of the land under their jurisdiction held for charitable purposes; in 1873 such land was allocated to the ownership of the Charity Commissioners. This difference in procedure will have nil or negligible results on our comparisons of changes in large estates in each county.

(iii) In the Eastern Counties Report of 1941, some of the figures of the amount of land held in large estates are given only as a percentage of total land area. Working back from the percentages to obtain the acreage involves small errors of approximation. (The maximum *possible* error on this account for any one county is 516 acres in Norfolk.) The differences are most unlikely to affect our figures of decline in large estates by more than 0·1 per cent if they affect them at all. All figures liable to this error of approximation are put in brackets in the following tables.

TABLE C2. *Huntingdon, 1873 and 1941. Estates over one acre*

Estate size (acres)	Owners 1873			Owners 1941		
	No.	Acreage	Acreage as % of total	No.	Acreage	Acreage as % of total
1– 5	734	2,044	0·9	292	990	0·5
6– 20	596	6,560	2·9	481	5,408	2·7
21– 50	281	9,362	4·2	258	8,354	4·2
51– 100	146	10,181	4·5	156	11,419	5·7
101– 150	75	9,162	4·1	88	10,918	5·5
151– 300	134	29,145	13·0	123	26,775	13·4
301– 500	48	18,204	8·1	65	24,382	12·2
501– 700	25	14,660	6·5	21	12,897	6·4
701–1,000	14	12,169	5·4	14	11,470	5·7
1,001–2,000	15	20,998	9·3	15	20,275	10·1
2,001–3,000	5	11,760	5·2	1	2,365	1·2
3,001–4,000	8	27,198	12·1	5	17,515	8·8
4,001–5,000	—	—	—	2	9,496	4·7
5,001–6,000	3	16,707	7·4	—	—	—
Over 6,000	3	36,608	16·3	4	37,814	18·9
Total over 1,000	34	113,271	50·4	27	87,465	43·7
Total over 2,000	19	92,273	41·0	12	67,190	33·6
Total of estates of 1 acre and above	2,087	224,759	100·0	1,525	200,078	100·0
Private estates over 2,000	18	88,713	39·5	N.A.	(42,216)	21·1
Other estates over 2,000	1	3,560	1·6	N.A.	(24,974)	(12·5)

N.A.=not available

Huntingdon, 1873 and 1941. Estates over 1,000 acres

From 1873 Return
Owners of estates of
1 acre and above

Number = 2,087 Extent = 224,764 acres*
Owners less than 1 acre
Number = 1,816 Extent = 399 acres
Estimated waste etc. = 796 acres

Difference in extent between
totals of 1 acre and
upwards 1873 and 1941

1) Absolute = 24,681 acres
2) Relative (i.e. percentage excess of 1873 over 1941) = 12·34%

Percentage Decline in Extent of large Estates, 1873–1941

Assumption	Estates over 1,000 acres	Estates over 2,000 acres	Private Estates over 2,000 acres
(i) Above	1·0	0·4	24·6
(ii) ,,	22·8	27·1	52·5
(iii) ,,	13·3	18·1	46·5

* The discrepancy of 5 acres between the total extent of estates of one acre and above recorded in the 1873 return and that derived from adding the acreage of estates in each size category is an error of printing or approximation.

Restatement of the Assumptions Utilized in Tables C2–C9 to show the percentage Decline in the Extent of large Estates, 1873 and 1941

(i) That the whole of the excess in acreage (for estates of one acre and above) of 1873 over 1941 consisted in 1941[1] of private estates over 2,000 acres.

(ii) That the whole of the excess in acreage (for estates of one acre and above) of 1873 over 1941 consisted in 1941 of estates below 1,000 acres.

(iii) That the whole of the excess in acreage (for estates of one acre and above) of 1873 over 1941 consisted in 1941 of estates of all sizes and categories in exactly the same proportion as the estates already analysed for that year.

[1] For Buckinghamshire substitute 1936 for 1941 throughout.

TABLE C3. *Bedfordshire, 1873 and 1941. Estates over 1,000 acres*

Estate size (acres)	Owners 1873			Owners 1941		
	No.	Acreage	Acreage as of % total	No.	Acreage	Acreage as % of total
1,001–2,000	22	30,686	10·7	27	36,927	15·1
2,001–3,000	13	32,170	11·3	3	8,309	3·4
3,001–4,000	2	6,438	2·3	3	10,541	4·3
4,001–5,000	3	13,863	4·9	1	4,085	1·7
5,001–6,000	—	—	—	1	5,055	2·1
Over 6,000	6	78,011	27·3	3	33,935	13·9
Total over 1,000	46	161,168	56·5	38	98,852	40·5
Total over 2,000	24	130,482	45·7	11	61,925	25·4
Total of estates of 1 acre and above	2,382	285,251	100·0	1961	244,099	100·0
Private estates over 2,000	23	127,488	44·7	N.A.	(37,591)	15·4
Other estates over 2,000	1	2,994	1·0	N.A.	(24,334)	(10·0)

From 1873 Return:
Owners less than 1 acre:
Number = 5,302 Extent = 825 acres
Estimated waste etc. = 1,127 acres

Difference in extent between totals of 1 acre and upwards 1873 and 1941

1) Absolute = 41,152 acres
2) Relative (i.e. percentage excess of 1873 over 1941) = 16·9%

N.A. = not available

Percentage Decline in Extent of large Estates, 1873–1941

Assumption	Estates over 1,000 acres	Estates over 2,000 acres	Private estates over 2,000 acres
(i) Above	13·1	21·0	38·3
(ii) ,,	38·7	52·5	70·6
(iii) ,,	28·3	44·4	65·5

TABLE C4. *Essex, 1873 and 1941. Estates over 1,000 acres*

Estate size (acres)	Owners 1873			Owners 1941		
	No.	Acreage	Acreage as % of total	No.	Acreage	Acreage as % of total
1,001–2,000	103	143,310	15·1	58	79,574	10·8
2,001–3,000	29	69,843	7·4	16	38,771	5·3
3,001–4,000	20	67,795	7·2	7	24,689	3·3
4,001–5,000	6	26,428	2·8	1	4,409	0·6
5,001–6,000	4	21,525	2·3	2	10,176	1·4
Over 6,000	11	96,244	10·2	6	51,207	7·0
Total over 1,000	173	425,145	44·9	90	208,826	28·4
Total over 2,000	70	281,835	29·8	32	129,252	17·6
Total of estates of 1 acre and above	7,472	946,401	100·0	5471	735,687	100·0
Private estates over 2,000	63	250,881	26·5	N.A.	(82,397)	11·2
Other estates over 2,000	7	30,954	3·3	N.A.	(46,855)	(6·4)

From 1873 Return:
Owners less than 1 acre:

Number = 14,833 Extent = 4,033 acres
Estimated waste etc. = 6,896 acres

N.A. = not available

Difference in extent between totals of 1 acre and upwards 1873 and 1941
1) Absolute = 210,714 acres
2) Relative (i.e. percentage excess of 1873 over 1941) = 28·6%

Percentage Decline in Extent of large Estates, 1873–1941

Assumption	Estates over 1,000 acres	Estates over 2,000 acres	Private estates over 2,000 acres
(i) Above	1·3	−20·6	−16·8
(ii) ,,	50·9	54·1	67·1
(iii) ,,	36·7	40·9	57·7

TABLE C5. *Hertfordshire, 1873 and 1941. Estates over 1,000 acres*

Estate size (acres)	Owners 1873			Owners 1941		
	No.	Acreage	Acreage as % of total	No.	Acreage	Acreage as % of total
1,001–2,000	50	70,347	18·4	35	47,823	16·5
2,001–3,000	18	44,413	11·6	12	28,655	9·9
3,001–4,000	5	19,005	5·0	5	16,986	5·8
4,001–5,000	1	4,863	1·3	1	4,201	1·4
5,001–6,000	—	—	—	1	5,655	2·0
Over 6,000	8	70,717	18·5	5	32,295	11·1
Total over 1,000	82	209,345	54·7	59	135,615	46·7
Total over 2,000	32	138,998	36·3	24	87,792	30·2
Total of estates of 1 acre and above	2,831	382,470	100·0	1876	290,413	100·0
Private estates over 2,000	32	138,998	36·3	N.A.	(51,403)	17·7
Other estates over 2,000	Nil	Nil	—	N.A.	(36,389)	(12·6)

From 1873 Return
Owners less than 1 acre

Number = 9,556 Extent = 2,339 acres
Estimated waste etc. = 5,302 acres

N.A. = not available

Difference in extent between totals of 1 acre and upwards 1873 and 1941
1) Absolute = 92,057 acres
2) Relative (i.e. percentage excess of 1873 over 1941) = 31·7%

Percentage Decline in Extent of large Estates, 1873–1941

Assumption	Estates over 1,000 acres	Estates over 2,000 acres	Private estates over 2,000 acres
(i) Above	−8·7	−29·4	−3·2
(ii) ,,	35·2	36·8	63·0
(iii) ,,	14·6	16·8	51·2

TABLE C6. *Norfolk, 1873 and 1941. Estates over 1,000 acres*

Estate size (acres)	Owners 1873			Owners 1941		
	No.	Acreage	Acreage as % of total	No.	Acreage	Acreage as % of total
1,001–2,000	110	149,842	12·2	81	114,013	11·0
2,001–3,000	43	107,222	8·7	34	86,597	8·4
3,001–4,000	19	66,614	5·4	16	55,441	5·4
4,001–5,000	13	57,059	4·6	10	44,887	4·3
5,001–6,000	7	36,778	3·0	—	—	—
Over 6,000	30	315,738	25·6	17	186,348	18·1
Total over 1,000	222	733,253	59·5	158	487,286	47·2
Total over 2,000	112	583,411	47·3	77	373,273	36·2
Total of estates of 1 acre and above	10,096	1,232,415	100·0	7,418	1,031,996	100·0
Private estates over 2,000	107	563,760	45·7	N.A.	(286,895)	27·8
Other estates over 2,000	5	19,651	1·6	N.A.	(86,378)	(8·4)

From 1873 Return
Owners less than 1 acre

Number = 16,552 Extent = 2,468 acres
Estimated waste etc. = 12,870 acres

Difference in extent between totals of 1 acre and upwards 1873 and 1941
1) Absolute = 200,419 acres
2) Relative (i.e. percentage excess of 1873 over 1941) = 19·4%

Percentage Decline in Extent of large Estates, 1873–1941

Assumption	Estates over 1,000 acres	Estates over 2,000 acres	Private Estates over 2,000 acres
(i) Above	6·2	1·7	13·6
(ii) ,,	33·5	36·0	49·1
(iii) ,,	20·7	23·5	39·2

TABLE C7. *Suffolk, 1873 and 1941. Estates over 1,000 acres*

Estate size (acres)	Owners 1873			Owners 1941		
	No.	Acreage	Acreage as % of total	No.	Acreage	Acreage as % of total
1,001–2,000	63	87,664	9·6	49	63,994	8·3
2,001–3,000	35	87,209	9·6	22	53,679	6·9
3,001–4,000	10	34,506	3·8	10	34,567	4·5
4,001–5,000	4	18,325	2·0	4	17,582	2·3
5,001–6,000	4	22,407	2·5	3	16,287	2·1
Over 6,000	21	224,804	24·7	11	103,702	13·4
Total over 1,000	137	474,915	52·2	99	289,811	37·4
Total over 2,000	74	387,251	42·6	50	225,817	29·1
Total of estates of 1 acre and above	6,765	908,764	100·0	5,130	774,573	100·0
Private estates over 2,000	72	382,406	42·1	N.A.	(193,252)	(24·9)
Other estates over 2,000	2	4,845	0·5	N.A.	(32,565)	(4·2)

From 1873 Return
Owners less than 1 acre

Number = 12,511 Extent = 3,673 acres
Estimated waste etc. = 7,831 acres

N.A. = not available

Difference in extent between totals of 1 acre and upwards 1873 and 1941

1) Absolute = 134,191 acres
2) Relative (i.e. percentage excess of 1873 over 1941) = 17·3%

Percentage Decline in Extent of large Estates, 1873–1941

Assumption	Estates over 1,000 acres	Estates over 1,000 acres	Private estates over 2,000 acres
(i) Above	10·7	7·0	14·4
(ii) ,,	39·0	41·7	49·5
(iii) ,,	28·4	31·7	40·8

TABLE C8. *Bedfordshire, Huntingdon, Norfolk and Suffolk combined,* 1873 and 1941 Estates over 1,000 acres*

County	Extent of estates in acres, 1873				Extent of estates in acres, 1941			
	of 1 acre and above	over 1,000	over 2,000	private over 2,000	of 1 acre and above	over 1,000	over 2,000	private over 2,000
Bedford	285,251	161,168	130,482	127,488	244,099	98,852	61,925	37,591
Huntingdon	224,759	113,271	92,273	88,713	200,078	87,465	67,190	42,216
Norfolk	1,232,415	733,253	583,411	563,760	1,031,996	487,286	373,273	286,895
Suffolk	908,764	474,915	387,251	382,406	774,573	289,811	225,817	193,252
Total	2,651,189	1,482,607	1,193,417	1,162,367	2,250,746	963,414	728,205	559,954

Difference in extent between the totals of estates of one acre and above for the four counties combined in 1873 and 1941 respectively:

(1) Absolute=400,443 acres

(2) Relative (i.e. percentage excess of 1873 over 1941)=17·8%

Percentage Decline in Extent of large estates (four counties combined) 1873 and 1941

Assumption	Estates over 1,000 acres	Estates over 2,000 acres	Private Estates over 2,000 acres
(i) Above	8·0	5·4	17·4
(ii) ,,	35·0	39·0	51·8
(iii) ,,	23·6	28·1	43·3

* These are the four counties in which the percentage differences between the total of one acre and above in 1873 and 1941 respectively, are least. In each case the difference is below 20%.

TABLE C9. *Buckingham, 1873 and 1936. Estates over one acre.*

Estate size (acres)	Owners 1873			Owners 1936		
	No.	Acreage	Acreage as % of total	No.	Acreage	Acreage as % of total
1– 5*	1,049	2,559	0·6	438	1,341	0·4
5– 20	776	8,225	1·8	485	5,577	1·6
20– 50	483	15,717	3·5	354	12,416	3·6
50– 100	328	23,761	5·2	328	24,553	7·1
100– 150	185	22,629	5·0	224	27,903	8·1
150– 300	206	43,892	9·6	301	64,494	18·7
300– 500	93	35,659	7·8	87	34,066	9·9
500– 700	46	27,439	6·0	27	15,593	4·5
700–1,000	35	29,759	6·5	21	17,615	5·1
1,000–2,000	39	52,510	11·5	29	41,024	11·9
2,000–3,000	23	53,229	11·7	13	32,011	9·3
3,000–4,000	10	32,588	7·1	5	16,303	4·7
4,000–5,000	4	18,023	4·0	5	22,925	6·6
5,000–6,000	4	21,424	4·7	2	10,981	3·2
Over 6,000	7	67,635	14·9	2	18,288	5·3
Total over 1,000	87	245,408	53·9	56	141,532	41·0
Total over 2,000	48	192,899	42·4	27	100,508	29·1
Total of estates of 1 acre and above	3,288	455,047	100·0	2,321	345,090	100·0

* 1 to 5 acres represents 1 acre and up to but not including 5 acres—and correspondingly. This is the basis on which the 1873 figures have been compiled for this table and is presumed to be the basis of the Buckinghamshire Survey.

From 1873 Return
Owners of estates of
1 acre and above

Number = 3,288 Extent = 455,056 acres*
Owners less than 1 acre
Number = 6,420 Extent = 1,153 acres
Estimated waste etc. = 2,942 acres

Difference in extent between
totals of 1 acre and
upwards 1873 and 1936

1) Absolute = 109,957 acres
2) Relative (i.e. percentage excess of 1873 over 1936) = 32·8%

* The discrepancy of 9 acres between the total extent of estates of one acre and above recorded in the 1873 return and that derived from adding the acreage of estates in each size category is an error of printing or approximation.

Percentage Decline in Extent of large Estates, 1873–1936

Assumption	Estates over 1,000 acres	Estates over 2,000 acres
(i) Above	—2·5	—9·1
(ii) ,,	42·4	47·9
(iii) ,,	23·9	31·4

STATISTICS OF OCCUPYING OWNERSHIP

Statistics of acreage owned by occupiers were collected for many years before the first World War in *Agricultural Statistics*. The following table shows the proportions of acreage owned by occupiers as quinquennial averages from 1890 to 1909 with 1910 and 1911 expressed as single years.[1]

TABLE C10. *Proportion of Acreage owned by Occupiers, 1890–1911*

	1890–1894	1895–1899	1900–1904	1905–1909	1910	1911
England	15·16	14·68	13·47	12·59	12·41	12·14
Wales	11·68	11·29	10·38	10·30	10·32	9·97
Scotland	12·58	12·48	12·49	12·25	11·92	11·76
G.B.	14·47	14·05	13·05	12·34	12·16	11·89

These figures show little variation except for a slight downward tendency, 1890–1912. However, this may be misleading in two respects.[2] First, owner-occupation can cover 'farms in hand'—where landlords themselves farm the land in default of a suitable tenant; this happened a lot in the severe agricultural depressions of the 1870s; as conditions improved it became possible to let the land—which would appear in the statistics as a decline in owner-occupancy. Second, there is evidence from reports of land agents all over the

1 *Agricultural Statistics*, 1911, Cmd. 6021, p. 10.

2 S. G. Sturmey, 'Owner Farming in England and Wales', 1900-1950, *Manchester School*, vol. XXIII, No. 3, September 1955.

country of an increase in owner-occupancy from 1909, mainly taking the form of purchases by tenants of estates put on the market. This increased owner-occupancy does not appear in the statistics, partly because of their general deficiencies (revealed in the consideration of post-war statistics, below) but also, Professor Sturmey suggests, because of a concealment of the fact of land ownership arising from the political campaign against land owners which characterized those years.

From and including 1912 the figures of occupying ownership published in *Agricultural Statistics* covered England and Wales only, the collection and publication of agricultural returns for Scotland being undertaken by the Board of Agriculture for Scotland.

The figures of occupying ownership for England and Wales 1912–1924 (with a break for war years) compiled from the annual *Agricultural Statistics* are set out in table C11.

TABLE C11

Year	Percentage of acreage owned	Percentage of holdings owned or mainly owned
1912	10·87	11·69
1913	10·65	11·19
1914	10·92	11·31
1919	12·32	11·68
1920	15·5	13·7
1921	20·0	16·8
1922	17·8	15·1
1923	24·2	21·4
1924	25·4	23·0

Unfortunately these figures are of very doubtful accuracy. They are based on the answers of farmers to a postal schedule. In the light of the significant changes which were taking place in the years immediately after the 1914–18 war, a detailed examination of the returns was carried out, and 'The examination showed a number of cases where the statements made by the same persons in respect of the same holdings were such as to give rise to doubt as to their accuracy, while in about one-third of the whole of the returns the question was unanswered.'[1] The report continues, 'In the majority of cases, where an occupier does not claim to be the owner, it is reasonable to assume that he is the tenant, but this is not, of course, necessarily the case. On the whole it was obvious that a considerable

[1] *Agricultural Statistics,* Pt.I, p. 13, 1924.

margin of error existed, and it is possible that the number of holdings owned or partly owned is larger than is shown.'

In *Agricultural Statistics*, 1925, no information on owner-occupancy was given. In 1926, although the returns were still unsatisfactory the acreage returned actually as owned was appreciably larger than before and *Agricultural Statistics*, 1926, concluded: 'Apparently at least 28 per cent of the total acreage of crops and grass in England and Wales is farmed by the owners of the land.' In the following year a particular effort was made to collect accurate returns on owner-occupancy: the conclusions, together with the comments in *Agricultural Statistics*, 1927, are of interest:

> 'For various reasons many occupiers have been reluctant to comply with the requirement to state whether they owned their holdings. Some occupiers apparently regard the schedule as having some connection with rating assessments. In other cases the existence of a mortgage gives rise to doubt in the occupier's mind as to whether he should describe himself as the owner. In a large number of schedules the question whether the occupier owns the holding has been left unanswered apparently on the assumption that no answer need be given unless it is in the affirmative.
>
> 'In connection with the returns of 1927, however, a closer effort was made to obtain more complete and reliable data in regard to ownership. Not only were the special instructions issued with each schedule with regard to the question, but the Ministry's Crop Reporters were requested to make the necessary further investigation in all cases where the information required was not given. In consequence about 99 per cent of the schedules were completed in this respect. The returns show that the acreage returned as in the ownership of occupiers in 1927 was . . . . over *36* per cent of the total land under crops and grass, the number of holdings owned being . . . *36·6* per cent of the total.'[1]

After 1927 data on owner-occupation were discontinued in *Agricultural Statistics*; reliable information on the subject is lacking until 1941. For that year it appears[2] that approximately *35* per cent of farmers could be classed as owners[3] or mainly owners and *33* per cent

[1] *Agricultural Statistics*, 1927, pp. 28-29.

[2] *National Farm Survey of England and Wales. A Summary Report*. 1946, pp. 18-21.

[3] 31·4 per cent of farmers owned 75 per cent or more of the land they occupied; 6·5 per cent both owned and rented between 25 per cent and 75 per cent of the land they occupied.

of the area of crops and grass in England and Wales was owned by occupiers. The report warns that a comparison between the figures for 1941 and those for 1927 cannot be regarded as a conclusive indication of a slight reaction against owner-occupancy, 'Because the Farm Survey figures refer to complete returns for holdings of 5 acres and above, while the 1927 figures are estimates based on incomplete returns from all holdings of 1 acre and above'.[1] This is, however, misleading comment, for although the 1941 Survey covered all holdings, the analysis was based on a 14 per cent sample.

Later figures of owner-occupancy derive from statistics collected as a result of the World Censuses of Agriculture, 1950 and 1960. After the second World War the Food and Agricultural Organization of UNO took over the responsibilities of the International Institute of Agriculture and proceeded with plans for decennial world censuses of agriculture to determine both the quantity of agricultural produce and the structural characteristics of agriculture in each country.

In so far as the information sought by FAO was supplementary to that collected from the normal agricultural censuses in England and Wales (and this applied to the questions of tenure) it was obtained by postal questionnaires sent to the majority of occupiers of holdings of over one acre; the remainder of occupiers, a stratified sample, were interviewed by Field Officers of the Ministry of Agriculture. Discounting some small and statistically insignificant holdings, the usable response rate on the postal questionnaire was 82 per cent whilst nearly 100 per cent of the stratified sample were in fact interviewed. The numbers and acreage of holdings owned and rented, taken from the census (published as a Supplement to *Agricultural Statistics, 1962–63, England and Wales*, Ministry of Agriculture, Fisheries and Food, HMSO 1965) are reproduced below.

[1] *Ibid.*, p. 20.

T

TABLE C12. *Numbers of Agricultural Holdings which were wholly owned, wholly rented or part-owned, part-rented, 1950*

Form of tenure	Size of holding (acres of crops and grass and rough grazing)											
	Under 5 acres		5–49¾		50–249¾		250–499¾		500 and over		Totals	
	'000	%	'000	%	'000	%	'000	%	'000	%	'000	%
Owned	40·9	53	58·6	38	33·3	27	4·6	25	1·3	24	138·7	36
Rented	32·7	42	70·9	46	68·3	55	10·3	56	2·8	52	185·0	49
Part-owned and part-rented	4·3	5	25·3	16	21·9	18	3·5	19	1·3	24	56·3	15
Total	77·9	100	154·8	100	123·5	100	18·4	100	5·4	100	380·0	100

TABLE C13. *Acreage of Agricultural Holdings which were wholly owned, wholly rented or part-owned, part-rented, 1950*

Form of tenure	Size of holding (acres of crops and grass and rough grazing)											
	Under 5 acres		5–49¾		50–249¾		250–499¾		500 and over		Totals	
	'000 acres	%	'000 acres	%	'000 acres	%	'000 acres	%	'000 acres	%	'000 acres	%
Owned	110·7	52	1,028·6	33	3,785·7	27	1,522·8	25	1,268·5	27	7,716·3	27
Rented	88·6	42	1,472·2	48	7,963·3	56	3,456·1	56	2,419·1	51	15,399·3	54
Part-owned	6·8	3	302·6	10	1,472·8	10	709·0	11	602·2	13	3,093·4	11
and Part-rented	6·6	3	265·0	9	1,026·1	7	467·8	8	439·3	9	2,204·8	8
Total	212·7	100	3,068·4	100	14,247·9	100	6,155·7	100	4,729·1	100	28,413·8	100

TABLE C14. *Numbers of Agricultural Holdings which were wholly owned, wholly rented or part-owned, part-rented, 1960–1*

Form of tenure	Size of holding (total area)										Totals	
	Under 5 acres		5–49¾		50–249¾		250–499¾		500 and over			
	'000	%	'000	%	'000	%	'000	%	'000	%	'000	%
Owned	37·2	65	66·5	50	45·2	39	6·7	36	2·0	32	157·6	47
Rented	17·6	31	46·4	35	48·6	41	8·6	44	2·6	41	123·7	37
Part-owned and part-rented	2·2	22	20·1	15	23·3	20	4·5	23	1·7	27	51·8	16
Total	57·0	100	133·0	100	117·1	100	19·7	100	6·4	100	333·2	100

TABLE C15. *Acreage of Agricultural Holdings which were wholly owned, wholly rented or part-owned, part-rented, 1960–1*

Form of tenure	Size of holding (total area)										Totals	
	Under 5 acres		5–49¾		50–249¾		250–499¾		500 and over			
	'000 acres	%	'000 acres	%	'000 acres	%	'000 acres	%	'000 acres	%	'000 acres	%
Owned	102·4	65	1,231·6	45	5,176·2	38	2,208·9	34	1,764·7	31	10,483·7	37
Rented	48·8	31	998·3	37	5,662·3	42	2,844·4	43	2,309·6	42	11,863·3	42
Part-owned	3·4	2	258·0	10	1,595·3	12	865·4	13	825·6	15	3,547·7	12
and part-rented	3·5	2	219·9	8	1,093·3	8	636·5	10	683·8	12	2,637·0	9
Total	158·1	100	2,707·7	100	13,527·1	100	6,555·2	100	5,583·8	100	28,531·9	100

Source of tables C12–C15: *Agricultural Statistics 1962–63*, tables 133–136.

Appendix D

A Calculation on the Growth of Action in Anticipation of Estate Duty by Private Businesses between 1922 and 1948

HYPOTHESIS

The Inland Revenue investigation for the Colwyn Committee[1] applied 1922 tax rates to a sample of estates of £10,000 and over liable to death duties in 1922 and examined the relationship between estate duty and non-trade assets for those estates with trade assets over £1,000. The Inland Revenue investigation of 1951[2] applied 1951 tax rates to a sample of estates of £10,000 and over liable to death duties in 1948 and also examined the relationship between estate duty and non-trade assets for estates over £1,000. To make possible a comparison between the two years, the 1951 investigators adopted the 1922 definitions for one set of calculations of non-trade assets by which all debts were charged against non-trade assets.

In 1922 little anticipatory action by private business against death duties would have been necessary because of the comparatively low rates of duty then applicable. We might therefore expect to obtain an indication of the growth of anticipatory action between 1922 and 1951 by applying 1951 tax rates to the 1922 estates and comparing with 1951 tax rates applied to 1948 estates. If there had been no increase in anticipatory action between the two dates, in view of the price rise and the increase in income tax, profits tax and surtax, we should have expected that the application of 1951 estate duty rates to 1922 estates would have shown a smaller proportion of cases in which non-trade assets exceeded estate duty liability than the application of 1951 estate duty rates to 1948 estates. In fact the opposite is true (see p. 114). Hence the suggestion that there has been a growth in anticipatory action. The purpose of this appendix is to make clear the limitations of the hypothesis and to indicate the method of making the comparison.

[1] Appendix 20, *Report of the Committee on National Debt and Taxation*, Cmd. 2800, 1927.

[2] *Estate Duty and The Family Business*, Cmd. 8295, 1951.

LIMITATIONS

Just as we have already indicated that we should expect the effects of inflation and of increases in other taxes to raise the proportion of the 1948 estates in which estate duty exceeded non-trade assets compared with 1922, so there may have been factors between 1922 and 1948 which worked in the opposite direction; in particular changes in the size structure or the pattern of ownership of private businesses or asset holding, quite unconnected with estate duty, which could have reduced the proportion of estates in which non-trade assets exceeded estate duty liability in 1948. We do not know whether this has happened and cannot readily test. We must therefore simply acknowledge that this possibility *could* invalidate our conclusion.

METHOD OF COMPARISON

The 1951 report published the figures of 1951 tax rates applied to 1948 estates; the difficulties lie in applying 1951 tax rates to 1922 estates to make the desired comparison.

In the 1922 data estates were arranged in value groups and classified according to the multiple that the non-trade assets bore to estate duty liability at 1922 rates in a series of divisions—thus, 'up to 1', '1·1 to 2', '2·1 to 3' and so on to 'over ten'. In order to obtain data in similar form for 1951 tax rates, the proportional increases of 1951 over 1922 rates have been calculated for each of these value ranges. But as each estate value range in the 1922 analysis was wider than the estate duty ranges of a particular tax band, and the percentage increases in tax were not the same for each band, the maximum and minimum increases in estate duty rates have been extracted and an average increase in rate calculated on the basis of equal weight for all estate values within each range. For the estate value range £500,000 and over a maximum capital value of estate of £2,250,000 has been assumed.

The figures of estate duty for 1951 (maximum, minimum and average) expressed as multiples of the estate duty rates of 1922 have then been applied to the 1922 estates in each division ('up to 1', '1·1 to 2', etc.). Thus, supposing estate duty rates had doubled between 1922 and 1951, then if there were 6 estates in the '4·1 to 5' range, all these estates would fall within a '2·1 to 3' range for 1951. It has been assumed that the numbers of estates within a division are evenly spaced so that, if estates from a division at 1922 rates do not fall into one division when 1951 rates are applied, they can be easily allocated between divisions. This assumption is not unreasonable in that the distribution of estates *between* divisions in 1922 is fairly regular and does nothing to suggest marked irregularity *within* a division.

The figures in each division based on the maximum and minimum tax increases can be thought of as the probable limits, the average as the most likely single figure. Because of the assumption of an even distribution of estates within a division the *conceivable* limits lie outside the figures indicated by our maximum and minimum tax increases. However, even on the most unrealistic assumptions, i.e. that where a category is divided, in the case of the minimum increase in tax rates no estates are included in the lower multiple division, whilst in the case of the maximum tax increase all the estates are included in the lower multiple category, even though the limits are wider the main conclusion would not be affected.[1]

The calculations, as outlined, have been made for each estate value range in the 1922 report and all ranges then combined and expressed both in terms of the total numbers in each division and the proportion of the sample with trade assets in each division.

To illustrate the method, calculations for one estate value range (£25,000–£50,000) are reproduced below, followed by the combined totals and percentages.

TABLE D1. *Value Range £25,000 to £50,000*

(a) *Rates of Estate Duty 1922 and 1951 and the Increases of 1951 over 1922*

Estate size £	Rates of estate duty (per cent) 1922	1951	1951 rate as multiple of 1922
25,000–30,000	8	18	2·25
30,000–35,000	9	21	2·35
35,000–40,000	9	24	2·67
40,000–45,000	10	28	2·80
45,000–50,000	10	31	3·10
Maximum increase of 1951 over 1922			3·10
Minimum increase of 1951 over 1922			2·25
Average increase of 1951 over 1922			2·63

[1] The number of cases where estate duty liability exceeds non-trade assets, on the basis of our 'reasonable' limits lies between 30 and 41; on the basis of the 'extreme' limits, this number lies between 27 and 54. The lowest conceivable figure, 27, is 7·2 per cent of estates over £10,000 with trade assets over £1,000, which compares with 6·2 per cent for the 1948 estates.

(b) *Relationship between Estate Duty Liability and Non-Trade Assets Number of Cases*

Multiple of estate duty of	Net assets (excluding trade assets), all debts charged against non-trade assets			
	1922	1951 maximum	1951 minimum	1951 average
up to 1	2	13	10	11
1·1–2	7	18	11	15
2·1–3	3	20	12	10
3·1–4	6	}	13	}
4·1–5	6	}	}	}
5·1–6	6	}	}	}
6·1–7	4	} 38	}	} 53
7·1–8	2	}	} 43	}
8·1–9	10	}	}	}
9·1–10	18	}	}	}
Over 10	25	}	}	}
Total	89	89	89	89

TABLE D2. *All Value Ranges, Relationship between Estate Duty Liability and Non-Trade Assets*

(a) Number of cases

Multiple of estate duty of	Net assets (excluding trade assets), all debts charged against non-trade assets			
	1922	1951 maximum	1951 minimum	1951 average
up to 1	12	41	30	36
1·1–2	11	68	54	59
2·1–3	15	43	37	37
3·1–4	27	51*	49*	62*
4·1–5	18	170*	6	12
5·1–6	22		8	167*
6·1–7	19		9	
7·1–8	16		162*	
8·1–9	22			
9·1–10	27			
Over 10	184			
Total	373	373	373	373

* Includes an indeterminate number of estates appropriate to a higher multiple of estate duty.

(b) Percentage of total cases

Multiple of estate duty of	Net assets (excluding trade assets), all debts charged against non-trade assets			
	1922	1951 maximum	minimum	average
up to 1	3·22	10·99	8·04	9·65
1·1–2	2·95	18·23	14·48	15·82
2·1–3	4·02	11·53	9·92	9·92
Over 3	89·81	15·25	67·56	64·61
Total	100·0	100·0	100·0	100·0

Index